THE WHICH?
GUIDE TO CAMERAS
AND OTHER
PHOTOGRAPHIC EQUIPMENT

THE WHICH? GUIDE TO CAMERAS

AND OTHER PHOTOGRAPHIC EQUIPMENT

Published by Consumers' Association
and
Hodder & Stoughton

First published in Great Britain by Consumers' Association
14 Buckingham Street, London, WC2N 6DS and Hodder &
Stoughton Limited, 47 Bedford Square, London WC1B 3DP

Editor	Quentin Deane
Consultants	Joe Franklin, Tom Ang
	Duncan Backhouse, Patrick Eager
	John Flewitt, David Fox
	Gordon Johnston
Design consultant	Jenny Mills
Illustrations	Tom Cross
All photographs and cover design	Behram Kapadia

Printed and bound in Great Britain by
Pindar Print Ltd, Scarborough

The publishers wish to thank the following manufacturers
for their help in making available materials and equipment
for photography in this book: Ilford Ltd, Kodak Ltd,
Nikon UK Ltd, Paterson Products Ltd, Pentax UK Ltd,
and Polaroid (UK) Ltd

The Which? guide to cameras and other photographic
  equipment
  1. Cameras–Catalogs
  I. Deane, Quentin   II. Consumers' Association
771.3'029'4   TR250

ISBN 0 340 35250 7

CONTENTS

CHAPTER ONE

WHICH TYPE OF CAMERA?

This chapter serves as an introduction. It explains how to go about deciding what type of camera you should buy, and gives you the basic background knowledge of photography you need

The main purpose of this book is to help you decide which of the many types of camera that are available on the market these days is the best choice for you. To a large extent, making the right choice of camera type is much more important than choosing the right brand – the differences between various types are much more marked than those between various models. If you buy a more sophisticated type of camera than you need, you could be spending more money than you need, and find yourself carrying around equipment which is bigger and bulkier than necessary too – a positive disincentive to picture-taking. On the other hand, a very simple type of camera may soon leave you feeling frustrated when you realise it is not able to take the kind of pictures that you had hoped to be able to produce.

So how should you go about deciding which is the right kind of camera for you? Start by reading this chapter. On pages 8 to 11 it describes the main characteristics of five types of camera. These aren't the only types available, but they are the only ones of importance to all but professionals or the most dedicated of amateurs (except perhaps for movie cameras, which this book does not cover). Pages 12 and 13 carry photographs showing you the sort of pictures each type of camera is suited to – not an exhaustive look at their abilities and limitations of course, but examples to whet the appetite.

The next five pages discuss some of the basic technical points of cameras. Many modern cameras are virtually foolproof – you can take a picture in almost any circumstances simply by pointing the camera in the right direction and pressing a button. So the discussion and explanation on these pages is kept as simple as possible.

To get the most out of some types of camera you do have to know more about the theory of how they work and what they do: you'll find this extra technical information only when you need it in order to help you make wise buys. If you want some basic landmarks before you start on those chapters, you'll find them on page 18 in an explanation of the anatomy of a camera. Finally in this chapter – as at the end of every chapter in the book – you'll find a *Buying guide* designed to summarise the important points so that you can quickly find your way to the information you need.

Use this chapter to gain an idea about which type of camera is most likely to suit you and the kind of photography you want to do. Then turn to whichever of the next five chapters discusses that type of camera in detail to learn all about your proposed choice: if you find that it doesn't suit after all, you can read one or more of the other of these chapters.

Chapters 7 to 11 cover aspects of photography other than the actual camera – and which are often just as important. For example, whatever type of camera you buy, it is no good unless you load it with film, which must be 'processed' before you can see the results of your picture-taking: Chapter 8 tells you about the different types and explains how to get the best out of whatever you choose. Chapter 10 describes flash lighting – it's easy and cheap to use these days, and greatly extends the scope of photography; Chapter 11 explains about the projector you'll probably want if you make much use of slide film.

Chapters 7 and 9, on lenses and filters, are a bit more specialised – something to read only if you've decided you want an SLR camera. You'd like to know what an SLR camera is, and how to decide whether you want one? Start overleaf....

Five types of camera

The cameras described in this book fall into five main types – but you can make a preliminary decision about which type is likely to suit you best by asking yourself just four questions:
- do you want to see the results of your picture-taking within minutes of pressing the shutter, rather than having to wait until your film comes back from the processors?
- are ease of use and a relatively cheap price your main considerations, even at the expense of the best picture quality?
- would you prefer good picture quality from a very easy-to-use camera, even if it costs rather more?
- do you intend to take photography seriously, regardless of cost or ease of use?

Do you want reasonable results from an easy-to-use, inexpensive camera?

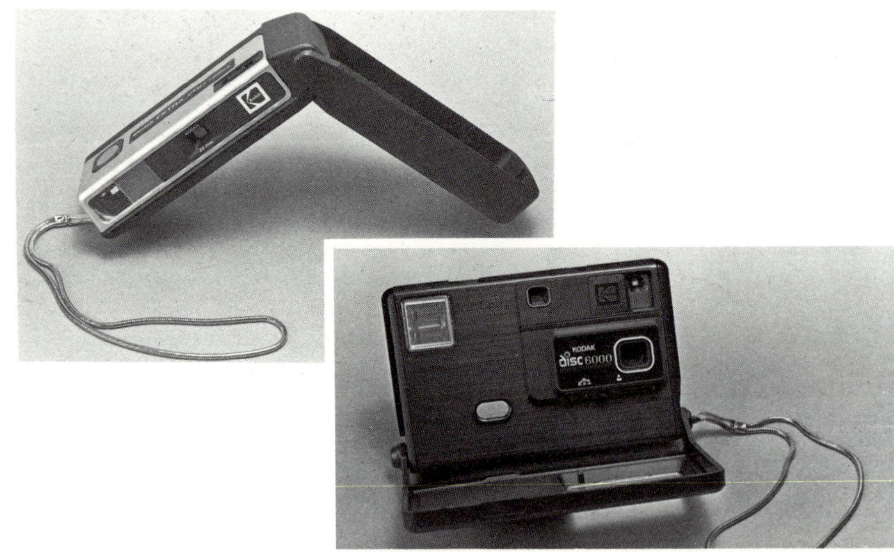

Do you want good results from a very easy-to-use camera?

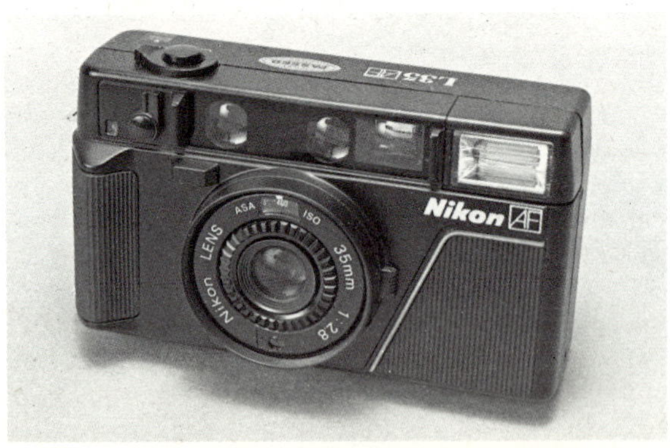

A couple of notes Costs given here and overleaf are guidelines in mid-1984: remember that many goods like cameras may *decrease* in price – even if only relative to other goods – rather than go up. *Print* and *slide* prices are those for a single picture, including film and processing: for an explanation of what prints and slides are, see Chapter 8.

The photographs shown here and overleaf are not to strict scale: the photographs in the following five chapters, which show the cameras in use, will give you a better idea of their actual size.

Your main choices are the **110 camera** and the **disc camera**. Both are small – they will fit into a large pocket or a handbag – can be relatively cheap, and are very easy to use.

Their basic drawback is the quality of the pictures that they produce, which is not of the best. The 110 camera is the poorer performer: many of them give good pictures only in reasonably bright, sunny weather. It has been almost totally superseded by the more modern disc camera.

The disc camera is, if anything, even easier to use than the 110. In a small trial conducted by *Which?* magazine, users with very little knowledge of photography found that it was very forgiving – few of the snaps they took turned out to be failures, though few of them counted as being very good pictures either.

The prints from a disc camera are a little more expensive than those from a 35mm camera (see below) but the camera is relatively cheap, so you would have to take a lot of pictures before this would become a drawback. For many people, who simply want to snap away on holidays and other odd occasions, a disc camera will be just the job – but don't bother saving a few pounds by buying one of the very cheapest models: treat yourself to something in the middle of the range, which will come equipped with automatic flash, film winding, and one or two other extra features that will make picture-taking easier.

Cost About £40 for a disc camera with a good range features. Prints are about 22p each: you cannot get slide film for a disc camera.

A **35mm non-reflex camera** is a little larger than a disc camera but, although beyond the pocket size, it is still reasonably light and easy to carry around. Its main virtue is that it takes 'standard' 35mm film (both prints and slides) which in itself is capable of professional results – which means in turn that most 35mm non-reflex cameras are capable of producing very good quality photographs.

There is a wide range of models of non-reflex camera: the fully automatic types are almost as easy to use as a disc camera; and in the *Which?* trial, a fully-automatic camera turned in many excellent pictures. Some automatic cameras can also be used in manual mode, so that you can exercise just that little bit of extra creativity over your photography.

Cameras that allow you to alter all the various settings yourself are also available and can be cheaper – but they are not as easy to use and, if you are prepared to put the amount of work into your pictures they require, you would probably be better off plumping for an SLR camera (see overleaf) which will give you more scope for your photography.

So, all in all, a good choice for someone wanting the possibility of very good pictures with the minimum of fuss is a fully automatic 35mm non-reflex camera.

Cost About £100 for a fully-automatic camera with a wide range of features. Prints cost about 15p each; slides about 13p each.

Do you intend to take photography seriously, regardless of convenience or cost?

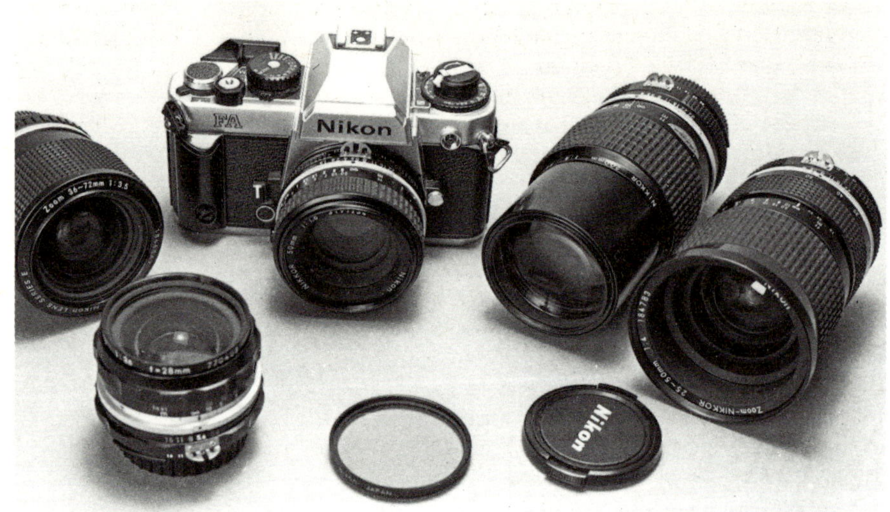

Do you want pictures available within minutes of taking them?

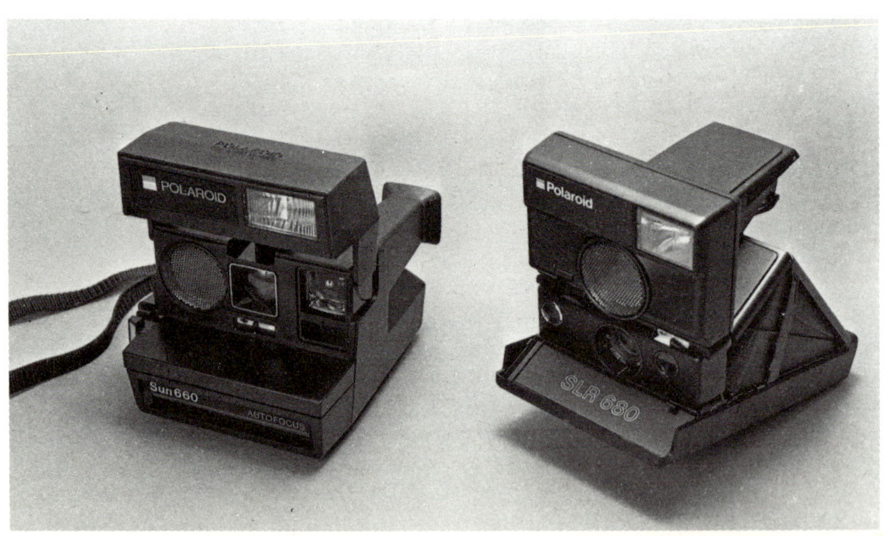

The ultimate choice for the amateur photographer (and widely used by professional photographers too) is the **35mm single-lens reflex (SLR) camera**.

This is a good quality camera that can give very accurate, sharp pictures. It has two advantages over the non-reflex type, which help you take a wider range of pictures and to compose your pictures better. The major advantage is that you can *change the lenses* – this makes it possible to take clear photographs of things far away that would appear only as small dots using an ordinary lens, or allows you to cram lots of a scene into your photo. (Interchangeable lenses aren't a feature unique to an SLR, but are rarely found on other types.) The other advantage is that you look *through the lens* at the scene and so you can see exactly what you are taking – this makes it easier to compose the picture and of course enables you to see clearly exactly what the results of using different lenses would be.

You pay for these extra features in two ways. First, an SLR camera is easily the most expensive type described here, especially when you have added all the extra lenses, separate flash unit and so on that make having an SLR worthwhile. Second, an SLR outfit is relatively bulky and heavy – and, particularly if you are gadget-prone, you'll find yourself having to lug enough gear to fill a suitcase every time you want to take a photograph.

There are some SLR cameras that are almost as automatic and easy to use as a non-reflex type. But if you intend to take photography seriously enough to justify buying an SLR, you will need to be able to adjust the various controls yourself at least some of the time, so go for an auto/manual type that allows you to do this.

The picture quality of an SLR is not inherently much, if any, better than that of a non-reflex camera but you have the scope to take good pictures in a greater range of conditions.

In summary, an SLR will allow you to take excellent pictures in a wide range of circumstances. But you can make use of this ability only if you are prepared to put quite a lot of work into your photography.

Cost Around £180 for an auto/manual camera, one lens and a flash unit; £130 for two additional lenses. Prints cost about 15p each; slides about 13p each.

An **instant picture camera** uses a special film which processes itself immediately after you have taken a picture. A colour picture is recogniseable in less than 90 seconds after you press the shutter, and is fully developed in less than 10 minutes.

They are great for family functions such as weddings and birthdays – you can have snaps of the event to give away to aunts and uncles before they leave; and if you find you've missed out an important member of the family in your picture rounds, you'll know and can put matters right before the festivities end. Most cameras have built-in flash and are very easy to use.

However, the cameras are bulky and the colours can be disappointing – not really suited, for example, to photographing landscapes. The prints are much more expensive than with other cameras, too. So, although an instant picture camera can be fun on occasions, it should not be your only camera.

Cost About £50 for a camera with reasonable performance, equipped with the main features we think desirable. Prints cost about 60p each, and you cannot get slides.

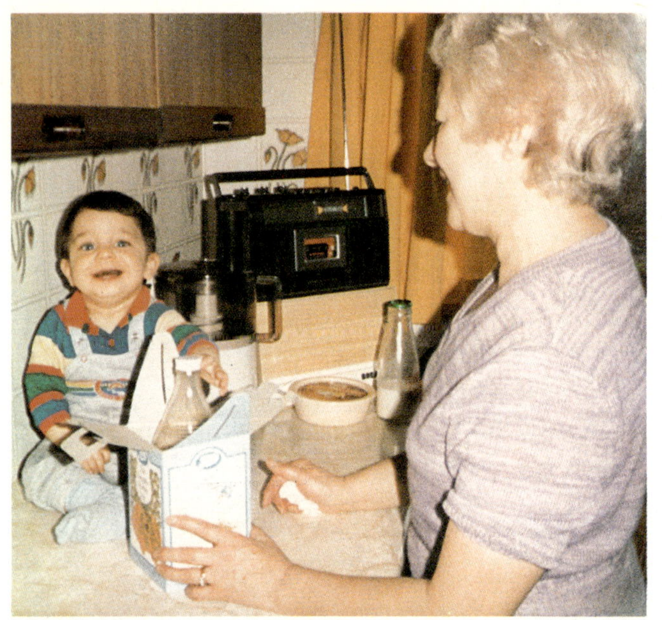

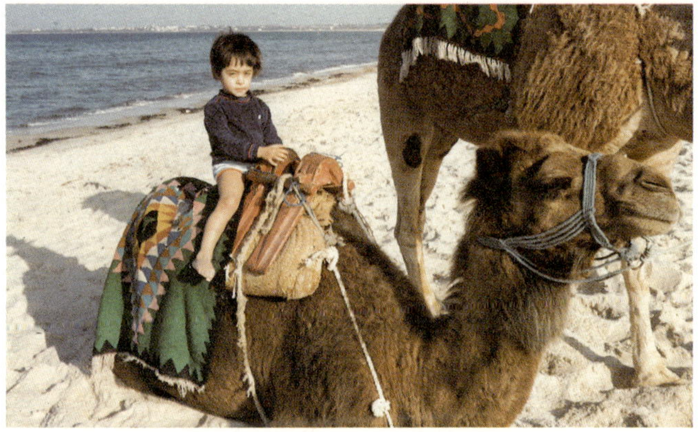

Left With the built-in flash on most disc cameras, you can take family snap-shots at a moment's notice

Below An automatic non-reflex camera is easy to use, and can give you very good-quality pictures

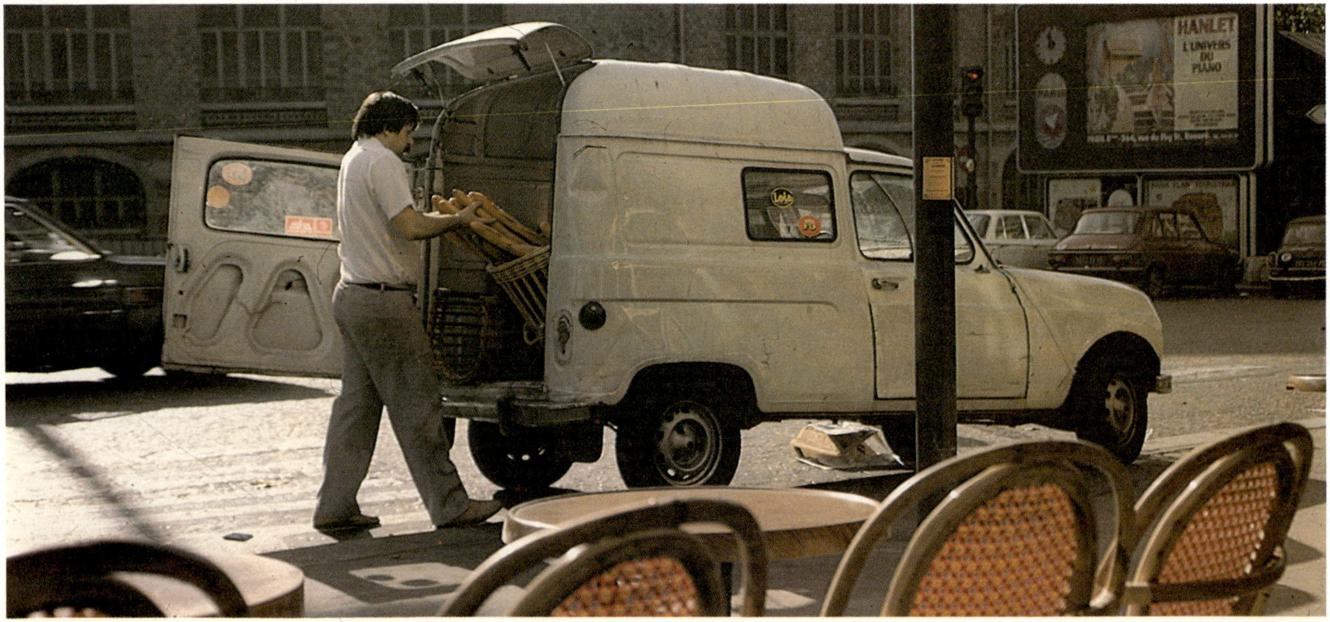

Left A 110 camera is easy to carry around, but most give good pictures only in bright, sunny conditions

Right By fitting the correct lens to an SLR camera, you can take clear pictures of subjects – like this deer – far in the distance: something that you can't do with most other types of camera

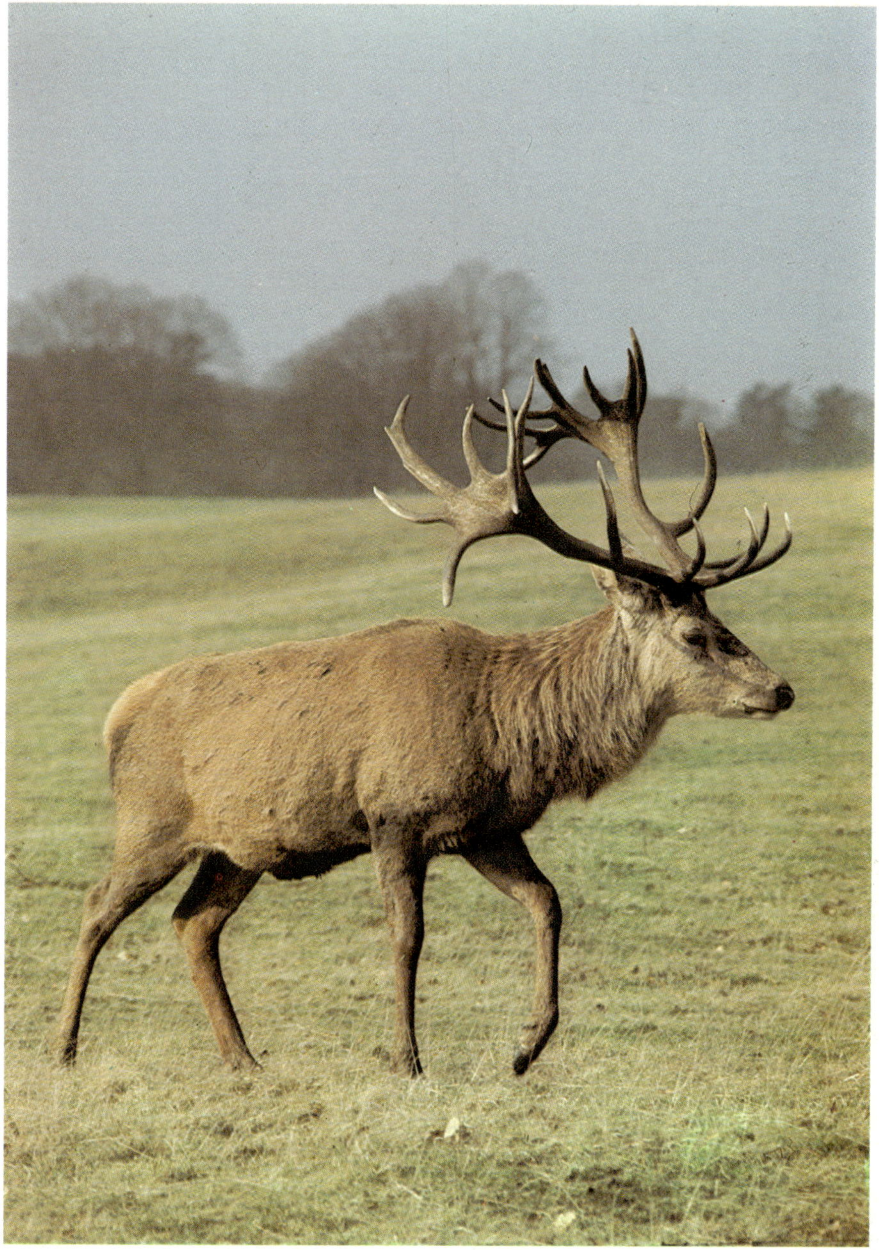

Below Children will love to see the results of your picture-taking straight after the event – for which you need an instant picture camera

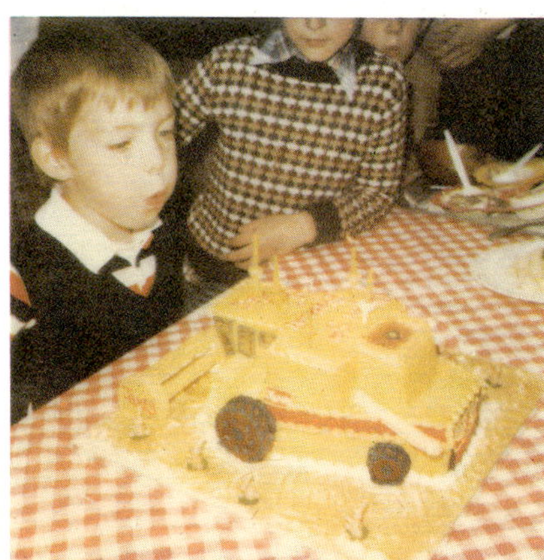

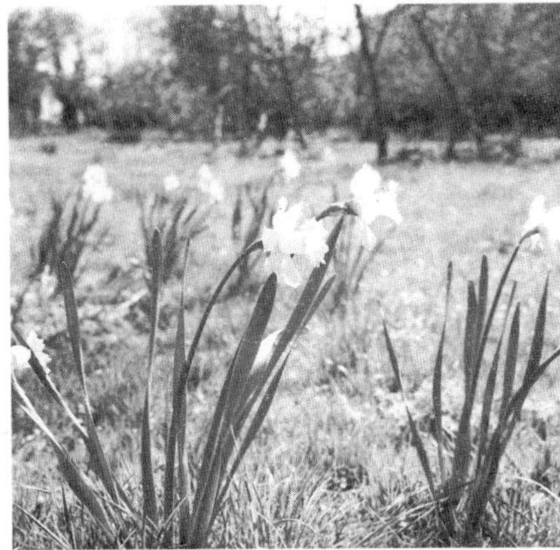

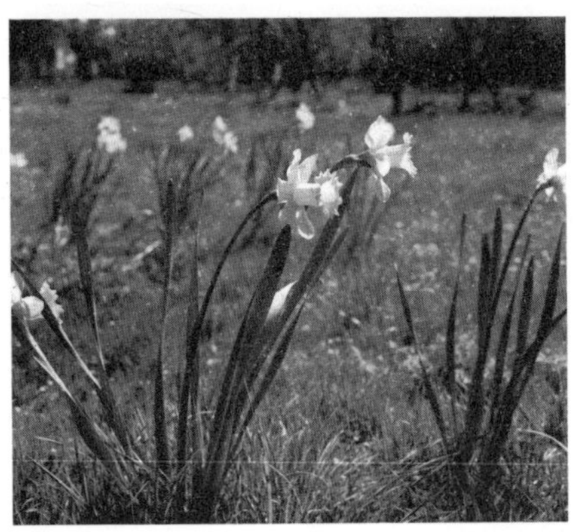

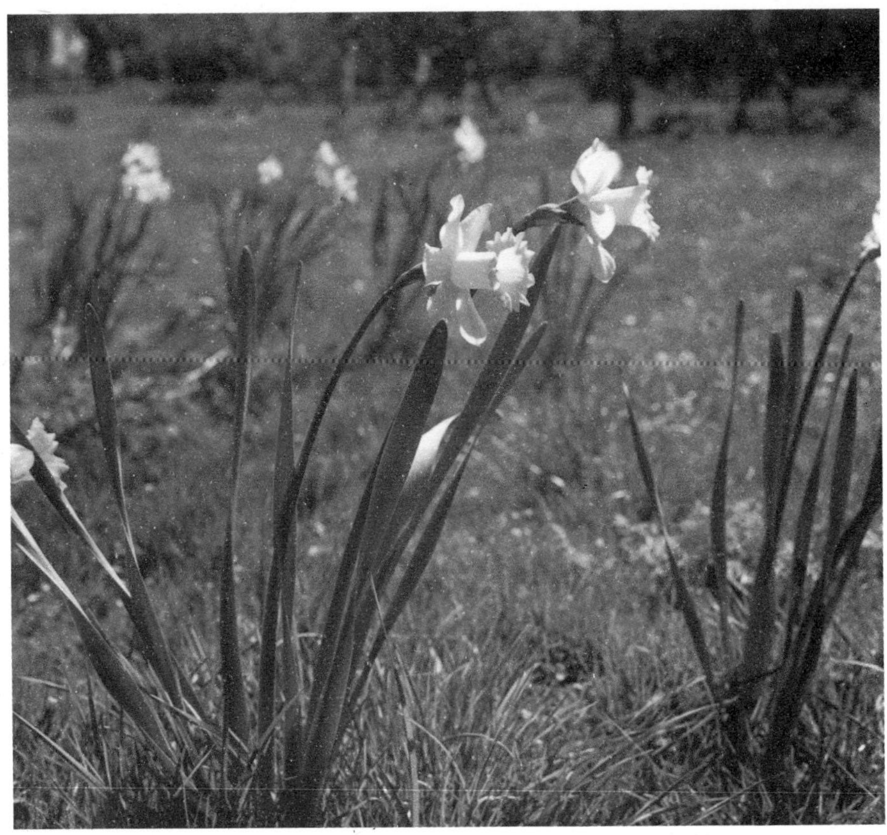

Exposure

The heart of a camera is not so much in the camera itself as in the photographic film it uses. The camera has three main functions:

● to provide a light-tight box to hold the film, so that the film isn't subject to light until you want it to be

● to provide a means of letting light in from a scene so that the film can record an image of that scene

● to control, in various ways, the light streaming on to the film.

One of the reasons the camera has to control the light is because it has to ensure the right quantity reaches the film so that the film is properly exposed. If you allow too much light on to the film, the result will be a photograph that is over-bright and washed out, as in the small picture *top left* on this page; this is **over-exposure**. If not enough light falls on the film, the photo will be dark and murky, or **under-exposed** (as in the picture *bottom left*). Either way, you will not be able to distinguish detail in the picture. Only when the film is correctly exposed (*above right*) will the picture appear correctly lit, with all the detail visible and the light and dark parts properly contrasted.

Depending on the type of camera, there may be no method of altering exposure – that is, exposure may be fixed which limits the range of light conditions in which you can take successful pictures – or exposure may be automatically adjusted by the camera, or adjusted by yourself before you take a picture.

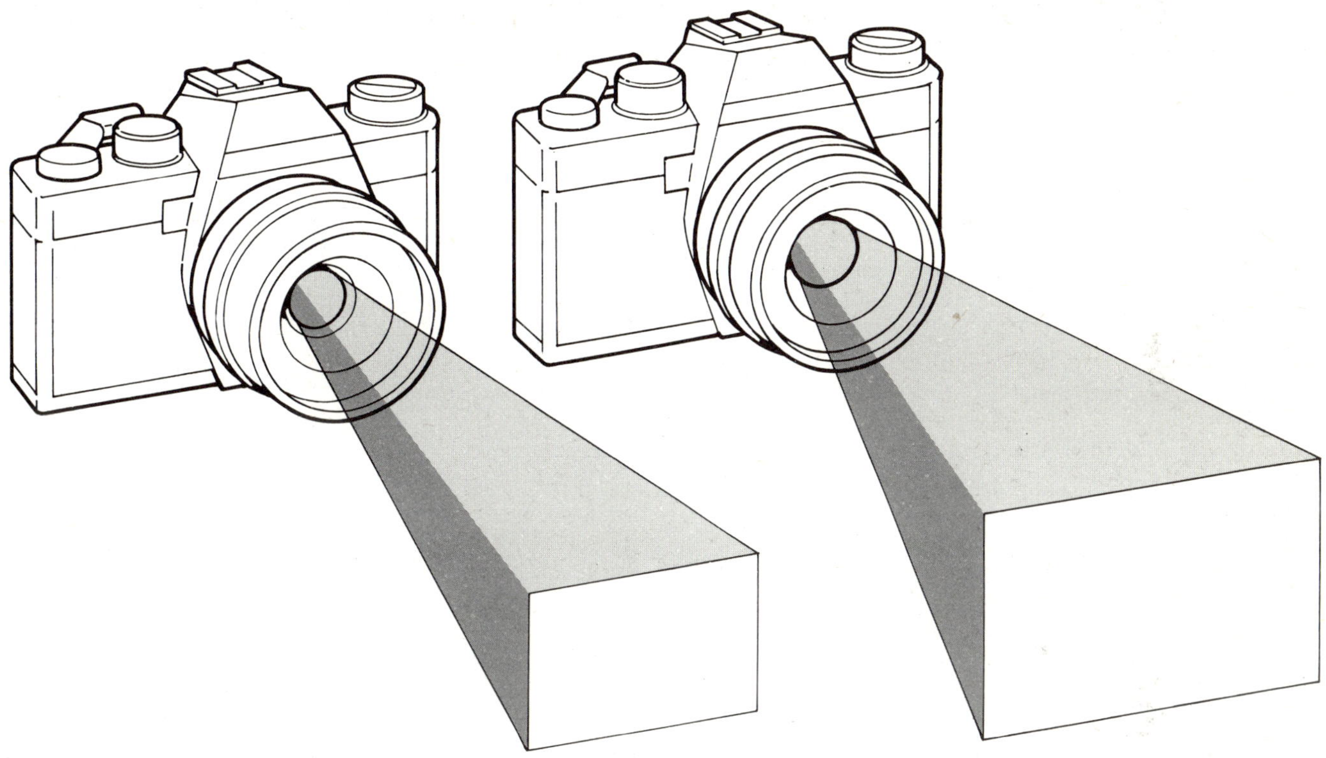

Angle of view

Stare straight ahead of you, and try to work out how far round the scene to each side you can see without moving your head – this is your normal **angle of view**. A camera similarly can 'see' only a limited side-to-side amount of the scene that is in front of it. However, unlike the human eye, a camera's angle of view can be varied, depending on the type of lens with which it is fitted.

There are many occasions on which it is useful to be able to have a choice about what angle of view your camera sees, and, therefore, how much of the scene from side to side and up and down is recorded on the film. For example, you may want to get a lot of the scene in front of you into your picture. You might be able to do this just stepping back, but often this is not possible – when you want to take pictures in a room, or in a narrow street, for example. In these cases, a camera lens with a wide angle of view would be useful. On the other hand, there may be occasions when you can't get close enough to your scene in order to be able to take in only the amount of the view that you want to photograph. In this case, a camera with a narrow-angle lens would be needed.

With some cameras – notably the SLR type – you can select any number of different angles of view by buying different lenses and interchanging them on the body of the camera. A few cameras have different lenses built in – you change the angle of view by sliding a lever or something similar. But many cameras have only one, fixed, lens and so only one angle of view.

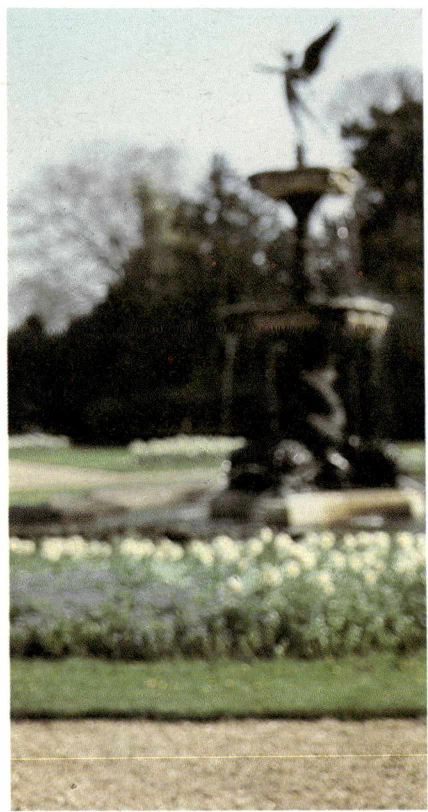

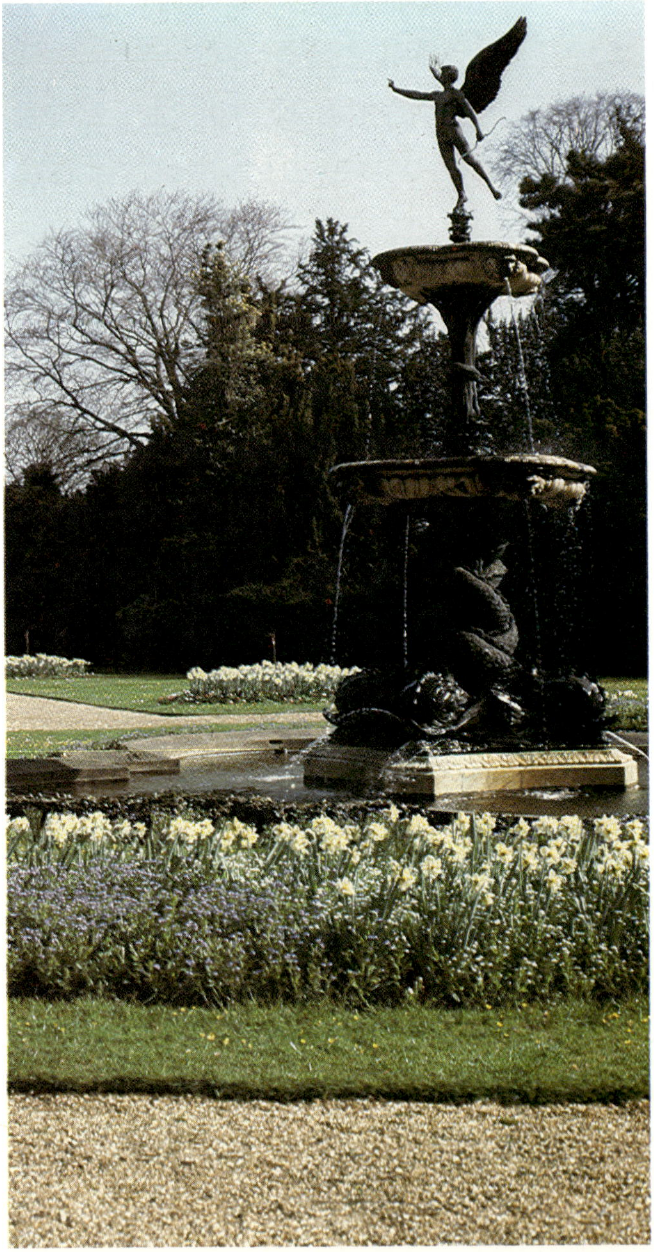

Controlling focusing

Another of the major functions of a camera (or, rather, of its lens) is to collect the light rays passing through it and to project them on to the film so that a sharp image is formed. If the image is blurred – as in the picture *above* – then it is said to be **out of focus**. When the edges of the images in the picture are sharply defined, and all the detail is clear – see picture *right* on this page – then it is **in focus**.

Although incorrect focusing is a major reason why a picture appears fuzzy and indistinct there are other causes of blurring, such as 'graininess' which is described in detail in Chapter 8.

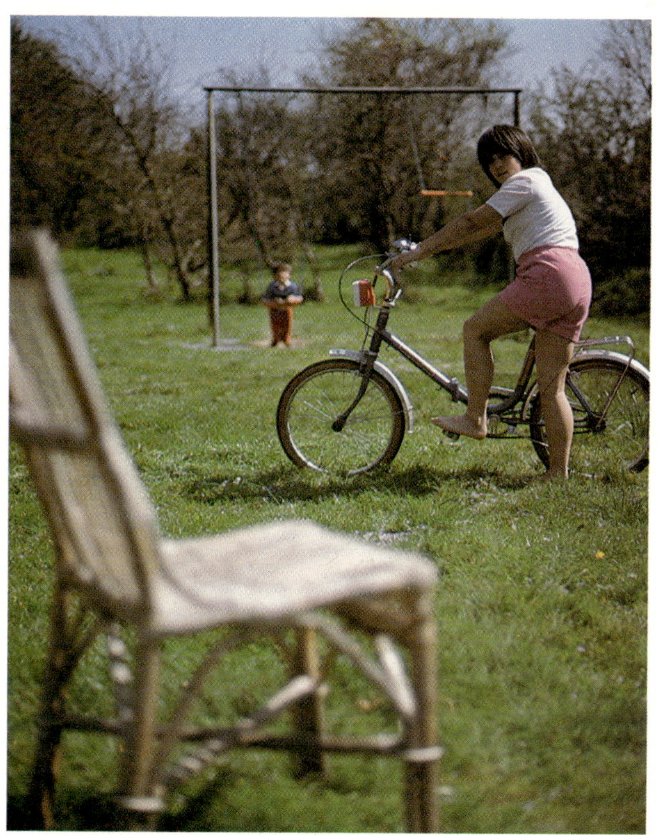

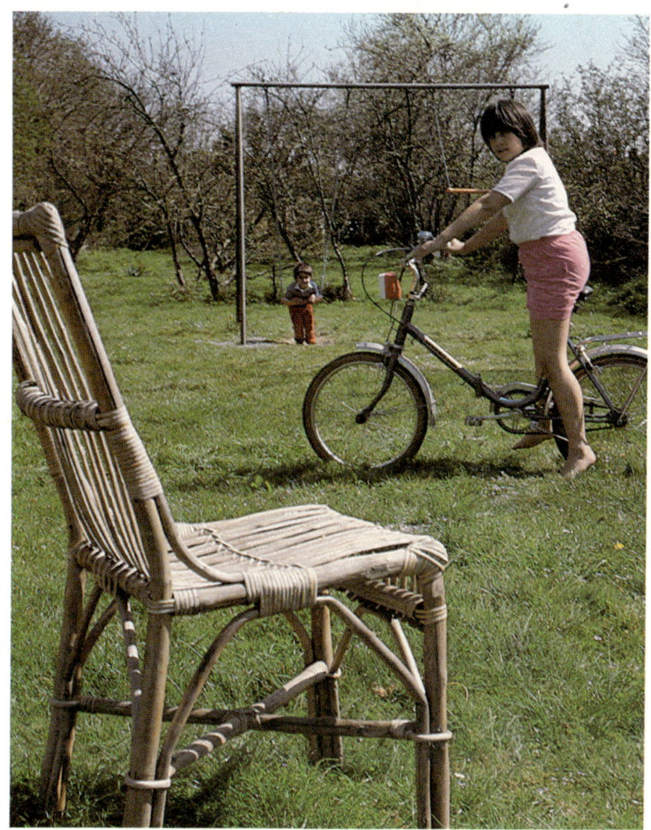

Depth of field

A lens is not capable of projecting a sharp image of every-thing it sees from very close by right up to the distant horizon. But although not every point of a scene will be in focus at one time, there is always a zone of depth over which the image is sharp: the distance from the nearest point of a scene that is in focus to the furthest point away that is still in focus is known as the **depth of field**.

The picture *left* has a very restricted depth of field – only the child with the bicycle in the middle-ground of the scene is sharply in focus; the swing in the background and the chair in the foreground are quite blurred. The picture on the *right* has an extended depth of field – everything from the front of the chair in the foreground to the trees in the distant background are sharply in focus.

The depth of field is fixed on many types of camera so that all points from, say, 0.5m (2ft) in front of the camera to the horizon will appear sharply in focus in your picture. This is normally what you would want for everyday snap-shots, so you need not usually bother about depth of field. But with more 'artistic' photographs you may prefer, for example, to have the background indistinct. And to allow for this you can vary the depth of field on some cameras as you wish – by changing lenses, or by altering the lens 'aperture'.

Inside a camera

Shutter release Press this to open the shutter when you are ready to take a picture

Film advance knob To wind on a section of film after it has been *exposed* (that is, after an image has been recorded on it), and so allow the next section of unexposed film into place

Viewfinder Lets you look at the scene in front of you, so you can see what it is you're taking a picture of

Film rewind knob Allows you to rewind the film into its light-tight cassette when you have exposed the whole reel – not needed with many types of camera

Aperture Another way of controlling the amount of light passing on to the film is by altering the size of hole, or *aperture* in the lens – again, not present on all cameras

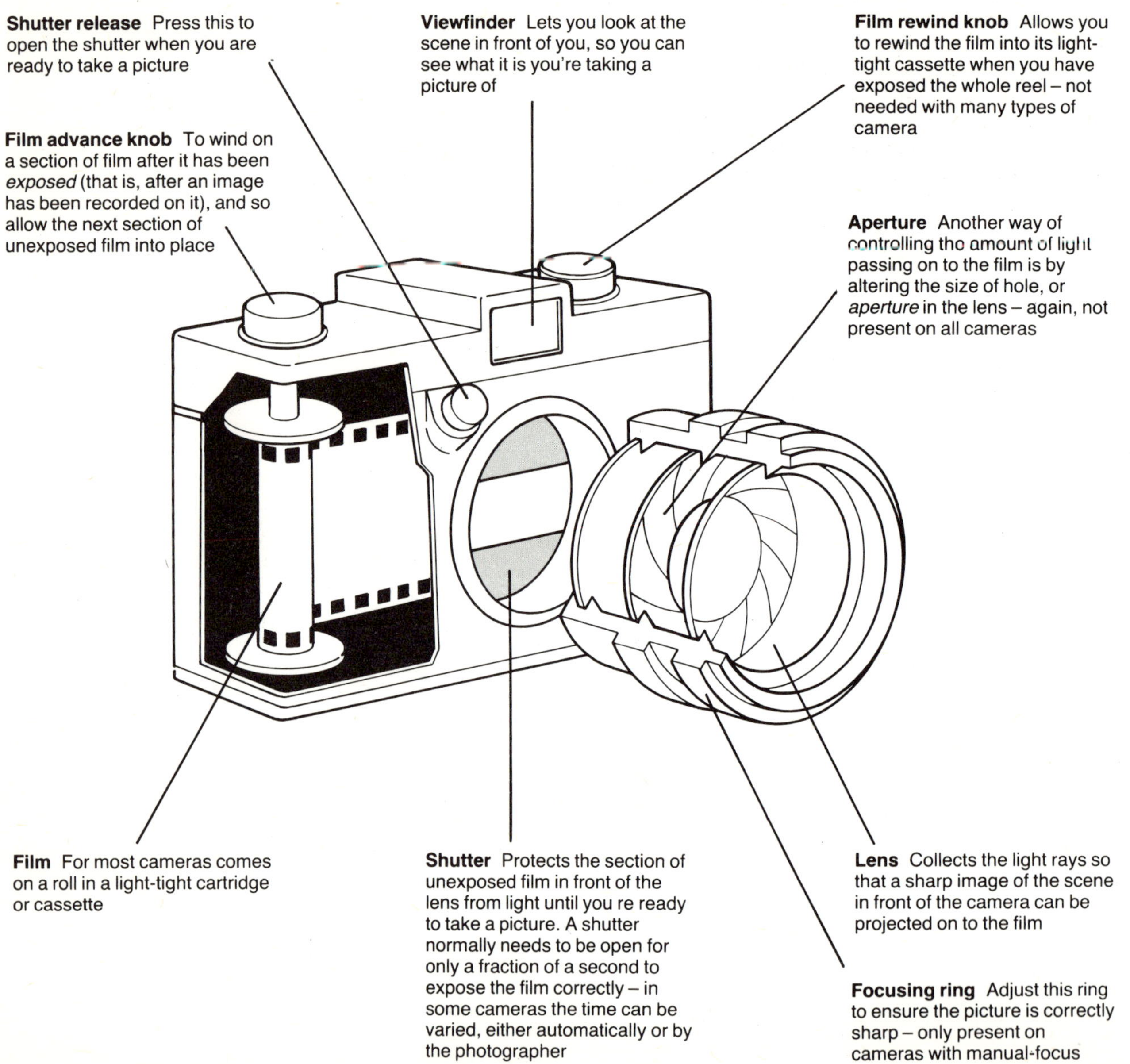

Film For most cameras comes on a roll in a light-tight cartridge or cassette

Shutter Protects the section of unexposed film in front of the lens from light until you re ready to take a picture. A shutter normally needs to be open for only a fraction of a second to expose the film correctly – in some cameras the time can be varied, either automatically or by the photographer

Lens Collects the light rays so that a sharp image of the scene in front of the camera can be projected on to the film

Focusing ring Adjust this ring to ensure the picture is correctly sharp – only present on cameras with manual-focus

≣≣≣≣ BUYING GUIDE ≣≣≣≣

Now that you've read this chapter you will have some idea of which type of camera is likely to be the best for you:

● if you want something simple and inexpensive for holiday and family snapshots, then either a 110 camera or a disc camera is likely to be your best bet

● for good results, but without too much work on your part, think about an automatic 35mm non-reflex camera

● if you want to see your pictures straight after you take them, you'll need an instant picture camera

● serious photographers, or those with special interests, will probably want an SLR camera.

The rest of this book describes all these types of camera in more detail so that you know exactly which to buy for your circumstances. And it explains about other pieces of photographic equipment that you may need.

CHAPTER TWO

DISC CAMERAS

Launched by Kodak for Christmas 1982, disc cameras are the latest attempt at making photography foolproof. But you pay in a number of ways for this convenience

A disc camera is a small, thin, machine with a minimum of controls. You buy your film as a disc and loading into the camera is simply a matter of slipping it into place and closing the back. All you usually have to do then (indeed, all you can do) is point the camera in the right direction, and press a button. Only print films are available – you cannot take slides with a disc camera.

Although many manufacturers have now launched disc cameras (though many of the 'different' brands are in fact identical) they are all very basic, with only one or two additional features available.

Exposure

Disc cameras have no exposure control – they are all **fixed exposure**, with one exposure setting for daylight pictures, another for flash. Different light conditions, and different distances from the subject when using flash, are taken care of by the very wide *exposure latitude* of the print film which permits corrections to be made when the film is printed.

The advantage of doing without exposure controls is that it makes the camera particularly small, easy to use, and cheap to buy. And, certainly for normal 'holiday' snaps, the range of light conditions in which you can successfully take pictures is quite wide. Even so, it can be helpful to have some way of increasing the exposure in very dull weather. If light is dull, switch to flash – it's not necessarily the flash itself that helps the picture so much as the fact that switching to flash automatically gives you extra exposure. With sensor flash cameras (see overleaf) the flash comes on automatically whenever the light level is low.

A tip worth considering for cameras that use separate flash bulbs, rather than a built-in flash unit. These cameras still give you extra exposure when you insert a flash bulb – even if the bulb is a 'spent' one – one you've already used. So if your

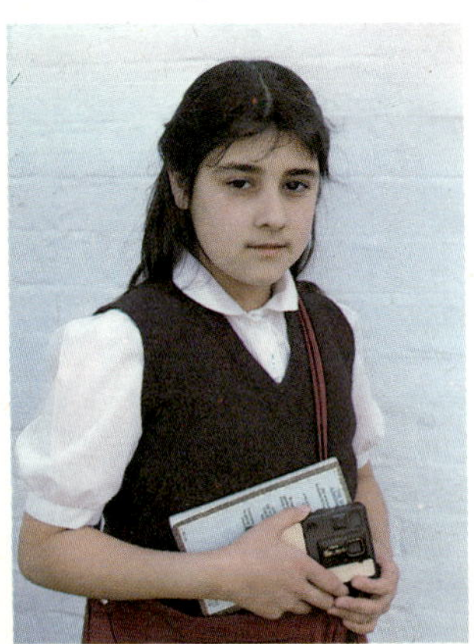
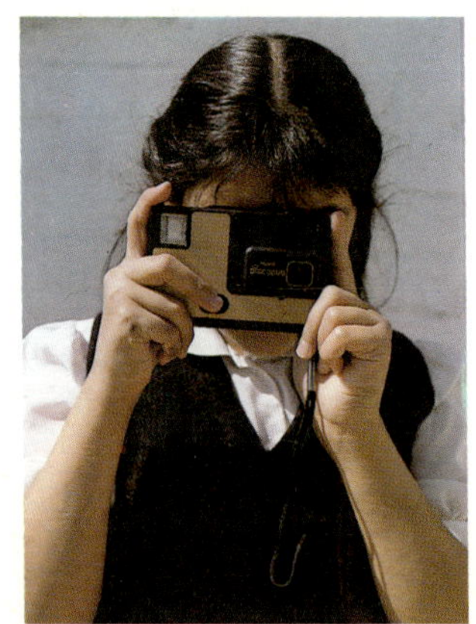
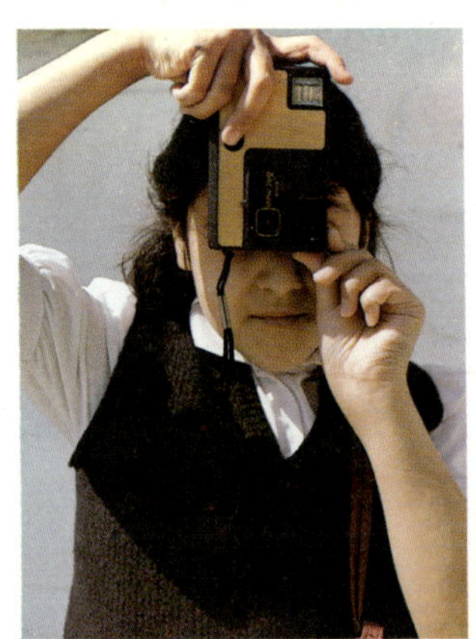
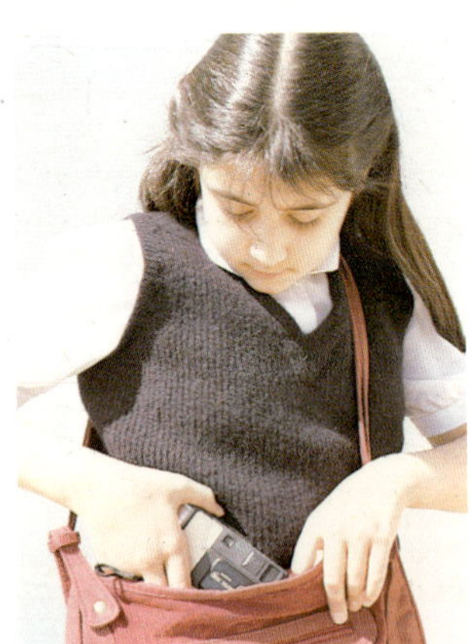

subjects are beyond the 'flash range' (see below) and would not benefit by the flash itself, use a spent bulb just to give you the extra exposure needed to cope with the dull weather.

Focusing

Again, there's little choice. All disc cameras have **fixed focus**. This is simple to operate (and, because there is no automatic mechanism, simple to build) and works quite well, making sure that *everything* in your picture that was about 1.2m (4ft) or more away from the camera appears sharp, not blurred.

If you want to take sharp pictures of objects closer than about 1.2m from the camera (head-and-shoulders portraits of people, say) you need a camera with a close-up control which moves an extra lens into place. You can also get a simple *auto-focus* disc camera, which lets you take close-up pictures without having to move any control by hand.

Flash

All disc cameras come with flash – either a **separate bulb** flash, or **built-in electronic** flash.

Separate bulb flash This is used on the very cheapest cameras. The unit used is called a *Flipflash*, and consists of a series of ten bulbs mounted in a special holder which plugs into a socket on the top of the camera. Plugging the unit the socket automatically switches you on to flash. As you take a picture, a bulb lights up, 'blowing' as it does so; when you take the next picture, the next bulb in the sequence fires. After five shots you unplug the unit, turn it upside down, and take the next five pictures. Then you throw it away.

Because a Flipflash unit is tall, you rarely get problems with *red eye* (people in your pictures appearing to have red pupils to their eyes; see page 119). But the unit is a nuisance to use, and roughly doubles the cost of your pictures.

Built-in electronic flash These are more convenient because they are always there, ready for work – but they do add slightly to the weight and bulk of a camera.

For a built-in unit, the flash is reasonably powerful, having

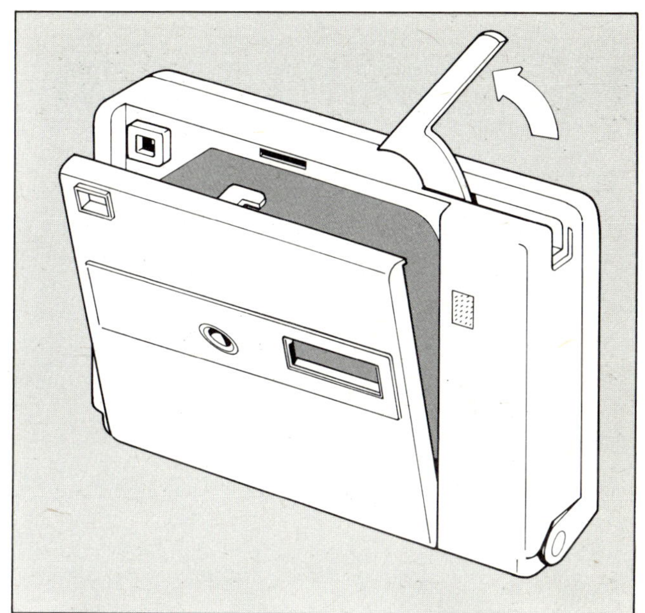

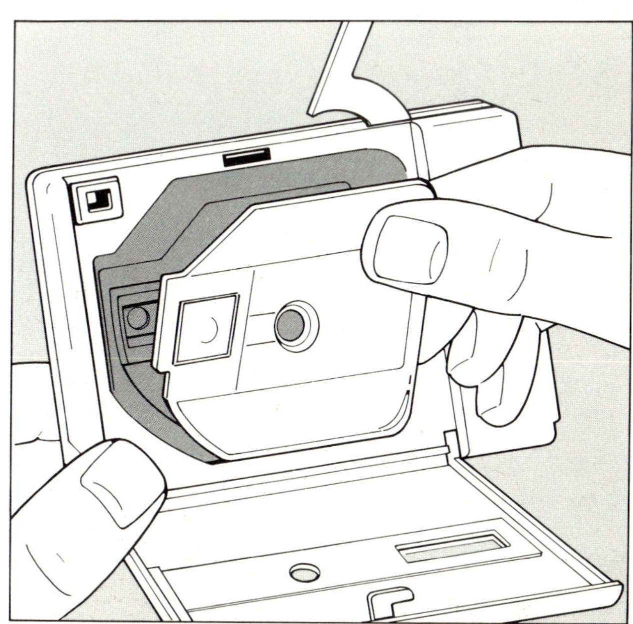

Right Loading a disc camera with film is easy – open the back and drop the film disc into place

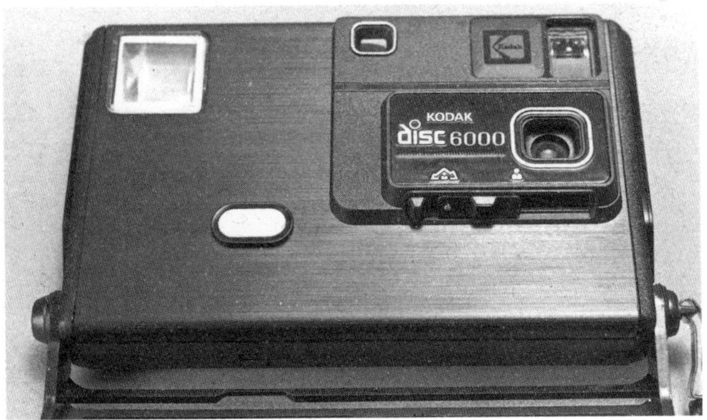

To use a built-in close-up lens, simply slide the lever on the camera to the correct symbol

a range of up to 5½m (18ft) – that is, subjects over about 5½m away from the camera will not be well lit and so will appear dark (that is under-exposed) in the photograph. Another problem is that many disc cameras tend to over-expose on close-up flash pictures; some warn you in their instructions not to take flash pictures closer than a couple of metres (6ft) but many do not.

Cameras with **sensor flash** are particularly easy to use because the flash turns on by itself if the light level is low.

If your camera does not have sensor flash, then it's useful for it to have a *low-light* warning indicator instead, so you'll know when to switch on the flash. But this isn't essential – the extra cost of using built-in electronic flash is negligible, so if in doubt switch it on.

Built-in flash (and the built-in motor drive – see below) uses batteries. These are not likely to need replacing more than every couple of years and add little to your cost. Some cameras have the new built-in **lithium batteries**. These are guaranteed to last five years without running down, and *Which?* tests have shown that they should live up to this claim and will probably last much longer. When they do run down, they have to be replaced by the manufacturer. Are they worth having? It's difficult to tell – no-one knows what the replacement cost will be! But they are unlikely to be more expensive in the long run than normal batteries, and of course there is the convenience of not having to think about the batteries in your camera for half a decade or more. Lithium batteries charge up the flash very quickly, and this tends to give a more consistent flash output.

Lenses

Most cameras have a single, fixed, lens – but others offer you more.

'Tele' lens A telephoto lens will make your subjects appear closer and larger, but at the expense of cutting down the angle of view you get in the final picture. Tele lenses are built into the camera and are simply slid into place in front of the film.

You need some way of being able to tell from the viewfinder what effect a tele lens will have on your picture: in some cases the viewfinder adapts automatically as you move the tele lens in place, so you're able to see exactly what the shot will look like with and without the tele lens. With other cameras the viewfinder doesn't alter, but marking lines within it give you an idea of what area the final picture will cover.

Close-up lens This is useful if your camera does not have autofocus (see above) and allows you to get everything down to about 0.5m (about 1½ft) in focus.

Motor wind

All but the cheaper disc cameras have a built-in motor drive to wind the film on after every shot (or, rather, turn the disc round). Professional photographers have found motor drive almost essential for some years – so that they can shoot many dozens of pictures in rapid succession, in the hope of catching that one fleeting moment of action, or person's expression, that makes an important news picture.

For once, however, this is a professional feature that point-and-shoot photographers can make good use of – it is a useful convenience and it can help you to keep the camera steady if you are taking more than one picture of the same thing. Most disc motors allow you to take a shot only every couple of seconds or so – though with a few, you can even emulate hardened news-hounds by loosing off several shots a second. If you're using flash, you are in any case limited in speed by the time the flash takes to get ready for firing.

Other features

There are one or two other features worth looking out for on disc cameras.

Viewfinder information   Because there are no controls for you to adjust, and so little for the camera itself to get wrong, there is little need for much in the way of information in the viewfinder. Most have a *bright frame* in the viewfinder to help you frame your shots; for cameras with a built-in close-up lens, the bright frame should move slightly so as to reduce any *parallax errors* (see page 36 for details of 'bright frames' and 'parallax').

Don't take these markings too literally – disc cameras usually give you *much* more in the final picture than the framing marks in the viewfinder tell you that you'll get as the picture opposite shows.

Self timer   This delays release of the shutter for a few seconds after you have set it – giving you time to race round to the front of the camera and get yourself into the picture. The main problem with this is that, having set the camera right for framing a group, it is tricky to press the shutter button without moving it off target – a camera with a sturdy *prop* or a socket for use with a *tripod* will help.

Time for another photo?   One expensive top-of-the-line disc camera even includes a built-in digital alarm clock.

Film

You buy your film as a disc, with each disc containing 15 pieces of film. Developed negatives are still fixed to the disc (so they're easy to store). The prints are about the same size as those you normally get from 110 or 35mm films, but they all include a date on the back, so you have a good record of when you took your pictures. There is a reference number too which matches up with a similar number on the negative disc, so you can easily locate a negative and get more prints made.

Note that the cost of pictures from disc cameras is dearer than from say, a 35mm camera – but the camera are a lot cheaper than their nearest equivalents, so you would have to take a lot of pictures before you would recoup the cost of buying the dearer camera.

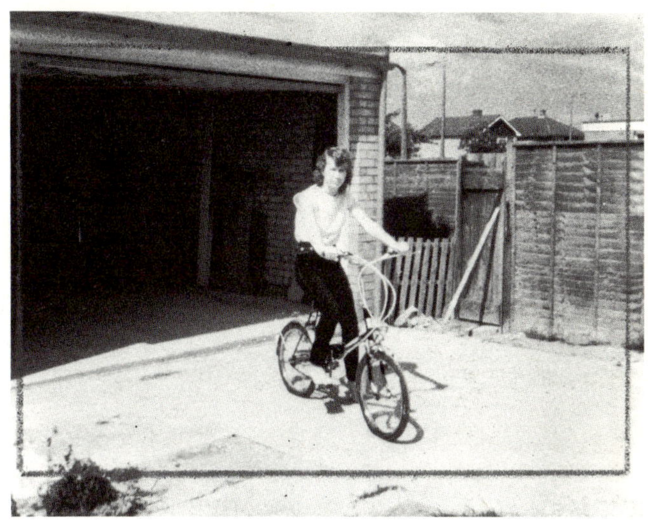

The finished picture often shows more than you see when looking through the viewfinder (shown by the marked border)

Ease of use

All disc cameras are relatively easy to use, because there are very few controls and adjustments to make, film loading is easy, and they are small and light enough to carry around easily.

Perhaps the major features enhancing ease of use are *sensor flash*, lithium batteries, and motor drive. Look for a cover that covers all the working parts – in particular the lens – and is attached to the camera body, so there's no prospect of losing it: some form useful handles when opened. Any lens cover should be designed so that it prevents you from releasing the shutter when it is closed.

Which? tests have shown that disc cameras are quite tough and should stand up to being battered about rather better than other types.

Picture quality

The major problem with disc cameras is that the pictures they give are not very good. This is mainly because of **grain**. A grainy picture looks slightly fuzzy and unsharp; you can see the individual minute particles which go to make up the

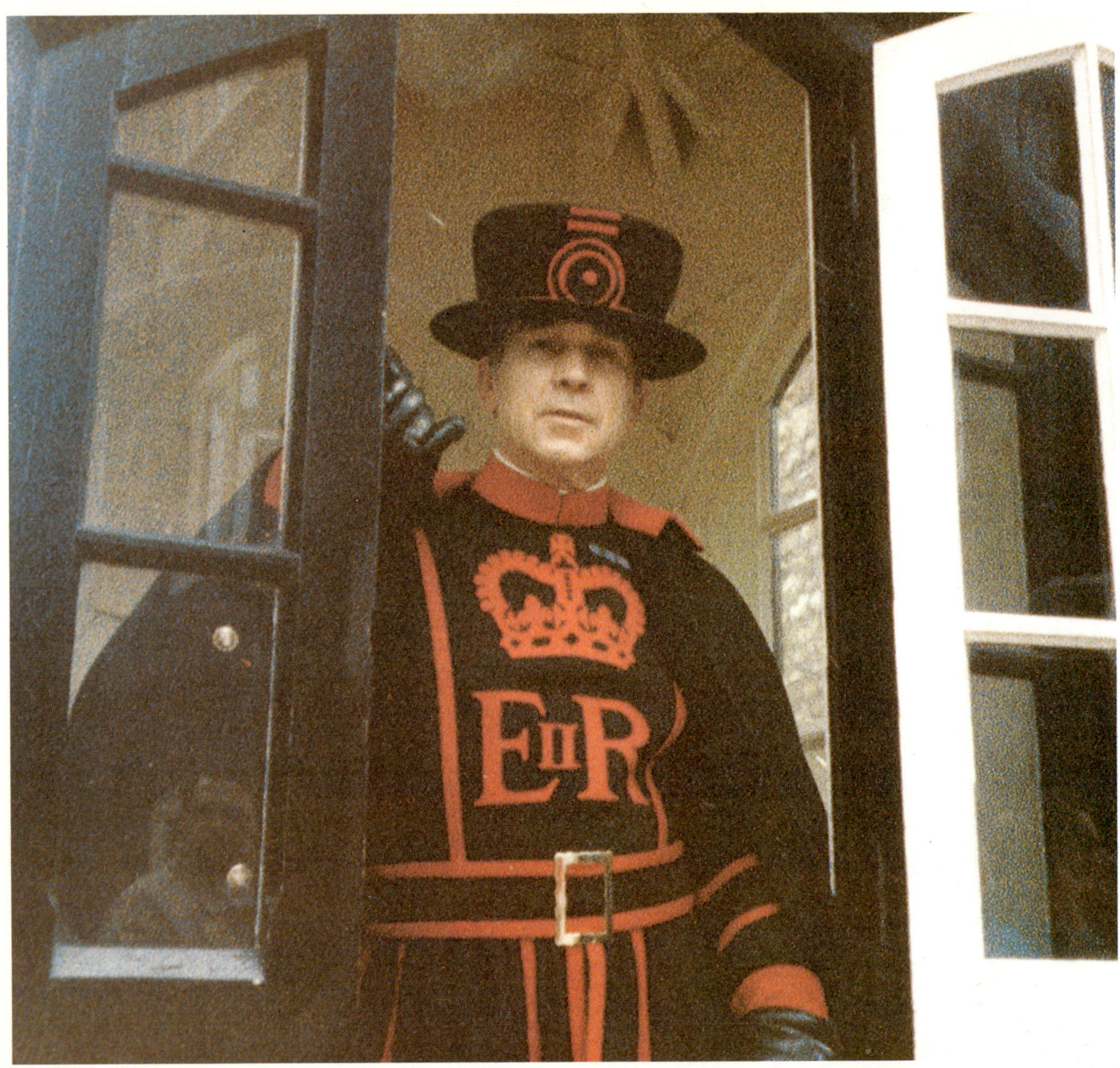

picture. Grain affects disc cameras particularly because the negative is very small and so a lot of enlargement is needed to make a reasonable-sized print. The extensive enlargement also means the picture is less likely to be perfectly sharp – even though the negative itself may be sharper than a negative from a 110 film, or even some 35mm films.

However, although the best disc pictures are not as good as the best pictures from a 110 camera, a disc camera is so easy to use and so much more tolerant of light conditions that the chances of your taking reasonable pictures are greater and your chances of total failure are very much lower – something that a small trial carried out by *Which?* confirmed.

BUYING GUIDE

A disc camera seems a good choice for a beginner. It's cheap to buy (though not the cheapest to run), very easy to use, and you can rely on it to give you reasonable results.

The cheapest cameras may look an attractive buy if you want something for only occasional use – but the initial saving is soon cancelled out by the cost of flash bulbs and the wastage with even relatively few poor shots, to say nothing of general dissatisfaction.

If you want reasonable pictures in a wide range of conditions, with the greatest convenience, go for a disc camera with sensor flash, a close-up lens, lithium battery, and motor drive.

For better-quality pictures, you need a different type of camera – the 35mm non-reflex is the obvious candidate. But it will cost you – the same level of convenience works out at roughly double the price.

Pictures from a disc camera are often marred by *grain* – the rough, dotty effect shown here on the Beefeater's face and in the background. (This photograph, taken by a disc camera, is enlarged here more than for a normal-sized print because the printing processes used for this book don't allow the grain to show up as clearly as it does in the original photograph)

CHAPTER THREE

110 CAMERAS

First introduced in 1972, the 110 or 'pocket instamatic' camera was one of the first pocket-sized cameras widely available. You can still buy them, but they have now been largely superseded

The main advantages of 110 cameras are size and simplicity of use. Most can fit easily into a handbag or a pocket, and to take pictures all you usually have to do is point and shoot. To change films you simply open the back, remove one film cartridge, and slot in another. Unlike disc cameras it is possible to find very sophisticated (and very expensive) versions in the 110 format, sporting many of the features you'd find on the more traditional types of camera.

Exposure

Different types of 110 camera use different methods of varying the exposure so that the pictures you take will appear correctly lit.

Fixed exposure   With the simplest 110 cameras the only method for varying exposure at all is to use films of different *speeds* – see pages 91 to 95. With the usual 100 ISO film a 110

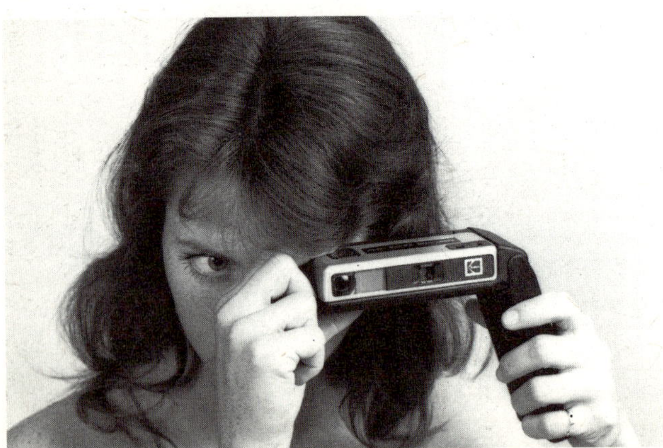

camera gives its best pictures only in bright sunny weather, but with the newer 200 or 400 ISO films this should be less of a problem.

Another way of getting better pictures in dull weather is to switch to flash – a trick which is explained more fully on page 20, in the chapter on disc cameras.

Manual exposure   Here you adjust the exposure with a control knob or slider to cope with differing light levels. To keep things simple, there are usually only two or three different exposure settings and the knob or slider is marked with easy-to-understand weather symbols (a cloud and a sun, for example). Even using this control properly you may still have problems taking good pictures in dull weather with 100 ISO film.

Automatic exposure   Automatic cameras adjust the exposure for you and, although the automatic control may not be perfect, it is generally very good. More than that – auto cameras usually have better lenses than the fixed or manual exposure models, and so can be used in a greater range of light conditions.

Focusing

110 cameras have either **fixed** focusing or **manual** focusing. Fixed focusing is simple and cheap and can give good results – anything further than about 1.5m (5ft) from the camera will be sharp and in focus.

With manual focus cameras you alter the focusing yourself to get a picture that's sharp. In the usual system, the camera has two or three focus settings marked with symbols (portrait, group, landscape, say) and you set to whichever symbol you think will give the best results. But you can't tell from looking through the viewfinder whether the picture you're about to take will be in focus or not.

Manual focusing is really no improvement over fixed focusing except for close-up work – many can focus on scenes as close as a metre (3ft) or less away, which makes them useful for portrait shots.

Flash

All 110 cameras can take flash pictures, but there are several different types of flash available.

Separate electronic Some 110 cameras have separate electronic flash units designed to clip or screw on to one end of the camera. The camera itself can be slightly smaller than a camera that has a built-in flash unit – but a separate flash is not as convenient to use.

Built-in electronic The easiest type to use. When you switch to flash, the camera adjusts automatically to the correct exposure. With some cameras a warning is shown in the viewfinder if there isn't enough light to take a picture without first switching on the flash. And there are some 110 cameras that switch over to flash automatically if it's needed. But built-in units are very small and, with 100 ISO films, they can light subjects only up to a couple of metres (6ft) away – faster films enable you to light up subjects further away.

Non-electronic bulbs Early cameras used **Magicubes** which fit into a special socket on the camera. Each cube has four flash bulbs and turns around automatically as you advance the film. Each bulb 'blows' as it fires, so after four flash pictures you throw the thing away. Magicubes can cause 'red eye' – people facing the camera appear to have red pupils. This can be solved by fitting an extender to raise the position of the flash cube, but this makes the camera a little unwieldy.

The type of bulb most often used now is the **Flipflash** (or **Topflash**) which plugs into the top of the camera (again into a special socket different from that on cameras which use Magicubes). You get five flashes, turn the unit over and get five more. Because a Flipflash unit is tall, you are less likely to get problems with red eye.

Bulb flash is quite expensive, and more than doubles the cost of each picture; electronic flash is the better choice.

Lenses

A 110 camera is usually fitted with a standard lens that gives much the same angle of view as that in a disc camera or SLR. You can use a telephoto lens (to make distant object appear larger, at the expense of having a narrower angle of view) with many cameras. There are three main types:

● **'tele' lens** You use a little slider to move a built-in telephoto-type lens in front of the film. The viewfinder adapts automatically, so you're able to see what sort of

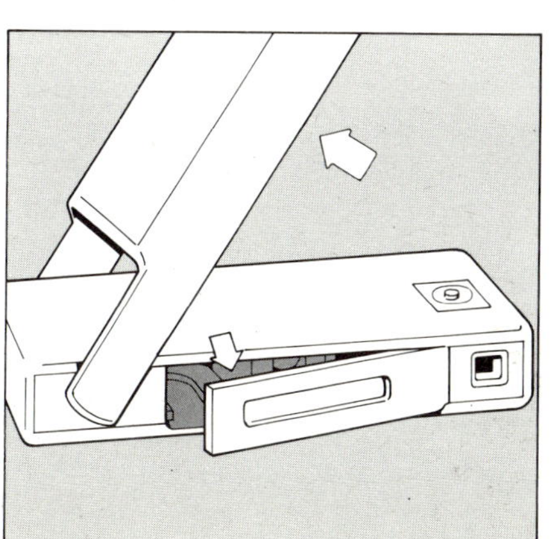
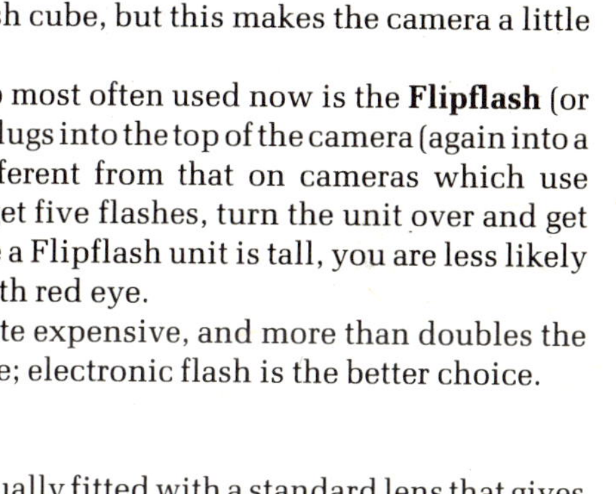
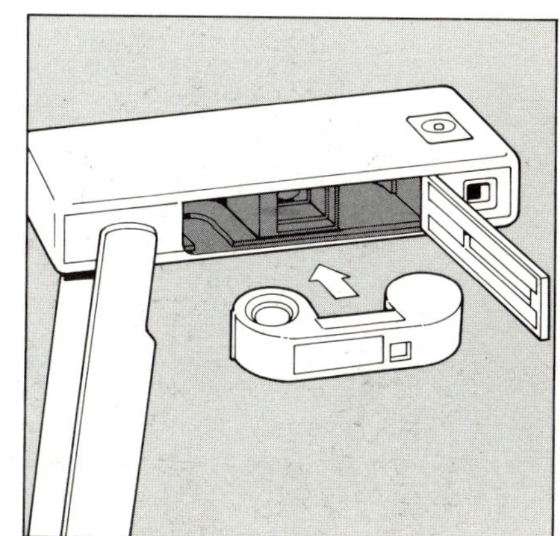

Film for a 110 camera comes in a cartridge – to load, you open the back of the camera and slip the cartridge into place

difference the tele lens will make to your shot

● **zoom lens**   This allows you to go progressively from a standard lens effect to a telephoto lens effect. The viewfinder alters progressively, too, so that you can always see what sort of a picture you will get

● **interchangeable lenses**   See 'System cameras', below.

You can also get 110 cameras with a built-in **close-up** lens to allow subjects close to the camera to remain in focus – again, useful for portraits.

Other features

There are relatively few additional features to look out for on 110 cameras.

Film winding   Winding on the film after each shot is usually very simple – you snap open and closed the camera body or push a little slider with your thumb. Some cameras have motor drive, but this doesn't move the film on any more quickly than the manual ratchet motion.

Date indicator   It may be useful to have the date, or other information, automatically added to the picture as you take it. It's important to be able to disconnect this feature though – a highly prosaic date would hardly grace a highly atmospheric photograph!

For Cousteau emulators   There have been weathertight 110 cameras available – with a sealed case for use in the rain, sandy or dusty places and so on, and even for underwater use (though not at very great depths).

System cameras   There is at least one 110 camera that behaves like a 35mm SLR (see page 11). You use the camera body as a base to which you add a whole range of accessories – interchangeable wide-angle, standard and telephoto lenses; flash units; motor drives and so on. It is a very specialised camera which is unlikely to be a good choice for the amateur.

Film

The usual film for 110 cameras is one for colour prints, rated at 100 ISO. This is relatively 'slow' and is one of the reasons why these cameras do not take good pictures in dull light.

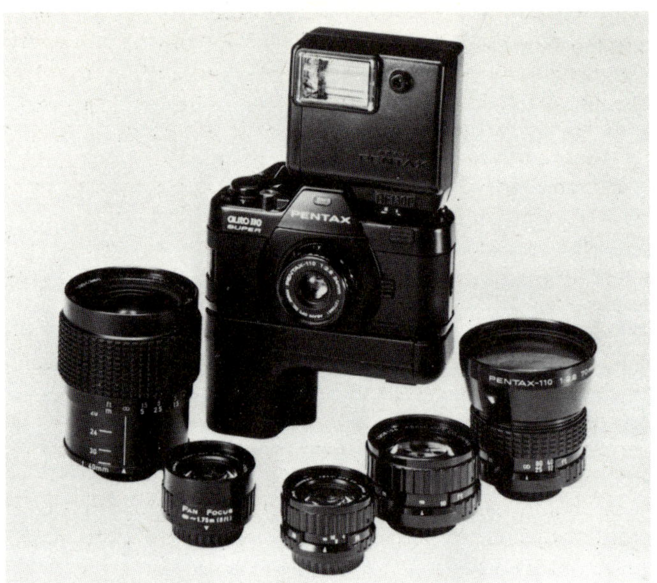

A 110 system camera, with flash, motor wind, and interchangeable lenses

The 200 ISO films are an improvement in dull weather, and should give just as good results in sunny weather.

Most cameras can also take a much faster film (400 ISO) for colour prints, and this *should* enable you to take pictures in much duller conditions or extend your range when taking flash pictures. However, there are some drawbacks:

● some cameras adjust to the faster film by sliding a filter in front of the lens – completely over-riding the value of having a faster film

● on cameras with fixed exposure, you'll certainly be able to take better pictures in dull conditions, but in very bright light (such as bright snow, beach scenes or close-up flash pictures) your photos may be over-exposed

● many automatic cameras also automatically adapt to the 400 ISO. Some don't, and with these you cannot ignore the low-light warning in the viewfinder or the shutter speed will be too low for hand-held picture taking

● the film is relatively 'grainy' (see page 24) and enlargements of prints won't be as acceptable as with 100 or 200 ISO film.

If you want the best from ISO 400 film use it in a cheap, manual camera, where you can set the exposure yourself. You'll need to experiment a bit to find out what exposure ratings give the best results – for example, on a camera having weather symbol adjustments, you should be able to set the weather to brighter than it actually is.

You *can* get slide film for 110 cameras, but it isn't a very good choice:
● slides are less tolerant of under- or over-exposure, and with the relatively poor exposure control on 110 cameras this is even more pronounced
● the slides are smaller than the conventional 35mm type. With a bit of know-how you can slip them into the frames of a conventional projector, but this exercise isn't always successful. Though there are some projectors specially designed for 110 slides, these projectors won't take 35mm slides as well
● because the slides are very small, they are enlarged greatly when projected on to the screen – this detracts from the quality of the image
● there are only a few 110 slide films available.

Ease of use

Perhaps the most useful feature of a 110 camera is its small size, but some models are relatively bulky. The type of flash used affects size quite a bit: if you hardly use flash at all, it's probably best to go for a camera that uses a separate flash. Otherwise, a built-in electronic flash is the most convenient system.

Most viewfinders include a 'bright frame' (see page 36) showing the actual extent of the picture area, but seeing the whole field of view can be difficult if you wear glasses. You might find some viewfinders easier to use with one eye than with the other. Information appearing in 110 viewfinders is limited – at best, all you will get is an over- or under-exposure warning.

Most cameras have a cover for the lens to protect it from dust and dirt. Make sure this is of the type that prevents you from pressing the shutter release when it is closed, and that it is fixed to the camera in some way: a separate lens cover can easily get lost.

Pocketing a 'pocket' camera is not actually a very sensible thing to do. Carrying one in a breast pocket is risky as it can fall out when you bend over; some cameras have a spring clip to prevent this. Sitting on a camera carried in a back pocket can break it irreparably.

Many 110 cameras seem rather less robust than they should be, given the conditions in which they're likely to be used. So treat them with some care.

Picture quality

Picture quality is not particularly good with a 110 camera. This is partly because of the small size of the film; partly because of the unsophisticated lenses; but perhaps mainly because very few 110 cameras can take good pictures in dull light. Don't necessarily believe what the manufacturers say on this – when *Which?* tested 110 cameras in 1980, few were capable of taking a correctly exposed picture outdoors on a cloudy day using the normal 100 ISO film – irrespective of whether the instructions said this would be possible or not. Results on tele lenses are often poor, too, with objects in the far distance not always in focus.

BUYING GUIDE

For most people, a 110 camera is not the best choice. For snapshots, a disc is easier to use, and more versatile; for 'serious' photography a 35mm camera will give better results and, if you go for a non-reflex type (see Chapter 4), need not be more cumbersome.

CHAPTER FOUR

NON-REFLEX CAMERAS

The 35mm non-reflex camera is often looked down on as inferior to the grown-up 35mm SLR. But there's no reason why it shouldn't produce equally good pictures – and it is smaller and cheaper

A 35mm non-reflex camera takes ordinary 35mm print or slide film – either colour or black and white. This film comes in a roll in a light-tight tin or *cassette*. Loading a 35mm camera with film used to be a bit tricky, but most newer models now have a *quick-load* film system which makes the job less painful.

Many of the modern cameras are of the 'point-and-shoot' variety, with automatic exposure and focusing to help give pictures that are correctly lit and always sharp. But the cheaper models rely on you doing most of the work, so they are less foolproof.

You can take extremely good pictures with a non-reflex 35mm camera, whether manual or automatic. The only important difference between a non-reflex and an SLR (single-lens reflex, described in the next chapter) is that you can't generally change lenses on the non-reflex so you're stuck with one angle of view. Another difference is that you don't see through the viewfinder exactly the same picture as the film sees through the lens. In fact, this *parallax* error is not important, except for close-ups: more details on page 36.

Non-reflex cameras have some important advantages over SLRs. Feature for feature, they are cheaper – anything down to half the price. They are quite a bit less bulky and heavy – again, half the weight or less. And they are quieter in operation, so there is less risk of scaring off the birds you're photographing, or of causing a disturbance if you are taking pictures during, say, a religious ceremony.

Exposure

There is a wide range of methods of varying the exposure so that the pictures you take will appear correctly lit, with the light and dark parts properly contrasted.

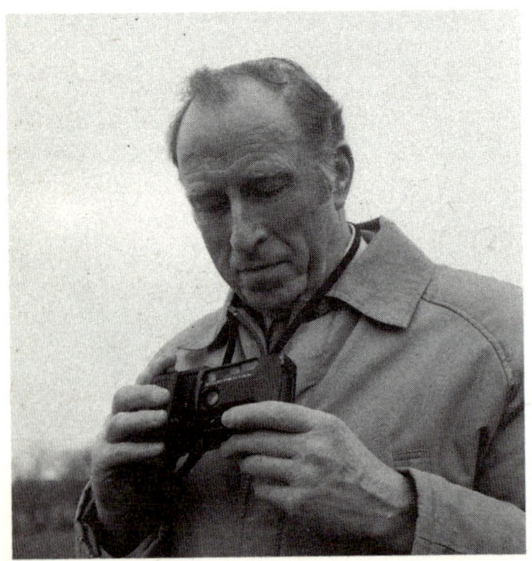
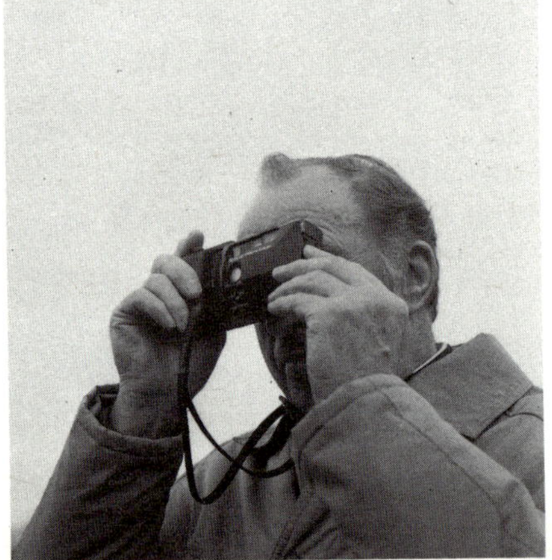
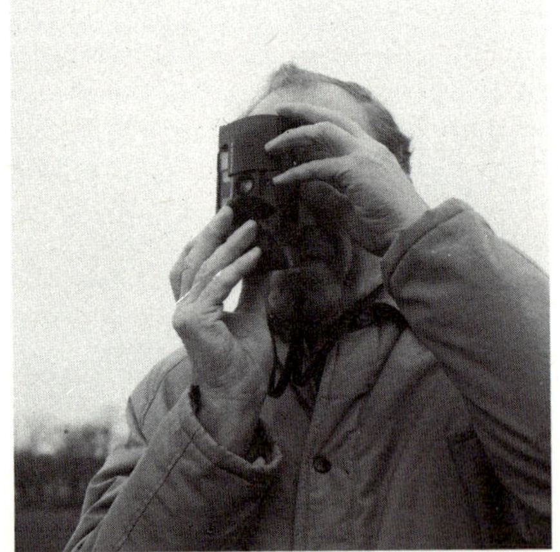

Manual – full control   Here you are able to adjust both the *aperture* and the *shutter speed* (see pages 42 to 47 for an explanation of what these are and what they do) as you like. Most cameras have a built-in *exposure meter* to give you an indication of whether your combination of aperture and shutter speed settings will produce a picture that is properly exposed, or under- or over-exposed.

The advantage is that you have full control over the picture you are to take: you can decide what *depth of field* you want (to control the range of things you want in focus); you can adjust shutter speed (for action shots); you can deliberately under-expose or over-expose; and generally make creative decisions about the look of your pictures. The drawback is that setting the controls is fiddly and you may make mistakes leading to poor pictures.

In general, if you want this level of creative control over your picture-taking you would be better off with an SLR camera, which offers even greater potential for this sort of thing, unless the small size or other advantages of the non-reflex type were overwhelmingly important to you.

Manual – symbols   Like the 110 camera (see Chapter 3) you alter exposure with a small control marked with weather symbols – cloud, sun, and so on. There is less chance of taking poor pictures with this arrangement, but you have very little control over the type of picture you get. These cameras are few and far between these days.

Fixed   The only method of varying the exposure with these cameras is to use films of different speeds, or to switch to flash – as with 110 cameras. Compared with other methods, this limits the ability of the camera to take pictures in a wide range of weather conditions. You will get best results if you use print, rather than slide, film because this has a greater tolerance to over- or under-exposing – much can be allowed for during printing.

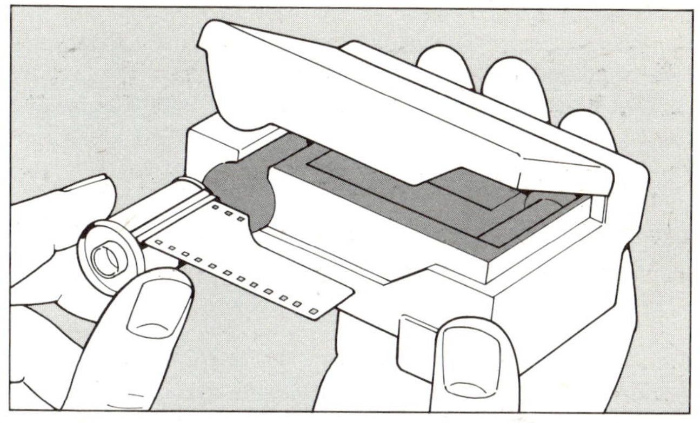

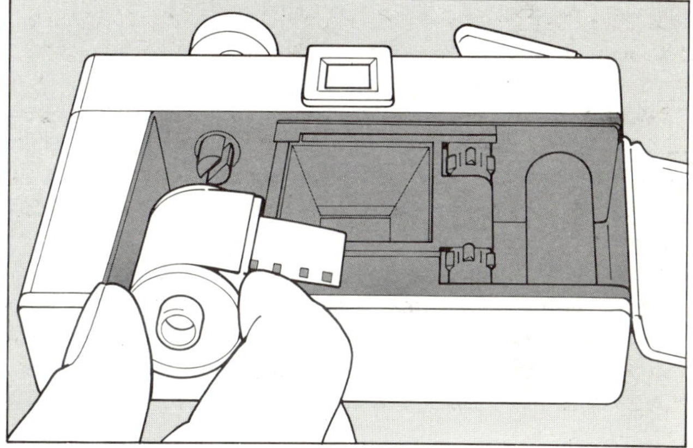

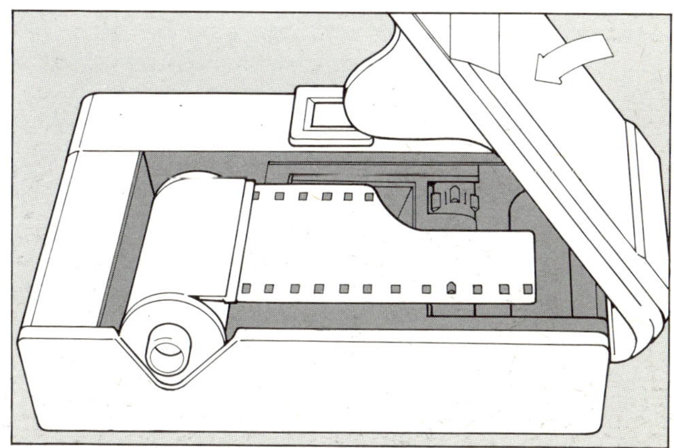

Right   Loading systems for non-reflex cameras vary – the one shown **top** is very easy: you just slip the film into a slot. The system shown in the other two drawings is a little less easy – after placing the cassette in the camera you must pull the end of the film out and place it over the cogs on the take-up spool

Automatic, programmed   These cameras do everything for themselves, selecting both the aperture and the shutter speed. Information in the viewfinder usually shows what has been selected. Together with autofocusing (see below) this produces a camera where all you have to do to get a good (99 times out of a hundred) picture is to point and shoot.

Automatic, priority   With this type of camera, you select *either* the aperture *or* the shutter speed you want, and the camera adjusts the other control accordingly. So you have got some control over what the camera is doing, as with manual exposure, but there is rather less adjusting for you to do. But again, if you are this interested in photography and don't absolutely need the particular advantages of a non-reflex camera, go for an SLR instead.

Other automatic mechanisms   There is a range of other types of automatic control in which you don't have to set anything to take a picture. They work by adjusting either the shutter speed or the aperture, but don't alter the other control at all (or only when you change film speed, or switch to flash). Though they are capable of giving good pictures in most conditions, they are not as good as a fully-automatic programmed camera.

Focusing

Non-reflex cameras may have either **fixed**, **manual**, or **auto** focusing.

Fixed focusing   This is the simplest and cheapest method and can give good results. The main drawback is that you cannot take close-ups: with some cameras, only objects more than 1.5m (5ft) away will be in focus, though many fixed-focus cameras give you acceptably sharp pictures down to a metre (3ft) away. (Strictly, this depends on the size of the aperture: if you can set the camera to a smalller aperture you will be able to focus more closely.)

Manual focusing   With these cameras, you alter the focusing yourself to get a picture that's as sharp as possible. Once the only type available, manual focusing is now fast disappearing, and is used mainly on specially small cameras, or those aimed at professional photographers.

There are two main systems:
● **symbol or scale focusing**   With symbol focusing, the focusing ring on the camera lens is marked with symbols (portrait, group, landscape, say) and you set to whichever symbol you think will give you the best result. With scale focusing, the focusing ring is marked in feet and metres, and you have to adjust the ring after estimating as accurately as possible the distance between the camera and the subject. You can't actually tell from looking at the picture in the viewfinder whether the picture you're about to take will be in focus or not – but some viewfinders show you what scale point or symbol the focusing is set to so you can check this without taking your eye off the picture
● **coupled rangefinder**   Here the viewfinder gives you an idea of what parts of the picture will be sharp. A small area in the centre of the viewfinder shows a double image until you adjust the focus to make the two images merge into one. Only a few cameras still use this system – it is expensive to manufacture.

Autofocus   Many cameras now have some form of automatic focusing. Most use a system which bounces a beam of infra-red (invisible) light off the subject. A few may still use a system which compares the image as seen by two sensors in the camera – this system is somewhat more easily fooled by dull subjects or those having a regular pattern (such as a brick wall).

One point to watch out for is that autofocus takes its measurements from the centre of the picture. This is usually fine, because this is the part you'll normally want in best focus – but there will be times when the main subject is to one side, and a central autofocus may put the background in focus leaving the main subject fuzzy (the pictures on page 34 show an example of this in practice).

To avoid this, without having to settle for boring centre-stage shots all the time, you need a camera with a **hold** facility. Here, you can point the camera at your main subject, press the shutter release half-way to hold the focus while you move the camera to compose your scene, and then take the picture. Some cameras have a separate control for the hold, which is a little less convenient. Usually, you can cancel the focus hold once you have set it; sometimes you cannot – a disadvantage.

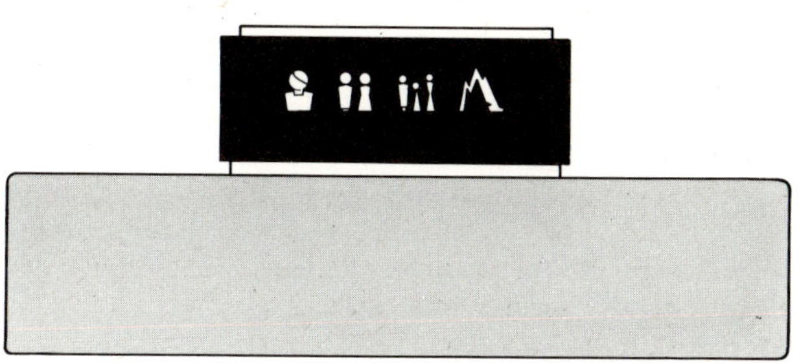

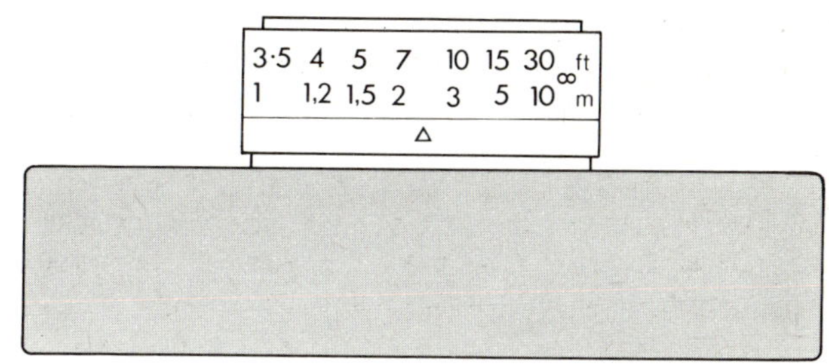

The focusing ring on the lens of this camera is marked with symbols...

...this one is marked in feet and metres

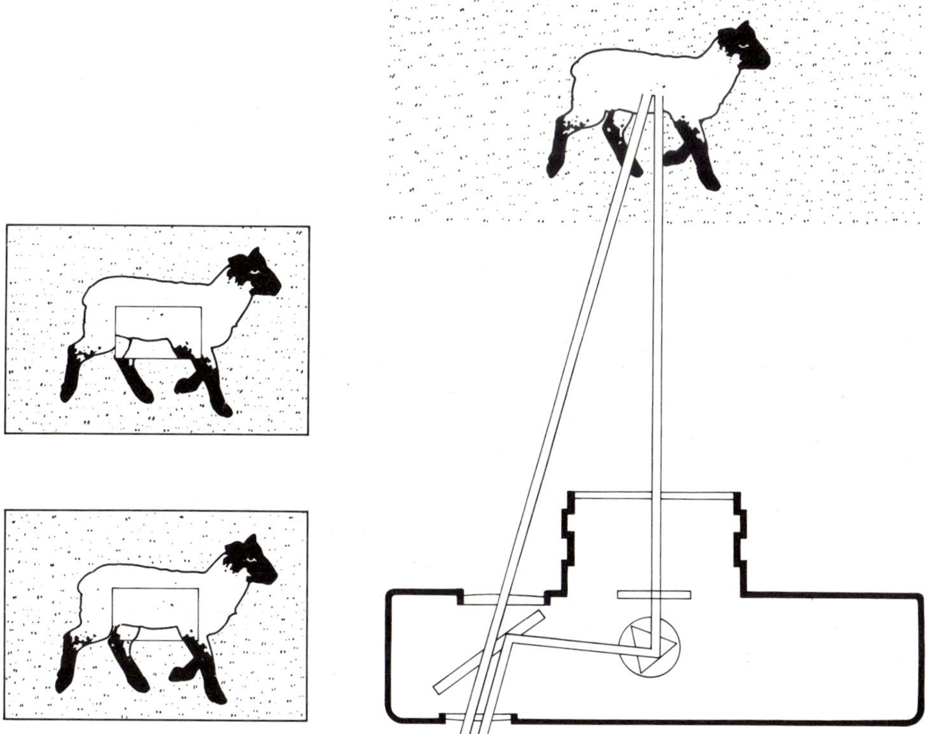

With a coupled rangefinder system, you can check through the viewfinder whether your picture will be sharp or not. Light from the scene in front of you enters the viewfinder both directly and via the lens. Until the lens is adjusted so that the picture is in focus on the film, the two paths create slightly different images – so the central part of the view in the viewfinder is offset from the surrounding part. Only when the picture is properly focused will the two views coincide to give you an unbroken image in the viewfinder

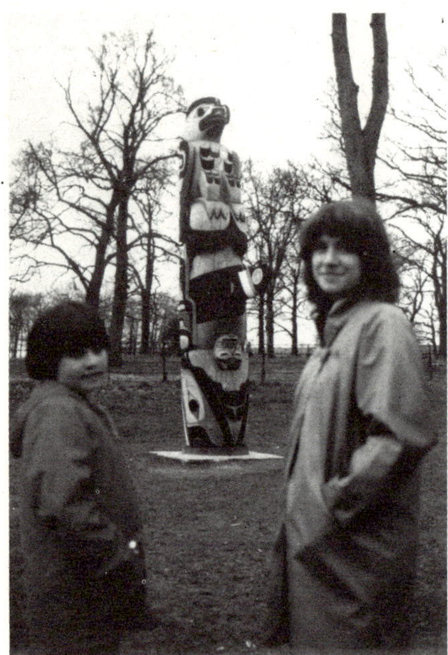

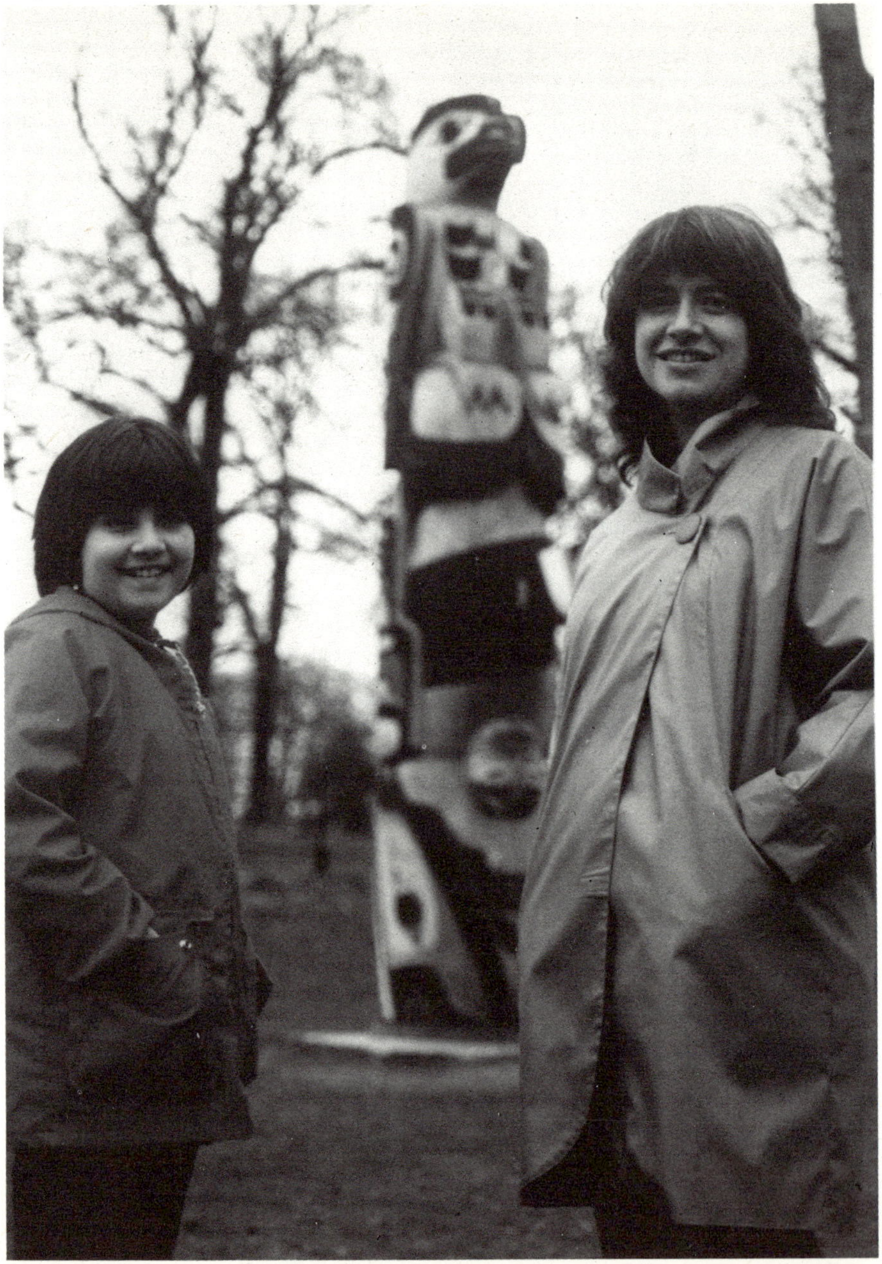

Above Autofocus systems take their cue from the subject in the centre of the scene, so if your main subject is to one side it could be thrown out of focus
Right A camera with a *hold* facility will allow you to make sure the main subjects are in focus wherever they are placed

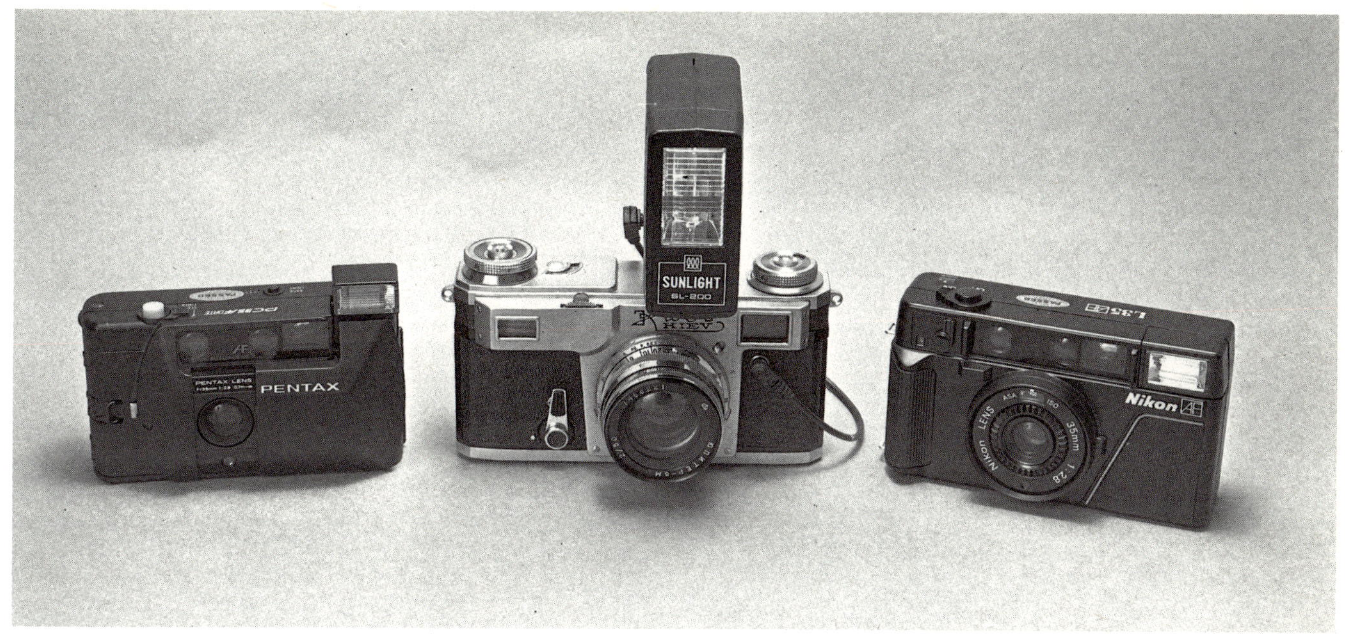

Different types of flash unit are available for non-reflex cameras. The middle one is a separate unit; the others are built-in

Flash

Most cameras these days have **built-in electronic** flash. Usually there is a *low light indicator* to show when there isn't enough light to take a picture without first switching on the flash: some cameras now have **sensor flash**, which turns itself on automatically whenever it is needed.

Built-in flash costs hardly anything to run, but the units are very small and they have a limited *flash range* – they can't light up subjects very far away. The best can manage a range of about 6m (20ft) but many can manage only half that and some even less. This is with 100 ISO film (see pages 91 to 95 for what this means). You could increase the distance by almost a half with 200 ISO film, double it with 400 ISO film, or increase it by over three times with 1000 ISO film.

Some 35mm cameras have a **separate flash** unit which you screw or clip on to one end of the camera. So the camera by itself can be smaller, and this makes it more convenient to use for the times when you know you won't need flash.

Separate flash units can be more powerful, too, and light up subjects further away. But however easy the units are to attach to the camera, you're never ready to take flash pictures quite as quickly as you are with a built-in unit – and there's the fag of having to carry around and remember about a separate piece of equipment.

Lenses

Almost all these cameras come with a fixed lens offering just one angle of view – you can't interchange lenses nor is there any built-in 'telephoto' lens as there is on some 110 or disc cameras. The lens is a slightly wider-angle type than that fitted to other cameras, so you can get a lot of the view into the picture. This is a good choice for point-and-shoot photography: it's useful for indoor pictures and for photographing buildings. And you can get away without accurate focusing – almost everything from relatively close by up to infinity will be reasonably sharp.

A few 35mm non-reflex cameras *do* have interchangeable lenses, but they are extremely expensive and not very easy to use – mainly for the professional photographer.

Viewfinder information

The most important piece of information a viewfinder can give you, of course, is a clear view of what it is you're about to take. Some cameras go a lot further than this, and include all sorts of detail on focusing, exposure, and so on visible within the viewfinder itself, so that you can check on all the data while you are composing your shot.

Of course, however interesting all this information is, it shouldn't get in the way of the image appearing in the viewfinder. With completely automatic (programmed) cameras, all you need to know is whether you can take the picture or not, and to be able to visualise exactly what it is that you are going to take. So you just need the minimum of information: anything else might lead to confusion.

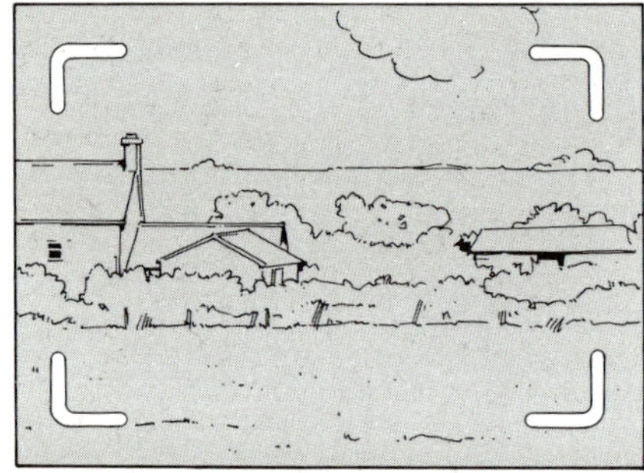

Bright frame

This is a clearly-marked border round the edge of the viewfinder which is supposed to show you just what will appear in your print or slide – no more and no less. Unfortunately, you tend to lose a bit round the edges of the picture when the film is processed – more so with prints than with slides. Most camera viewfinders are designed to allow for this, so that you don't chop off Aunt Edna's head by mistake. However, they often go too far, and you'll get more in your picture than you bargained for – your nicely composed shot will come back from the processors showing a lot of road in front or a telephone pole at the side, and the people in the middle will be smaller than you thought they would be. On some cameras, the viewfinder is not correctly centred, so what you thought was right over at the edge of the picture may be some little way towards the centre. *Which?* has even tested a camera where the lens and viewfinder were pointing in slightly different directions.

It is a good idea to experiment with a new camera before you start to take serious pictures. Set up shots with easily-recognisable (and memorable) landmarks – a telephone pole, the eaves of a house roof and so on. (To avoid errors from parallax – see below – keep about four metres or more back from your landmarks.) Take pictures with these landmarks coinciding with the bright frame borders in your viewfinder. When your pictures come back from the processors check how they correspond with the views as you composed them – remember the differences and try to compensate for them when you take important shots.

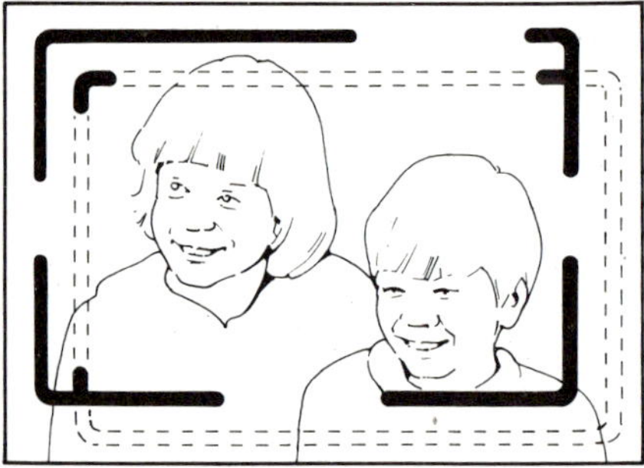

Parallax lines

The viewfinder lens that you look through is at a slightly different position from the one that the film 'looks' through. This means that what you see and what the film sees are slightly different images – this is **parallax error**. The pictures opposite show how this occurs, and demonstrate the effect it can have on your photographs.

Because the two lenses are so very close together, however, the two versions of the scene are very similar, and at distances beyond a couple of metres (6ft) there is no need to worry about this effect – the bright frame marks could be positioned to reduce most of the error.

However, in close-up work the effect of parallax is greater, and there is more of a danger that you will unwittingly chop off heads in your pictures. So some viewfinders have extra markings showing which of the close-up parts of the scene you can see through the viewfinder should actually appear on the photo (at least in theory – again, many viewfinders' close-up markings are rather inaccurate, and you would be well advised to experiment with your camera to find out how it behaves in practice).

Right To help you check on the accuracy of your camera's viewfinder, pick a subject with strong lines in it – such as this building with its steps in front. Make a sketch of how it appears in the viewfinder and compare this with the print you get back from the film processors

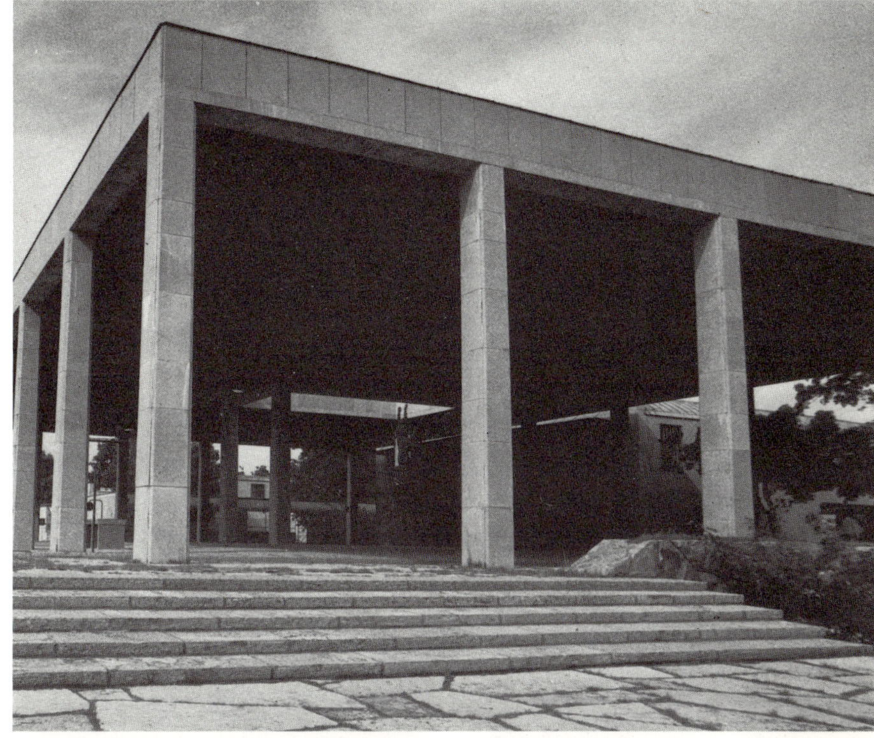

Below The viewfinder and lens see slightly different parts of the scene in front of the camera, which affects close-up shots. The viewfinder shows that your photo of the boy should be nicely composed (**centre**); the picture you get back from the processors (**right**) shows that the lens has sliced off the top of his head

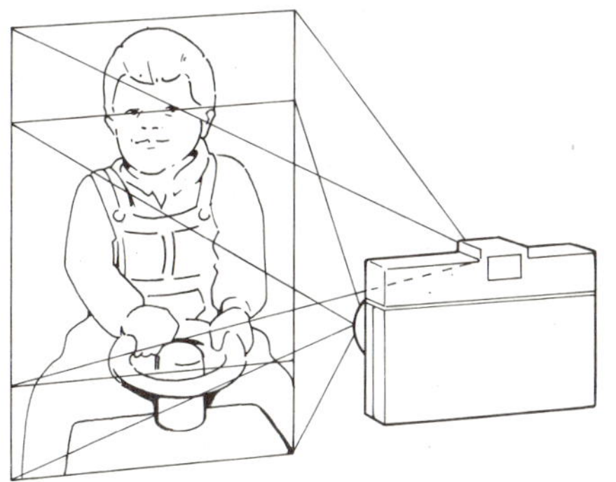

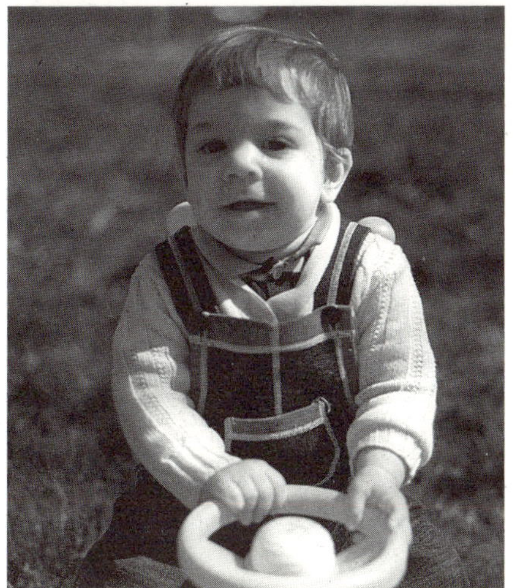

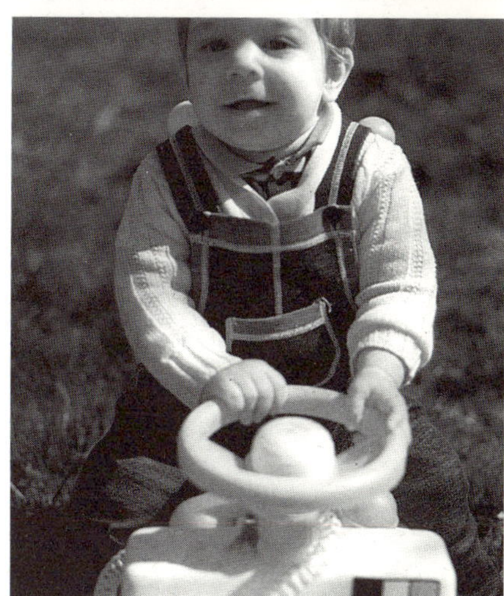

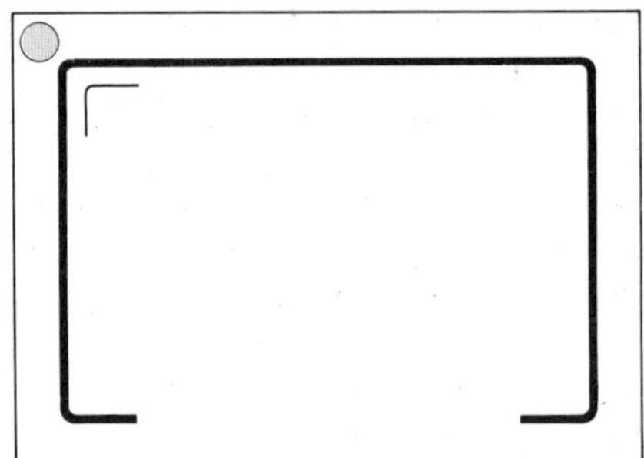

Flash

When flash is turned on – either manually or automatically – you have to wait a few seconds (the time gets longer as the batteries run down) until a *flash ready light* in or near the viewfinder comes on. If you are not in a hurry to take your picture, it is a good idea to wait 15 seconds or so longer after the light comes on to be sure that you will get the brightest light possible from your flash. Some cameras have interlock mechanisms to prevent you pressing the shutter release for a flash picture until the ready-light comes on. If there isn't an interlock and the light isn't actually in the viewfinder check that it is close enough for you to be able to see it without taking your eye away from the viewfinder.

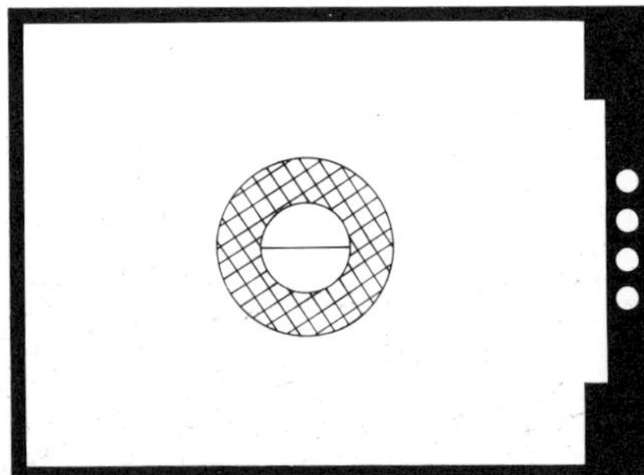

Exposure

With non-auto cameras, or auto cameras that can be operated manually, you need an indicator of some sort which will tell you how you have to alter the aperture or the shutter speed to get a properly-exposed picture. With a fully-auto camera, there is no need for this, but even an auto camera will run out of adjustment in very bright or very dull light, so you need some indication of whether the picture you are about to take will come out at all: most auto cameras have an over- and under-exposure warning indicator to tell you this. Some give an audible warning (one even speaks!) and with some, the shutter locks so that you cannot take a picture. It's important, though, that the camera allows you to over-ride this shutter lock – there are times when you may deliberately want an under- or over-exposed picture, either for artistic reasons or because the shot is so important that any picture is better than none.

If you haven't set the shutter speed yourself, you need to know when you are about to take a picture that will involve a long exposure time – when camera shake or movement of the subject could cause blurring. So an indicator to tell you when the exposure time is longer than about $\frac{1}{60}$ second is useful.

Automatic cameras with aperture priority or shutter priority are intended for more serious photography and you need information on what aperture or shutter speed the camera has selected for you. Usually these cameras also indicate simple over- or under-exposure.

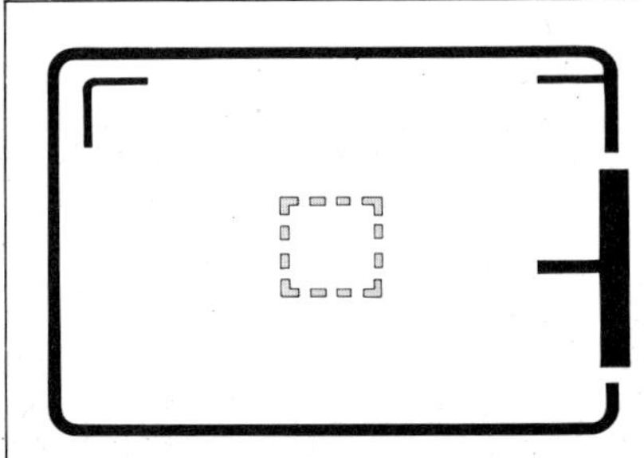

Focus

Cameras with autofocus indicate the area for which focusing is correct by means of a frame in the viewfinder known as the autofocus spot. With manual focus cameras, the focus distance may be indicated by symbols, or shown by a range-finder system (as described earlier in this chapter).

Date marking   With some cameras the date appears in the viewfinder. You set this yourself and it appears in reverse order – so that 4 August 1984 becomes 84 8 4. You can if you wish use a code number of some sort instead. Check whether the date or code will appear on the picture itself – and if it does, whether you can switch this feature off.

Other features

There are relatively few additional features to look out for on a 35mm non-reflex camera.

Film loading   Loading a 35mm cassette into a camera has traditionally been tricky – you have to slot the end of the film into the take-up spool and make sure it is held securely and the film is lying correctly before closing the back. Then you have to 'take' two or three waste pictures to move on the start of the film that was exposed to light as you loaded the camera. Many models now have 'quick-load' systems (see the drawings on page 31) that do away with much of this hassle. Systems vary, and not all are equally easy to use.

Unloading a 35mm film is easier than loading it. Usually you simply wind the film back into the cassette using a little handle (there's a safety button that prevents the handle from having any effect normally, so it's difficult to wind the film back accidentally). Once the film is completely back in the cassette, you simply open the camera back and lift it out. Some quick-load systems make the job easier by providing a motor to rewind the film for you.

Film winding   A manual-wind camera is not difficult to operate – after you have taken a picture, you move on to the next unexposed piece of film by operating a lever or turning a knob. With a motor wind, a built-in motor moves the film on automatically as soon as a picture has been taken: if you are not using flash you can take the next shot after little more

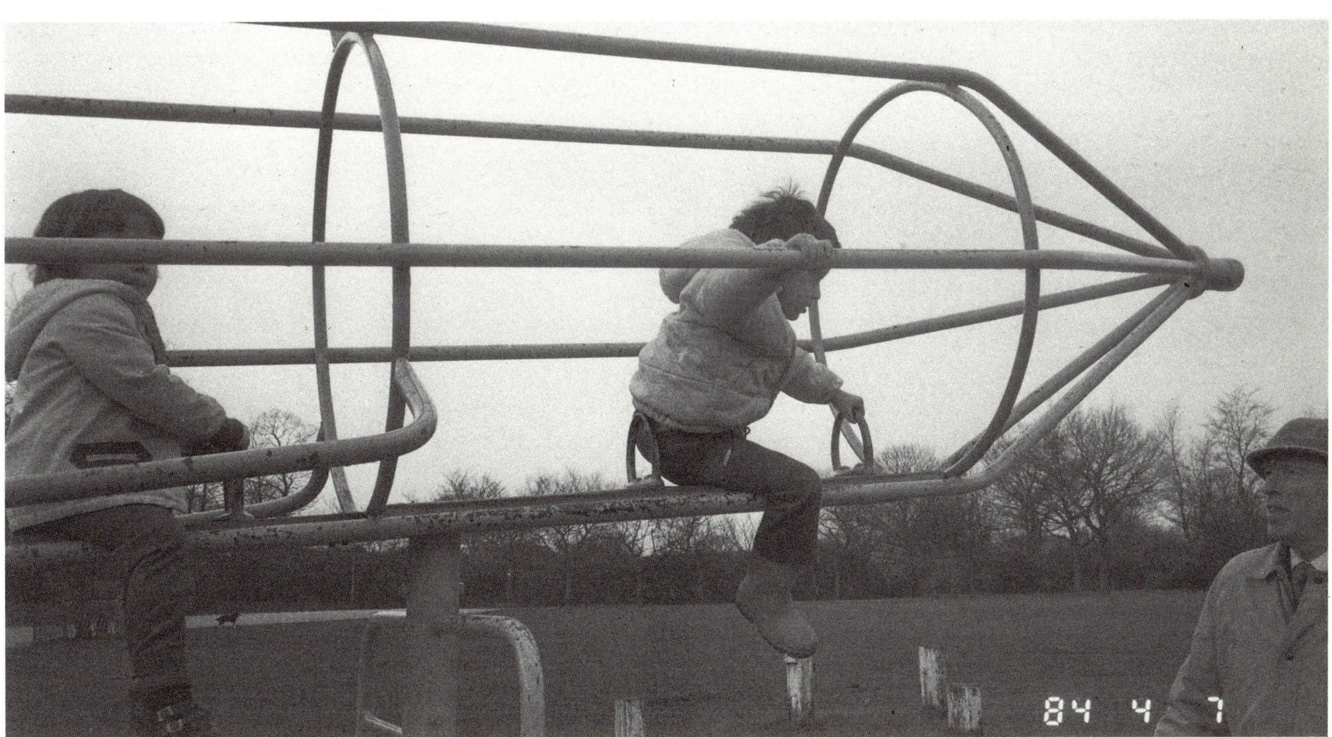

Date-marking your pictures makes it easier to recall the occasion on which you took them

With motor-wind you can shoot a series of pictures easily and quickly and pick out the best for enlargement later

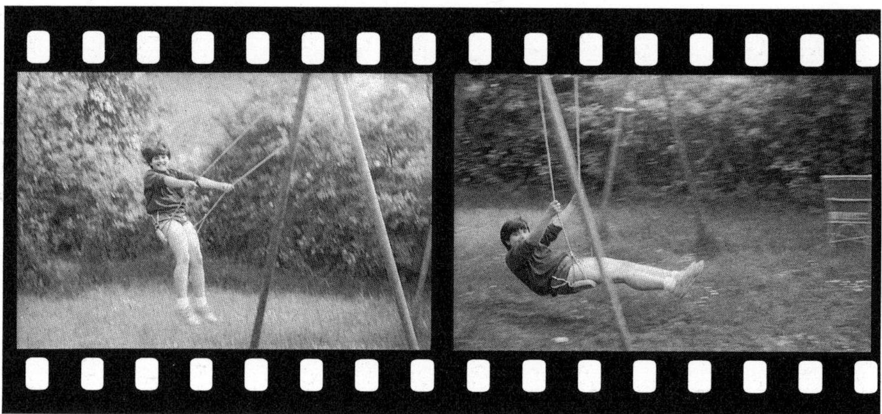

than a fraction of a second. Though point-and-shoot photographers don't really need motor wind for its ability to take tens of pictures a minute it is a useful convenience. In any case, almost all cameras with quick-loading systems also have motor drive.

Film

One of the advantages of 35mm non-reflex cameras is that they can use many of the wide range of 35mm films available. However, not all cameras have the right *film speed settings* to benefit from the total range, though in practice you can get by with a very restricted range of films – less even than the most basic cameras offer. There's more details of film types in Chapter 8, but briefly:

● you need settings for at least 100 ISO and 400 ISO films plus 200 ISO if you want to use slide film – all cameras are likely to have these, except the very cheapest which may not have 200 ISO

● some cameras can adjust to any film speed between their upper and lower limits. Others can be set only to discrete settings – these often miss out a 200 ISO setting

● settings for 64 ISO and 1000 ISO film are quite useful

● you are unlikely to need to use 25 ISO slide film but, for the more advanced photographer, a setting for this film is quite useful with faster film (for example, Kodachrome 64) if you are taking pictures with the light coming from behind the subject. This makes the camera give the extra exposure that the subject needs (see page 52 for the how and why of all this).

Similarly, at the other end of the scale, many cameras do not have settings for the new 1000 ISO print and slide films, but you can get good results from the print film with cameras that have only 800 ISO, and often only 400 ISO, settings because there is wide 'exposure latitude' with print film.

Ease of use

Though a non-reflex camera is smaller and lighter than an SLR, it is still a bit larger than the 110 or disc format, and most cannot be carried in a pocket or handbag. There are extra-small versions available that are just about pocketable – but check that you do not lose out on other worthwhile features if you choose one of these.

If you really need small size, look for a camera with a separate flash unit – but remember that this will not be as convenient to use for flash, and, unless you take very few flash pictures, you're probably better off sacrificing very small size for convenience in other departments.

If you carry a camera around a lot, it's important to protect it (particularly the lens) from dust and dirt. Most cameras have a cover for the lens – make sure it is of the type that prevents the shutter releasing when it is closed, and that it is fixed to the camera in some way: a separate lens cover can easily get lost. Cameras usually come with a case or pouch – these vary in quality but all sorts of separate camera bags can be bought if you need something better.

Ease of use is largely dependent, with these cameras, on how automatic they are. So look for fully automatic exposure

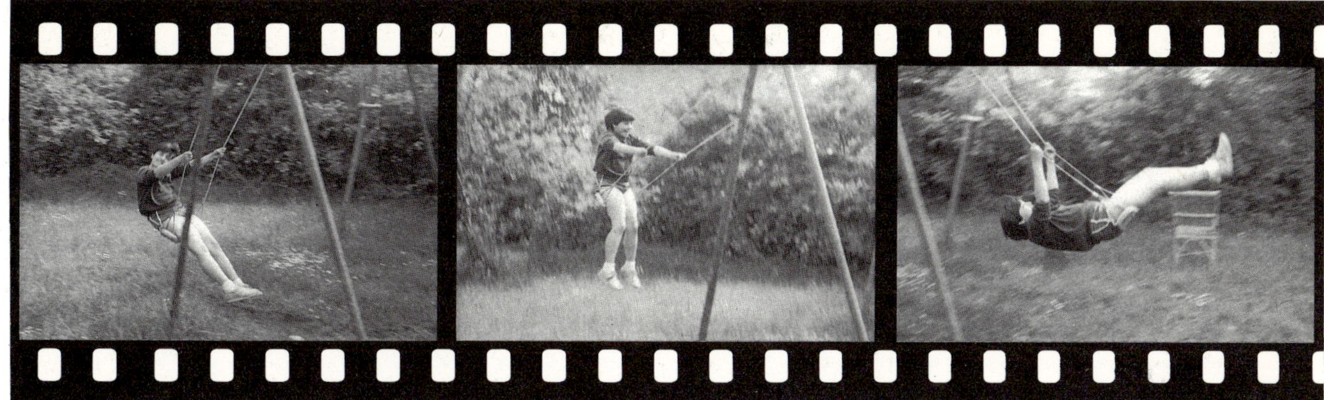

and focusing, motor wind and a quick-load system.

Check what information you can see in the viewfinder. If you wear glasses, some cameras will be easier to use than others. This depends on you to some extent, so check before you buy.

Picture quality

The best 35mm non-reflex cameras should be capable of producing pictures every bit as good as most 35mm SLR cameras – they use the same film, and the quality of the lenses in the two cameras can be equally good.

A fully automatic camera *can* produce high-quality pictures – but not under all conditions, so you are a little bit limited as to what you can do. Similarly, the fact that you cannot interchange lenses limits the type of shot you can take, and the effects you can get. It is impossible to describe exactly what would be possible, and what not – in general you can certainly take high-quality family album shots in a reasonable range of lighting conditions, but you may come unstuck when you try to take more 'artistic' types of picture.

If you feel the need to be more adventurous with your picture-taking, you could buy a manual camera – being able to set exposure, focusing and depth of field for yourself will certainly increase the types of shot you can take. *But* if you want this amount of flexibility, you probably also want the ability to change lenses, so you really should go for an SLR camera.

A compromise might be an automatic non-reflex camera which also allows you to set the shutter speed or the aperture while the camera sets the other control. With one of these, you could still take shots relatively easily, and at the same time familiarise yourself with techniques – how to take action shots; what depth of field is all about; how to compensate for particular light conditions. This sort of camera might appeal to someone who wants good pictures easily, but still wants to learn something about the art of photography.

BUYING GUIDE

If you want good pictures easily, then a 35mm non-reflex camera is a good choice. For the greatest convenience (though at a price) get one with all the automatic features:

- built-in flash
- auto exposure and focusing
- quick-loading system
- motor wind and rewind.

For good pictures from something reasonably easy to use but with you still in control, think about an automatic camera where you can set either the aperture or the shutter speed. If you must be fully in control, a non-reflex camera is not the best choice – read about SLRs. A manual non-reflex makes sense only if you need something small that still is capable of taking excellent pictures.

CHAPTER FIVE

SLR CAMERAS

Used by professionals and amateurs alike, the 35mm single lens reflex offers enormous scope for creative photography. But it is expensive and can be complex to use

The 35mm SLR camera has two main features:
● you can **interchange lenses** so that you can alter the angle of view, depth of field and perspective of your shots. This greatly increases the scope of photography, taking it out of mere 'picture-taking' and into the area of creativity
● you can view the scene you're about to take **through the lens** being used to take the picture. This gives you an accurate image of the scene – an image that will change, of course, depending on the type of lens you are using.

These features are not unique to the 35mm SLR – there are cameras which take other sizes of film that use the SLR principle to show you the view through the lens; and there are some non-reflex cameras that offer something in the way of interchangeable lenses. But it's only in the 35mm SLR that you get the potential for such high quality pictures at a reasonable price (compared with more 'professional' types of camera); such a wide range of cameras, lenses and many other accessories; and the choice between fully-automatic and fully-manual operation (with all the steps in between).

However, SLRs are fairly bulky and cannot be carried in the pocket. On their own, they are relatively heavy – and if you are lured by the possibilities of the available accessories, you could easily find yourself carrying around a small suitcase full of gear. Compared with other 'amateur' format cameras they are relatively expensive – you could get a good-quality non-reflex camera (but of course without the potential for changing lenses) for about half the price of an SLR. Although modern SLRs are available that are fully automatic, you won't be getting the best out of the format unless you are using manual operation frequently, which makes them complex to use. And film loading (though getting easier on the latest models) is a little fiddly.

To make the most of the potential of an SLR camera you need to know rather more about the theory of photography, and how you can control the various elements that go to make up a picture, than you do for using the other types of camera covered in this book. This chapter gives you the necessary information – mostly in the section 'Controlling exposure', below.

Controlling exposure

Most SLRs have some means of automatically controlling exposure so that just the right amount of light falls on the film to give a picture that is correctly lit. But being able to set exposure manually is an important part of creative picture-taking: to understand why, you need to know a little about the mechanics of exposure control and their effects.

Light from the scene you are photographing reaches the film in your camera through – putting it very crudely – a hole in the front of the camera, and the amount of light falling on to the film can be controlled in two ways:
● by regulating the **time** during which the light is allowed to reach the film
● by altering the **quantity** of light reaching the film during this time.

An SLR camera allows you to use both these methods of controlling exposure. It has an adjustable *shutter* covering the 'hole' which can remain open for different periods of time, and an adjustable diaphragm or *aperture* which can vary the size of the hole – see the drawing on page 18.

The length of time for which the shutter is open is known as its shutter *speed*. There is a set of standard speeds forming a progression in which each speed represents roughly half as much time as the previous setting: the shorter opening times

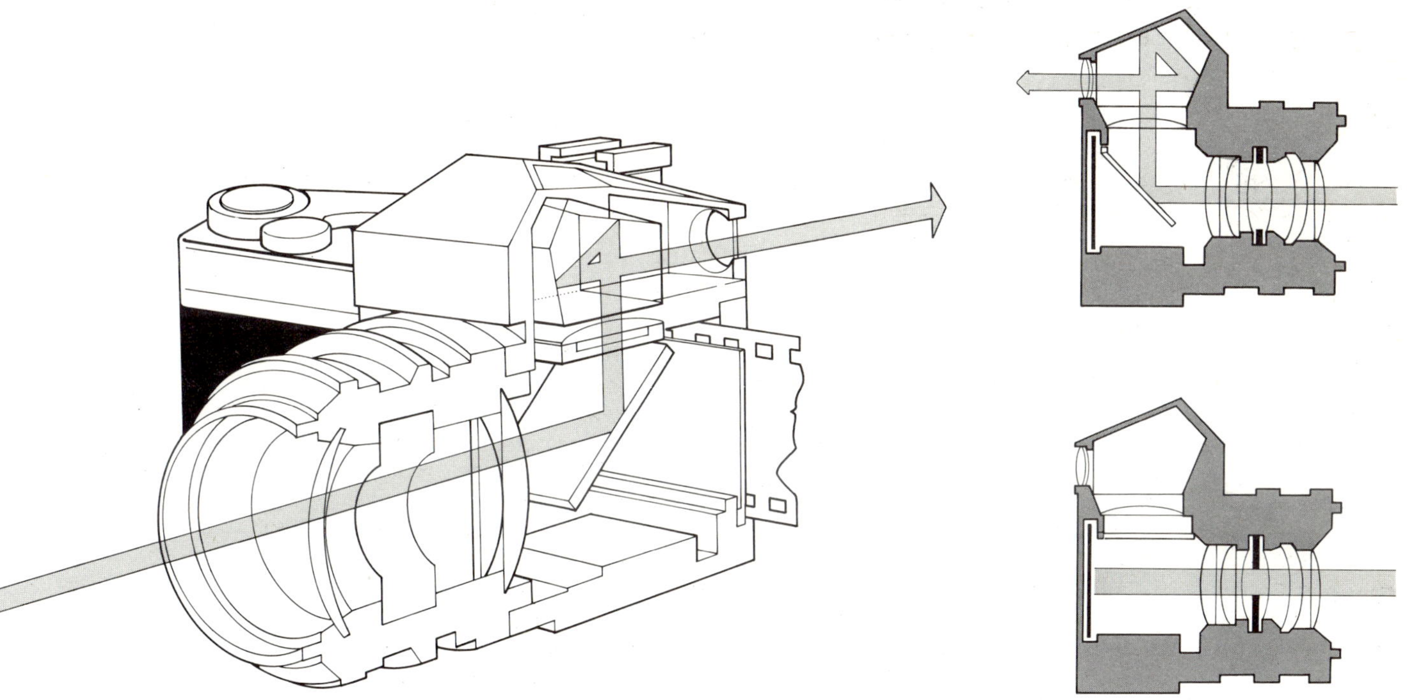

In a *reflex* camera, you see an image of scene as it is focused on to a ground glass screen – in the same way that an image is focused on to the film. With a single-lens reflex camera, the image you see passes through the same lens as that used to take the picture. A mirror placed in front of the film reflects the image towards your viewing screen. The main advantage of this arrangement is that you see the same image that the film sees, irrespective of the angle of view of the lens being used. It also ensures that there is no *parallax* error (see page 37). The image reflected from the mirror is reversed from left to right – to correct for this, the light rays are passed through a *pentaprism* which reverses the image again. The pentaprism also provides the viewing screen

When you press the shutter release, the mirror springs out of the way of the film, the shutter opens to expose the film to light, then shuts. Then the mirror drops. During the time the mirror is moved, you can't see the image in the viewfinder – but as shutters are usually open for only a fraction of a second this is not a major disadvantage

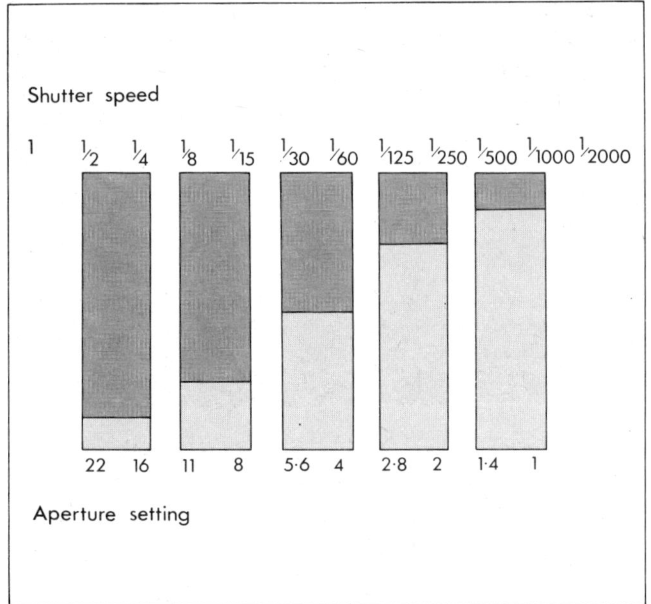

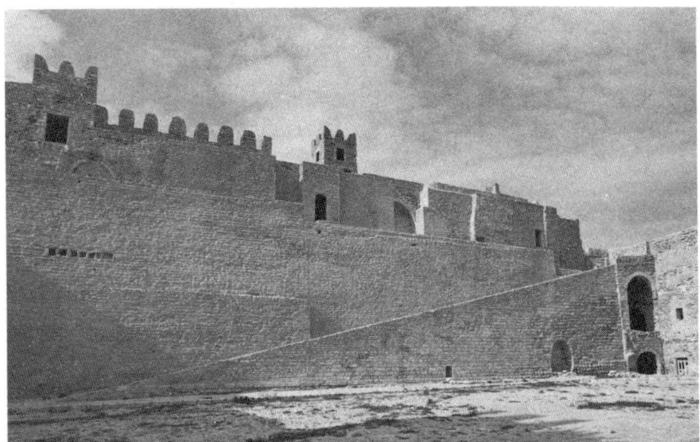

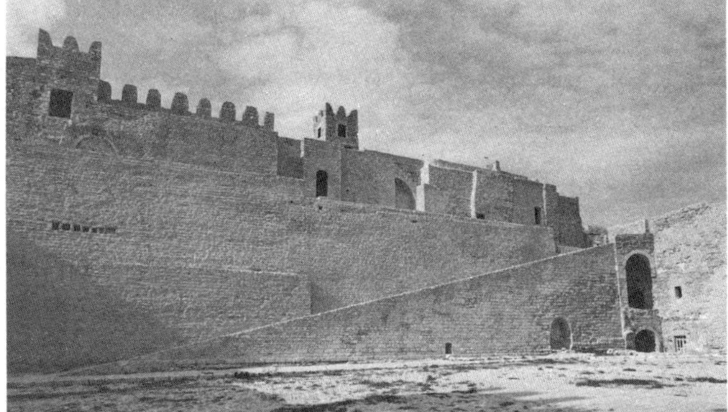

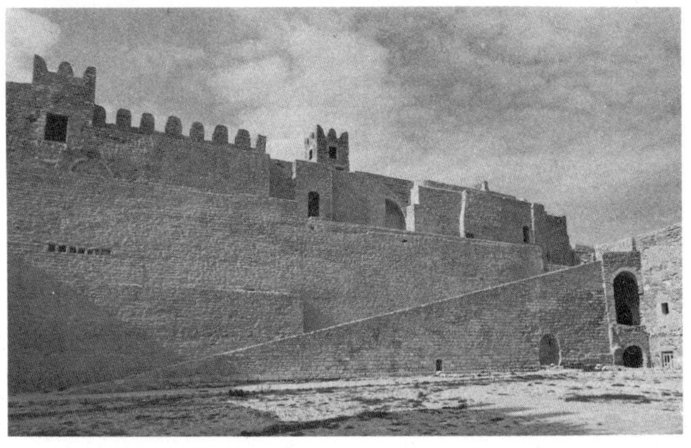

are sometimes referred to as *fast* shutter speeds; and the longer ones as *slow* speeds. These standard settings are shown in the drawing above.

The size of hole cannot be expressed simply as, say, its diameter because the quantity of light transmitted depends on other things as well. Instead, aperture sizes are described in terms of *f numbers* – a given f number always implies the same quantity of light reaching the film in a given amount of time. Again, there is a standard set of f numbers forming a progression in which each number implies roughly half the quantity of light as the previous number. Note that f numbers run backwards – the bigger the number, the smaller the amount of light (that is, the smaller the aperture).

The difference between one standard setting and the next (whether shutter speed or aperture setting, and whether an increase or a decrease) is called a 'stop'. So, for example, increasing the exposure time by changing the shutter speed from 1/30 second to 1/15 second is called something like 'giving one stop more exposure'; decreasing the exposure time by changing the aperture setting from f5.6 to f11 might be called 'stopping down by a couple of stops'.

Left These photos were taken with different combinations of shutter speed and aperture size. The **middle** one used $\frac{1}{250}$ second at f11. The **top** one used *half* the speed and *twice* the aperture size – $\frac{1}{500}$ second at f8. The **bottom** one used *twice* the speed and *half* the aperture – $\frac{1}{125}$ second at f16. In each case, the same total amount of light has fallen on the film, and as you can see, each one looks the same

Right These photos were also taken with different shutter speeds (and so, to get a properly-exposed picture, with different aperture sizes). But, as you can see, this time there is a difference between them. The **top** picture uses a very fast shutter speed so that the moving car is 'frozen' in its tracks – good if you want a sharp picture, but it doesn't convey any sense of movement. The other two pictures use a slower shutter speed to help give this impression. In the **middle** picture, the car has travelled a short distance while the shutter was open so it presents a blurred image on the film. In the **bottom** picture the camera is moved from right to left, tracking the car, so the car remains sharp in the photo but the background is blurred. To use this *panning* action successfully, start tracking your car before you press the shutter release, and carry on following it for a short while afterwards

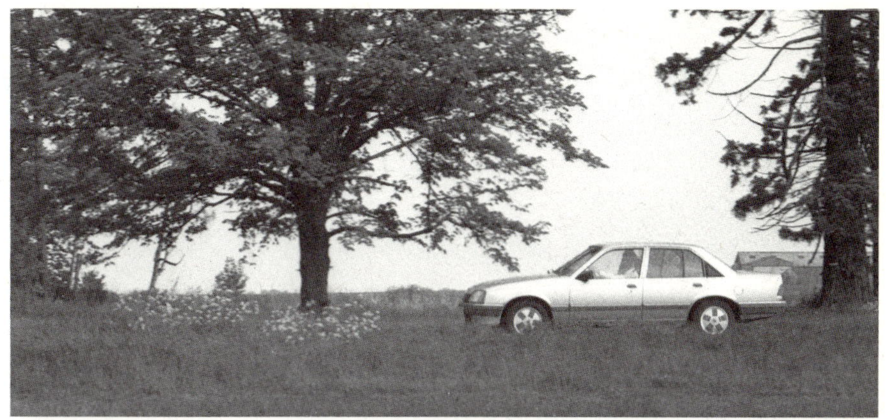

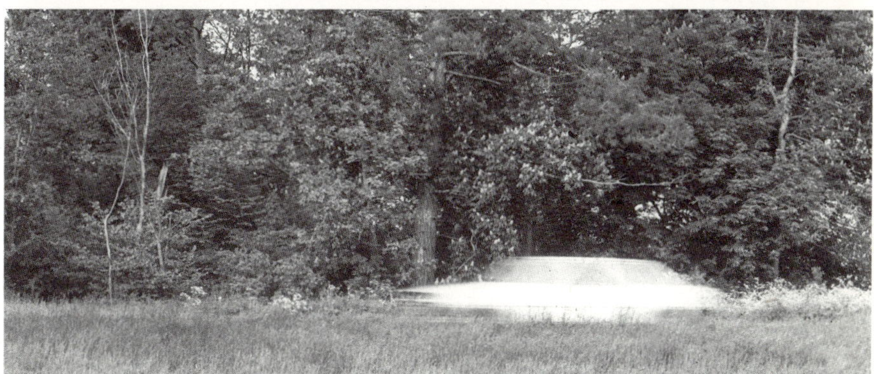

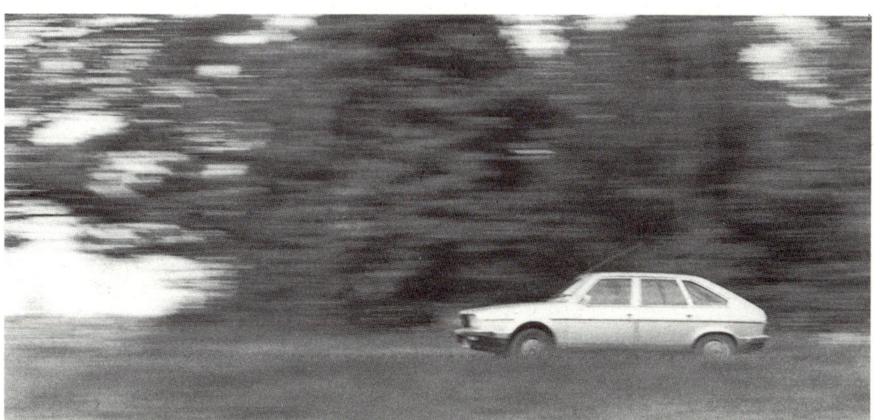

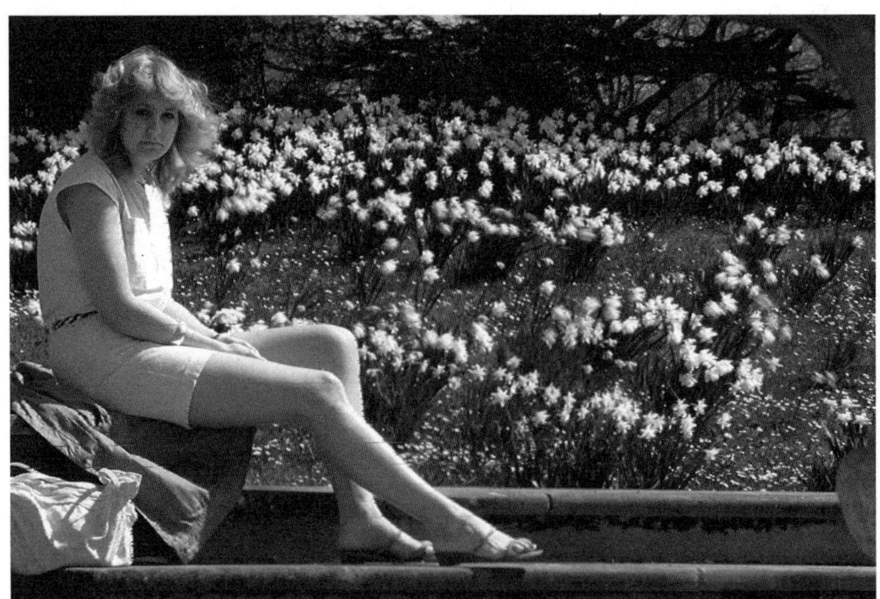

This pair of pictures shows an effect of using different *aperture* settings (varying the shutter speed according, of course, to get a properly-exposed picture). The **top** picture uses a small aperture to give an extended depth of field – everything in the front of the picture is sharply in focus. But by using a large aperture (**below**) the depth of field is very restricted – careful focusing on the main subject then ensures that the main subject is sharply-defined and the background disappears into a blur

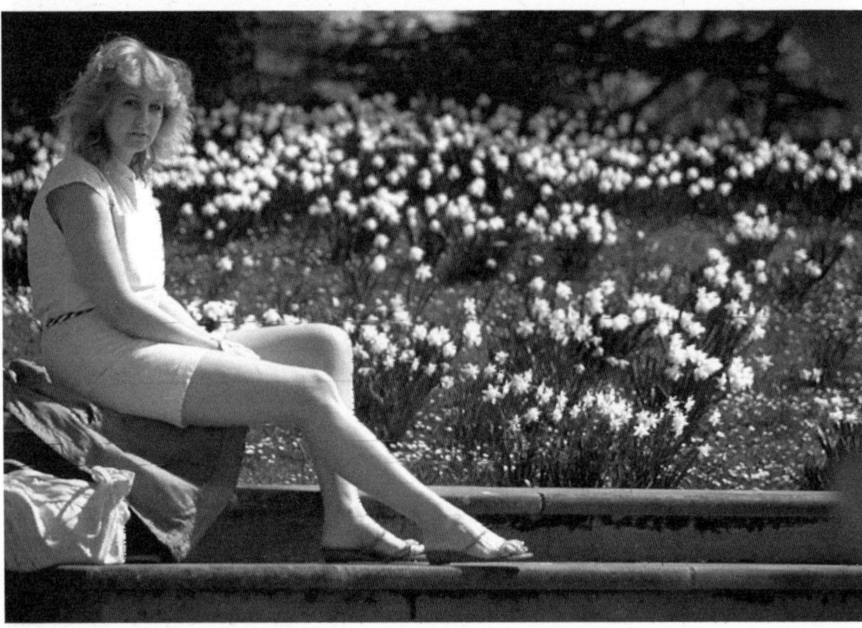

You can use this single term – *stop* – for both aperture settings and shutter speed, and link it directly to overall exposure in this way, because the total amount of light reaching the film is a combination of the shutter speed setting and the aperture size setting – and because each change in either setting doubles or halves the amount of light reaching the film. So you can select many combinations of the two settings that will let the same amount of light through on to the film. And from the point of view of exposure, it doesn't matter what combination you select.

One of the thrills of photography, however, is that the different combinations *do* have an effect on other aspects of your picture – and it's being able to control these effects, while still being able to take a picture that is technically correctly exposed, that is the start of the creative aspect of picture-taking.

The effect of different **shutter speeds** is apparent in photographs of moving objects: use a fast shutter speed and you can 'freeze' the object, so that it appears stationary against a stationary background; use a slow shutter speed and the object will appear blurred, giving an impression of movement. It's up to *you* to choose how you want the object to appear.

The effect of different **apertures** shows up as differences in the *depth of field* (how much of the picture is in focus: see page 17). The larger the aperture (that is, the lower the f number) the shorter this depth of field will be. However, note that depth of field also depends on:
- **focal length** of the lens – see page 72
- **distance from subject** – the closer to the lens that the scene is sharp, the shorter is the depth of field.

In short, the ability to alter aperture and shutter speed separately greatly increases your ability to take a wide range of creative pictures. But remember that to get a picture that's properly exposed you can't have everything your way: if you want a small aperture you must use a relatively slow shutter speed; if you want a larger aperture, you must use a faster shutter speed. (Though there is one other factor you can change which will help: you can use films of different speeds – see pages 91 to 95.)

Types of exposure control

Only the very cheapest SLRs now offer only **manual** exposure setting. These have a built-in *exposure meter* – the meter's needle tells you how much light is falling on the camera and what combinations of shutter speed and aperture size will give you the correct exposure. You then set whatever speed and size you want (you can even ignore the settings on the meter entirely if you wish).

Much more common are semi-automatic and automatic systems – auto systems are further divided into automatic priority and automatic programmed types.

A simple exposure meter has a needle indicating how much light is falling on the film, and helps you decide what combinations of shutter speed and aperture setting you would need to get a properly-exposed picture. The heart of the exposure meter is a photo-electric cell built into the camera, which receives the light reflected from the subject. There are various types of cell but, in practice, the quality of a camera depends more on other factors and you should not worry too much about the type of photo-cell fitted

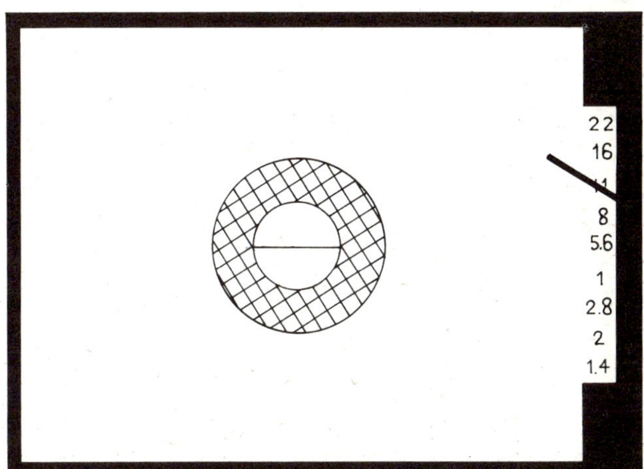

Automatic exposure mechanisms

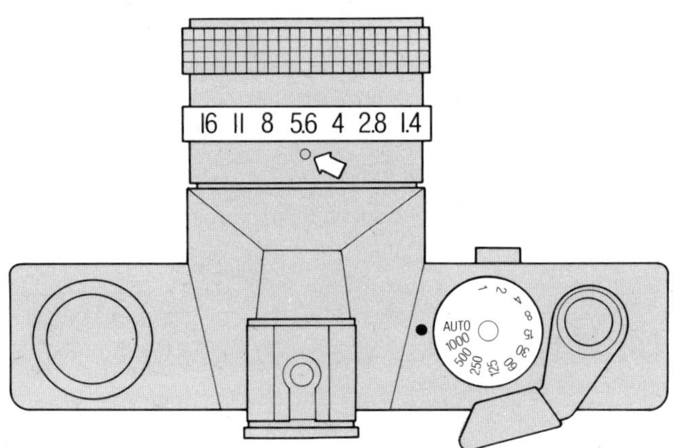

Aperture priority

You decide   What aperture setting to use
The camera sets   The corresponding shutter speed

Semi-automatic   The first advantage of these over manual cameras is that the exposure meter is visible in the view-finder, as a meter needle or row of lights or something similar: this in itself makes taking a picture much easier. More importantly, the meter registers the actual amount of light falling on the film – as you alter the shutter speed or aperture size the position of the needle (or whatever) will alter. When the needle is in line with a mark at the side of the viewfinder, your exposure is correct.

It's up to you to decide which of the different combinations of speed and size that will give the correct exposure you want to select: unless you are after a particular effect – such as an impression of movement as shown on page 45 – you would normally set for a middle-of-the-range speed (say $\frac{1}{125}$ second in normal light conditions) and then set the aperture accordingly; or you could set a reasonable aperture setting (perhaps f16) and then alter the speed to give the right exposure. And again, you can ignore what the meter says entirely if you wanted to go for a picture that (theoretically at least) would be over- or under-exposed.

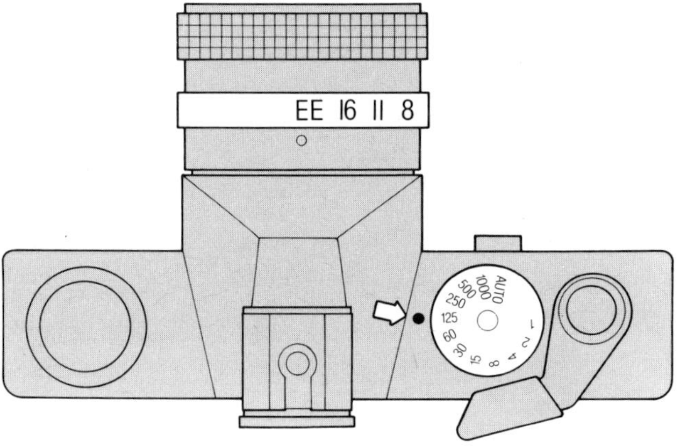

Shutter priority

You decide   What shutter speed to use
The camera sets   The corresponding aperture setting

Automatic, priority   With this type of camera, you decide on one setting and the camera automatically adjusts the other to give a correct exposure. There are two types – aperture priority and shutter priority.

With an **aperture priority** camera, you start by setting the aperture yourself – it's up to you to make a judgement about what sort of aperture size is suitable for the light conditions and the type of shot you're taking. Once selected, this aperture remains the same until you change it (which goes for any of the other, less automatic, types of camera as well). You then point the camera at the scene and it automatically adjusts the shutter speed to give the correct exposure. A scale in the viewfinder will show you what value this is – if you would prefer something slower or faster you can decrease or increase the aperture size before pressing the shutter; on some cameras there is also an indicator in the viewfinder to show you what size aperture you have selected.

If there is too little or too much light for the aperture you have selected (so that your shot would be under- or over-exposed no matter what shutter speed the camera were to

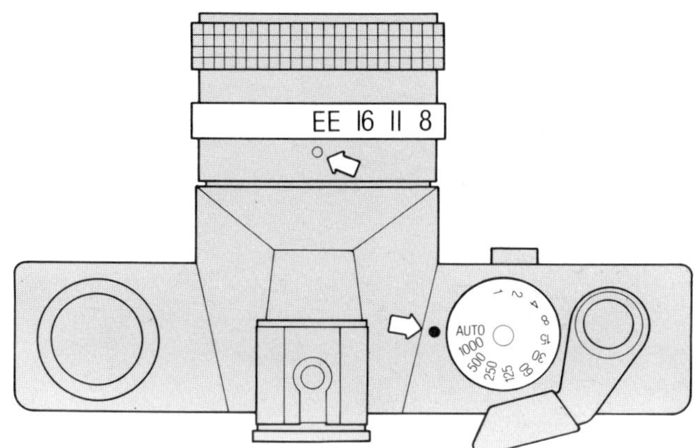

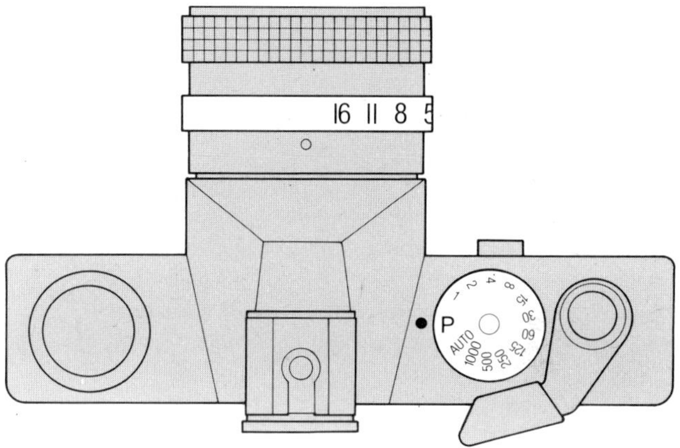

Dual priority

You decide *Either* aperture setting *or* shutter speed
The camera sets The corresponding shutter speed or the aperture setting

Automatic, programmed

You decide Nothing
The camera sets Both aperture setting and shutter speed

select) that fact will be shown in the viewfinder, and on some cameras the shutter locks so that you can't then take a picture. But assuming the light is satisfactory, you simply press the shutter.

A **shutter priority** camera, as you might guess, works in exactly the same way except that *you* set the shutter speed and the *camera* works out the aperture size.

Deciding whether to go for aperture or shutter priority is really a matter of personal preference – though there are some types of shot where one system has the edge over the other. For example, if you want to take freeze pictures of fast-moving objects you would want to be able to demand a fast speed, so a shutter priority camera would be the better bet. If you want to take pictures requiring a great depth of field you will want to demand a small aperture, so the aperture priority type would be better. On the whole, though, you'll want to take a mixture of shots, so the choice is little more than a toss-up – but note that skilled photographers tend to prefer aperture priority, and that with shutter priority you cannot take automatic time exposures (that is, pictures

requiring very long exposure times of the order of seconds).

One way out of the dilemma of which to choose is to buy a camera with **dual priority** – which you can decide to use as either a shutter or aperture priority machine. These are relatively expensive.

Automatic, programmed These cameras do everything for themselves, selecting both the aperture and shutter speed. Apart from focusing (auto focusing isn't yet available on SLRs) the programme exposure SLR is suitable for simple point-and-shoot picture-taking, leaving the photographer with very little to do.

The latest SLRs offer you a choice of programmes – to give emphasis either to a fast shutter speed or a small aperture. However, having more than a couple of programmes is rather self-defeating: by the time you've worked out which one to use, you could have set the controls manually.

Making your own decisions The whole essence of photography at the SLR level is that you can alter all the factors that

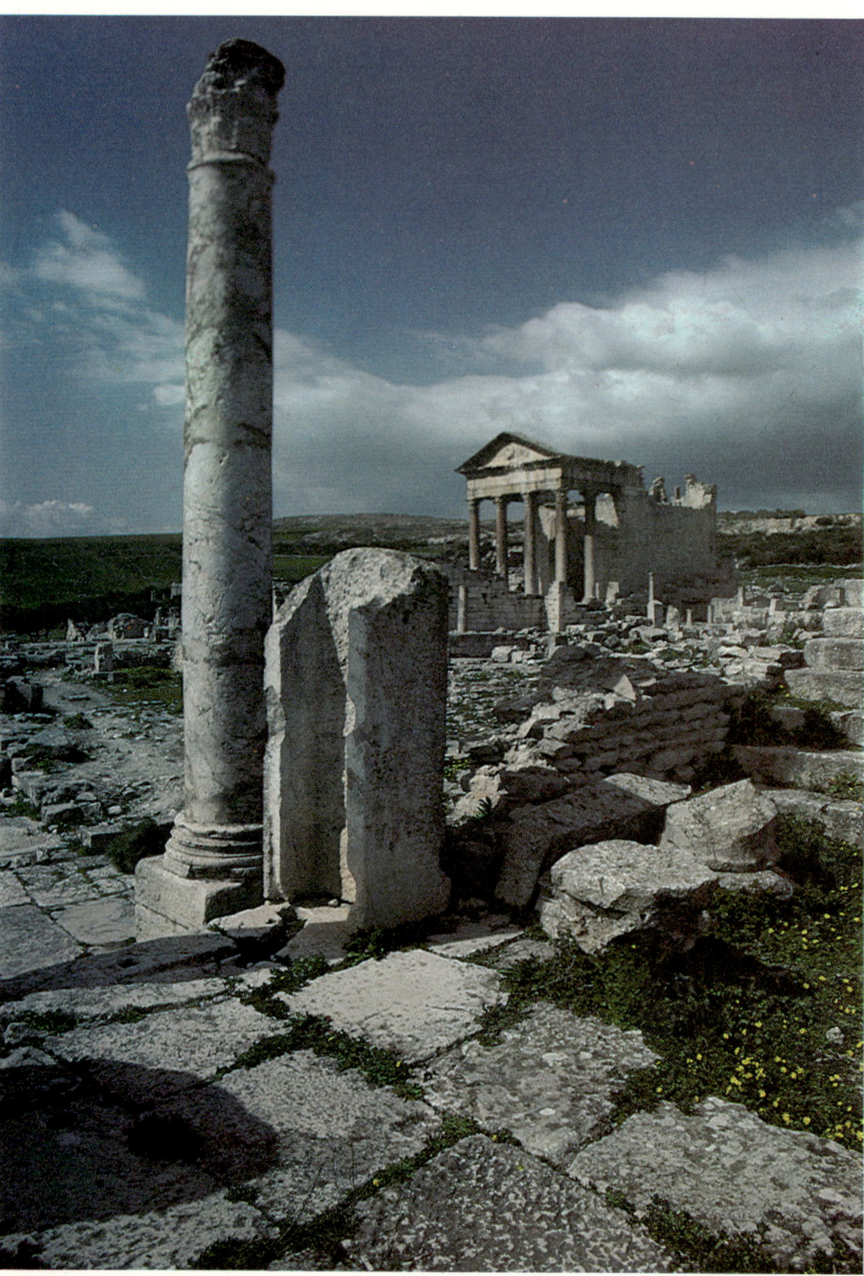

Left An extended depth of field was needed for this picture, so that everything from the fore-ground to the background would be sharply in focus. You need to control the aperture size yourself for such a shot – so an aperture-priority camera would be needed

Right The correct choice of shutter speed for photographing moving objects is a creative decision that you, rather than your camera, must make – so a shutter-priority camera is needed

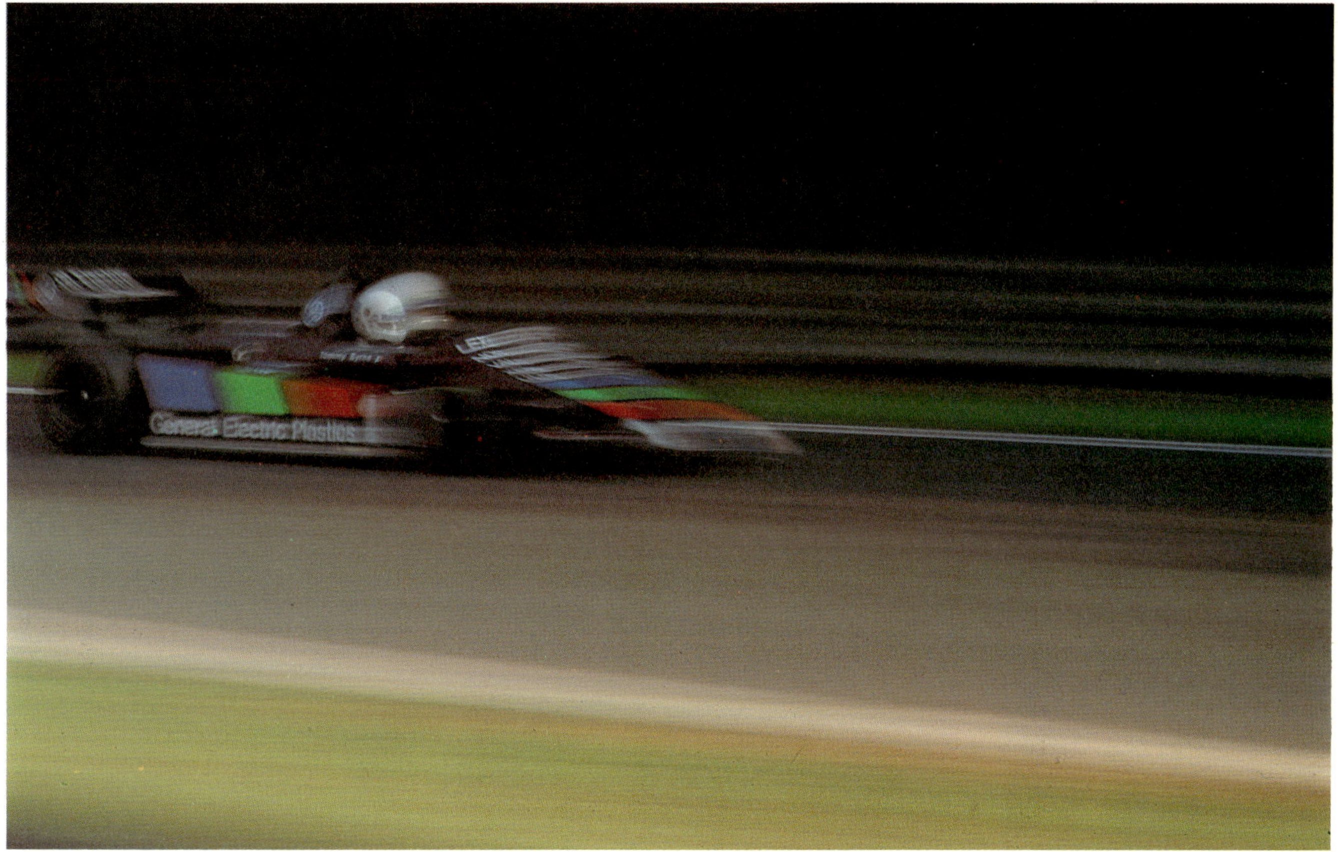

go to make a picture to achieve the effect you want. Automatic systems rob you of that ability. So most auto cameras, of whatever sort, allow you to over-ride the automatic settings, and let you select the speed and aperture directly for yourself – irrespective of whether this would result in a theoretically wrongly-exposed picture.

Beware of **automatic-only** cameras, where you are not allowed to over-ride settings (except by altering the film speed) because they are very restricting. If you really think you'd never use an SLR except on auto, you're probably wasting your money buying one – and, unless you've a good reason for needing to use different lenses, you would be better off buying a non-reflex camera instead.

Meter type

The amount of light being reflected from a scene varies across the scene, depending on how bright or dark the various sections of it are. So it's often tricky for a (human) photographer to know how long to expose the film, to ensure that the very brightest parts of the picture are not over-exposed, and the darkest parts are not left completely black. And it's much more difficult for a single photo-cell to work out exposures and to get them right no matter what type of shot you are taking.

There are a number of different metering techniques, some more successful than others at getting round this problem of deciding what exposure value to select.

Whole-field metering Gives each part of the picture as much importance in working out what the 'average' amount of light falling on the film is. This technique rarely reflects reality – pictures usually consist of an important subject somewhere close to the middle, with land in the bottom half, sky in the upper half and not much of importance around the edges. Whole-field metering has been abandoned.

Selective metering, centre-weighted This takes most account of the light values in the middle of the scene, and gives less and less weight to the areas of the picture getting closer to the edges. So, for example, the presence of a bright sun in one corner of the picture will not have enough effect on the total meter reading to close up the aperture and so render the centre of the picture under-exposed – as might well have happened with whole-field metering.

Selective metering, centre and foreground-weighted This takes most account of the centre, but in turn the lower part of the picture (that is, the foreground) is given more weight than the upper part (usually the sky). This is the sort of meter-weighting which is most common these days, largely because it corresponds in practice to the type of pictures people are most likely to take.

Spot metering This measures only the light reflected from the centre of the scene (an area which may be shown in the viewfinder as a small rectangle). This weighting is particularly suited to highly-contrasted subjects when you want to expose the subject correctly and leave the background under- or over-exposed.

Spot metering on its own would not be a very good plan because it evaluates only a small part of the scene. So it is usually an addition to selective metering. It's a helpful addition, especially if you spend a lot of time in 'creative' photography, but it is not essential for a couple of reasons:
● it still won't tell you exactly how to expose for a difficult shot – to be certain about this you need lots of experience, or luck, or to take a series of shots with different exposures (called *bracketing*: see overleaf)
● there are other ways of correcting for selective metering readings that you think won't give the exposure you are after: see below.

Exposure correction methods

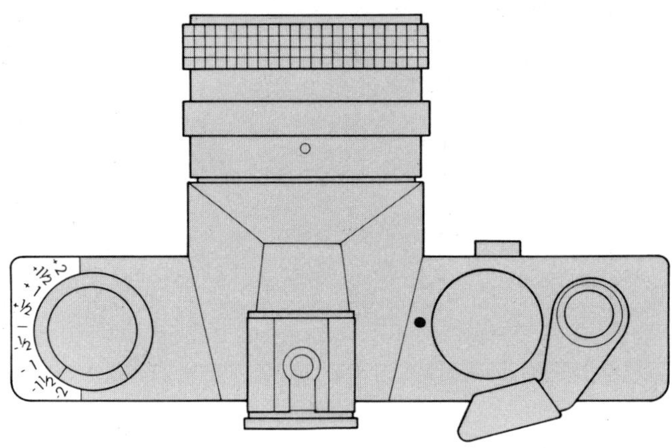

Type of control Exposure compensation
What it does Increases or decreases amount of exposure a little, after you have set the level according to the exposure meter
What you do Adjust the knob for the amount of compensation you think necessary

Correcting exposure

Although automatic exposure control systems are usually very good, they don't give best results in all circumstances. Light coming from behind a subject will usually cause the camera to reduce the exposure, so the subject may appear as a silhouette (which may or may not be the effect you are after). If you are taking a snow scene, the camera will try to make the snow grey – it doesn't know that snow is supposed to be very bright. In both these cases, you need to increase the exposure by one or two 'stops'. Conversely with a spotlit figure against a dark background, you will need to *decrease* the exposure by one or two stops.

You can do this one way or another on almost any camera. Many cameras have a special **exposure compensation** knob, next to the film speed selection dial. This is usually marked in units of ½ stop up to plus or minus two stops. You alter the exposure in the normal way for whatever type of camera you have, until the camera says you'll get a properly exposed picture. Then, using your skill and judgement, you decide

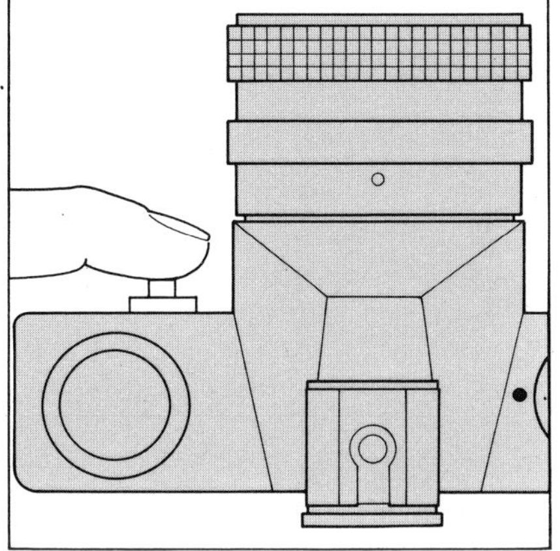

Type of control   Exposure memory
What it does   Allows the camera to set exposure from a selected part of the scene
What you do   Point the camera at the selected part and hold the memory button

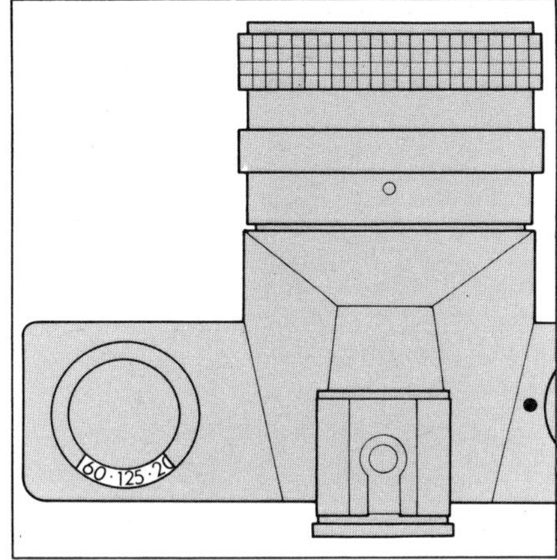

Type of control   Film speed dial
What it does   Fools the camera into thinking it is using a different speed film
What you do   Alter the film speed setting by the amount you think necessary

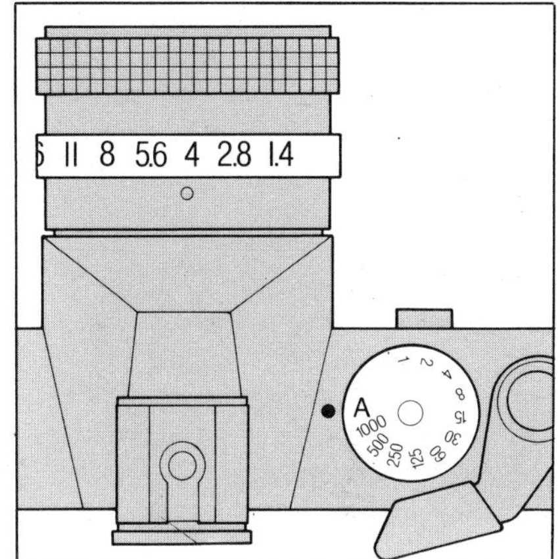

Type of control   Semi-auto operation
What it does   Over-rides automatic settings from the levels camera advises
What you do   Alter shutter speed or aperture setting as you think necessary

how much you should increase or decrease the exposure to give what *you* think will be the best setting, and alter the compensation knob accordingly.

Some compensation knobs do not allow you to go beyond the speed range of your camera. So, for example, if you are using 25 ISO film and this is the slowest setting on your camera you cannot use the compensation knob to give extra exposure. In this case, or on a camera that is not fitted with a compensation knob, you could simply alter the film speed control, to fool the camera into thinking it is using a slower or faster film than it actually is – which is all a compensation knob does anyway. (To increase exposure times, set for a *slower* film; to decrease, set for a *faster* film. A doubling or halving of the ISO film speed number is equivalent to a change of one stop in exposure, as Chapter 8 explains.)

Alternatively, after you have adjusted for the 'correct' exposure, simply re-adjust the shutter or aperture to allow for more or less exposure (on some cameras, you'll get a rude bleeping to tell you the exposure's not properly set). All you

are doing is using the camera as a semi-automatic type – something you should be able to do on any SLR.

Exposure memory   This is really another method of correcting a camera's automatic exposure setting. You have to get close enough to the scene you're shooting so that the part of the subject you want to be correctly exposed fills the whole frame. You then allow the camera to set the exposure and press a memory button. Then you step back and compose your picture as you want – the part of the scene you have selected will come out correctly exposed, no matter how much of the picture it occupies, where it is positioned, or how different the lighting in the rest of the picture is.

Exposure memory is easier to use than exposure compensation because you don't have to guess at the amount of exposure correction to give. But you do have to be able to get close enough to the important part of the scene so that you can measure it correctly. (Though if the problem is caused by a bright sky behind your subject you can sometimes use a

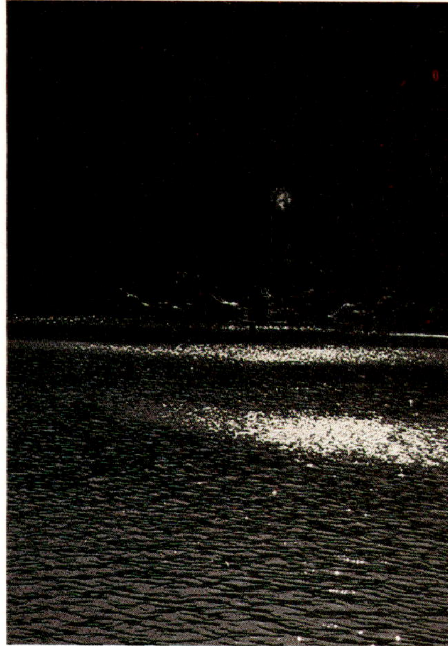

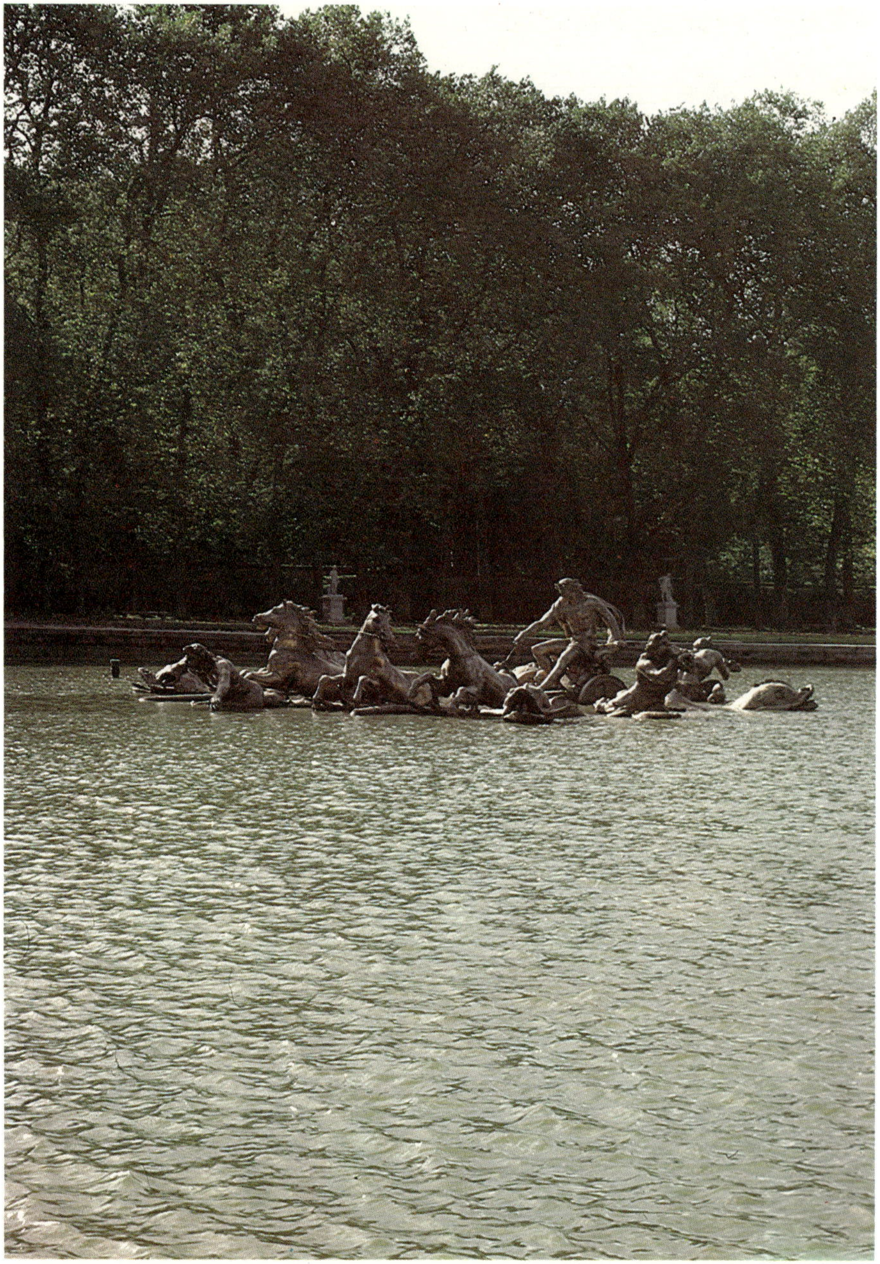

Highly-contrasted pictures can fool a camera's auto-exposure systems: in the photo **above** the camera has taken its readings from the very bright reflection on the water, and so completely under-exposes the much darker fountain and trees in the background. By adjusting the exposure yourself (**right**) you can make detail in the fountain and trees properly visible: though the fore-ground is now over-exposed, that only reinforces the feeling of how bright the actual reflection was

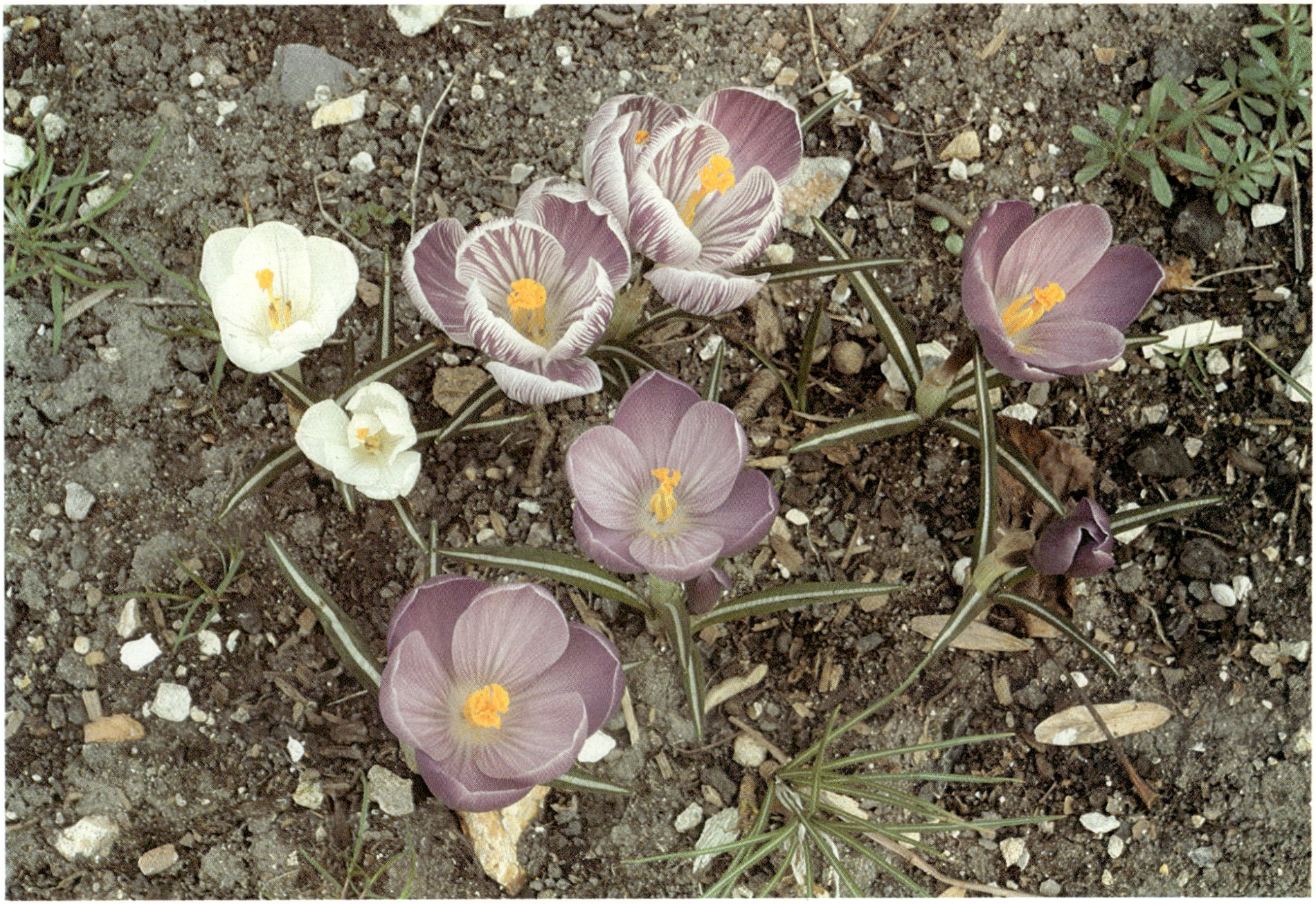

Professional photographers can't take chances with exposure, so they will often take three shots (**right**) of each scene with a half-stop or one-stop difference in exposure between each one – called *bracketing*. After studying the results, the best shot (**above**) can be printed up as an enlargement

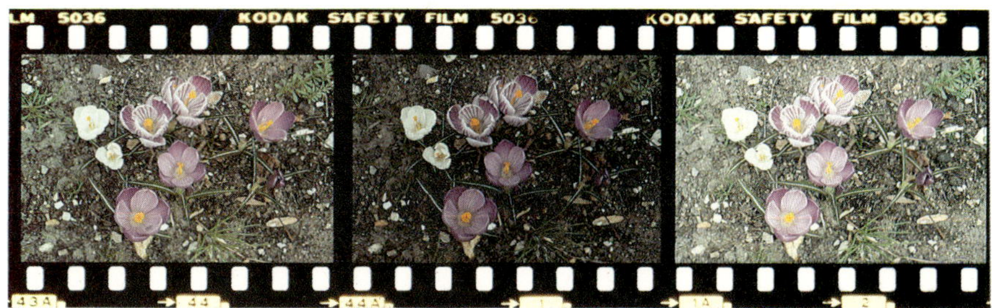

Correcting exposure
Some examples of the types of
picture needing manual
correction to an automatic
exposure setting, and the effects
of that correction

Very light background
1 Automatic setting
2 One stop extra exposure (too
little)
3 Three stops extra exposure
(the best result)

Light background
1 Automatic setting
2 One stop extra exposure (not
enough)
3 Two stops extra exposure
(the best)

Dark background
1 Automatic setting
2 One stop less exposure (not
quite enough)
3 Two stops less exposure (a
little too dark)

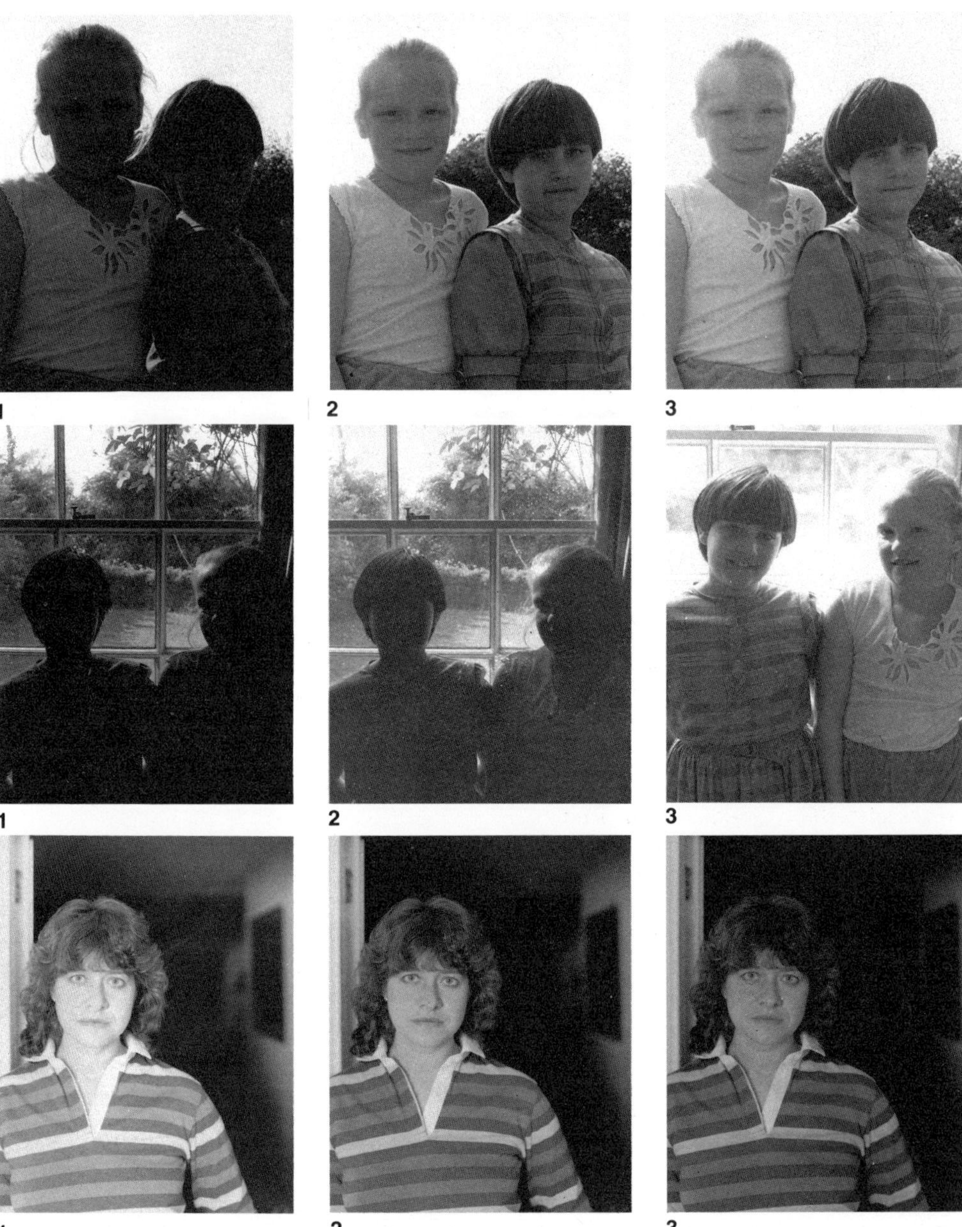

The viewing screen includes three areas to aid focusing. When a picture is out of focus (**right**) the outer area shows the picture as generally fuzzy; in the annular microprism area the image will be broken up; and in the central rangefinder area the picture, though sharp, will not be in alignment over the two halves. When the picture is properly focused (**far right**) the viewing screen will show a single, sharp, image

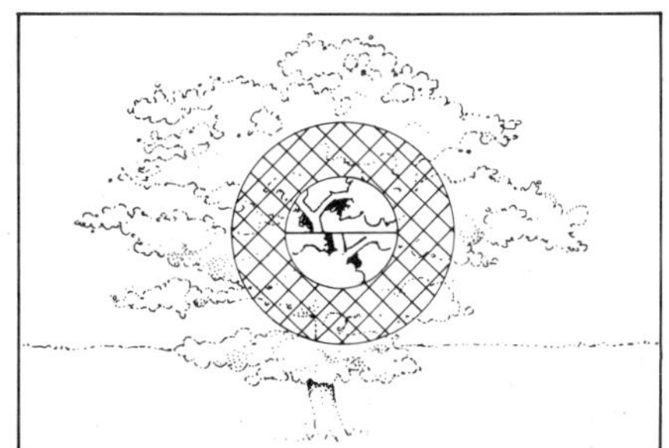 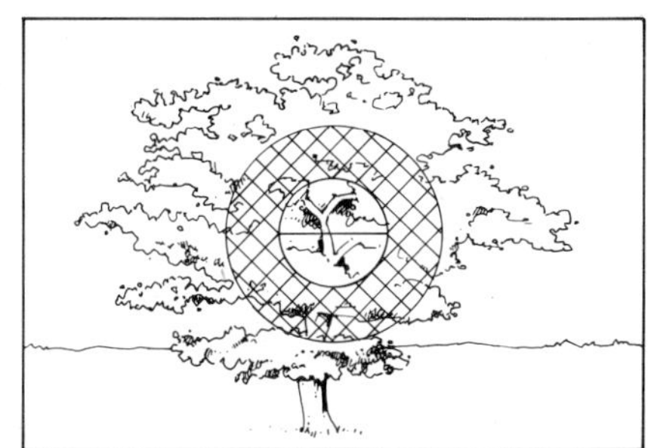

memory button by pointing the camera downwards to cut out the sky, then holding the button as you raise the camera up again: this saves you having to get close to your subject, but the compensation may not be so accurate.)

Focusing

The only method of focusing available on most SLRs is manual – you rotate the scale ring on the lens (which actually moves the lens slightly towards or away from the film) until the parts of the scene that you want to be sharp are focused on the film. How can you tell this? SLRs have good focusing aids to help you.

The basic focusing aid is the ground glass **viewing screen** that forms the main part of the viewfinder – it's here that the image from the mirror in front of the film is thrown. The distance from the mirror to the screen is the same as from the mirror to the film, so any part of the image that is in focus on the screen will be in focus on the film.

But the screen is rather small, and it is often difficult to tell if a picture really is as sharp as it can be. So SLRs usually have two other, more accurate, focusing aids: a *microprism area* and a split-image *rangefinder*.

Microprism Within the microprism area, the image appears sharp if it is in focus, but breaks up into lots of little prism areas – along the lines of the sort of thing that you might see in a kaleidoscope – if it is out of focus. Using the microprism area is difficult when the light level is low.

Rangefinder Here, the image is divided into two half-circles, usually one on top of the other. The image remains sharp, whether in or out of focus, but until the focus is precise

the two halves will be out of alignment, with the top half offset to the left or right of the bottom half. Focusing with a normal split-image rangefinder is difficult if there are no vertical guidelines in the centre of the picture – on some cameras, the split-image circle is divided diagonally, so that you can use something with a vertical or horizontal edge to focus on, without having to turn the camera round. Instead of an optical rangefinder, a few camera use *electronic indicator lights*.

Checking depth of field During focusing, the lens aperture remains fully open, irrespective of what aperture setting you (or the camera's automatic system) have selected. This is because at anything less than full aperture the image on the viewing screen would not be very bright, and so would be unnecessarily difficult to see. Further, because at maximum aperture the depth of field is very limited, it is possible to focus more precisely – you can be sure that what you do see in focus really will be sharp in your final picture. When you press the shutter, of course, the aperture reduces (or 'stops down') to the size selected.

The only drawback is that it is impossible to see through the viewfinder what the actual depth of field of your composition will be – what amount of fore-ground and back-ground will be blurred, and what depth of the scene in between will be in focus. There are two ways round this.

Many lenses have a *depth scale* on them, showing the distance of the nearest and furthest points in focus for different aperture sizes, but unless you're good at judging distances you won't find this of much help. However, some cameras have a *depth of field preview* button on the lens which stops it down to its working aperture while you're

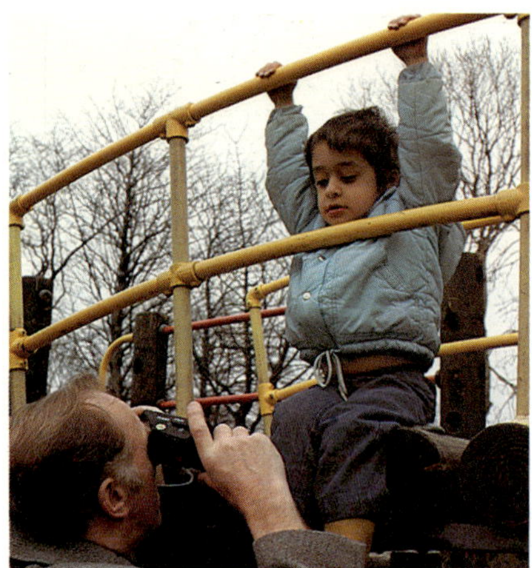

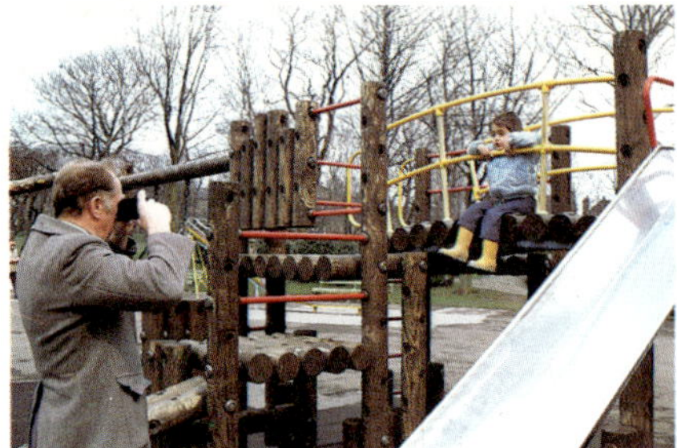

To use an exposure memory button, first close up on your subject (**top**) so that the area you want the camera to take its exposure reading from fills the viewfinder. Then step back (**above**) and compose your shot. Result (**right**) is a correctly-exposed picture, despite difficult lighting conditions

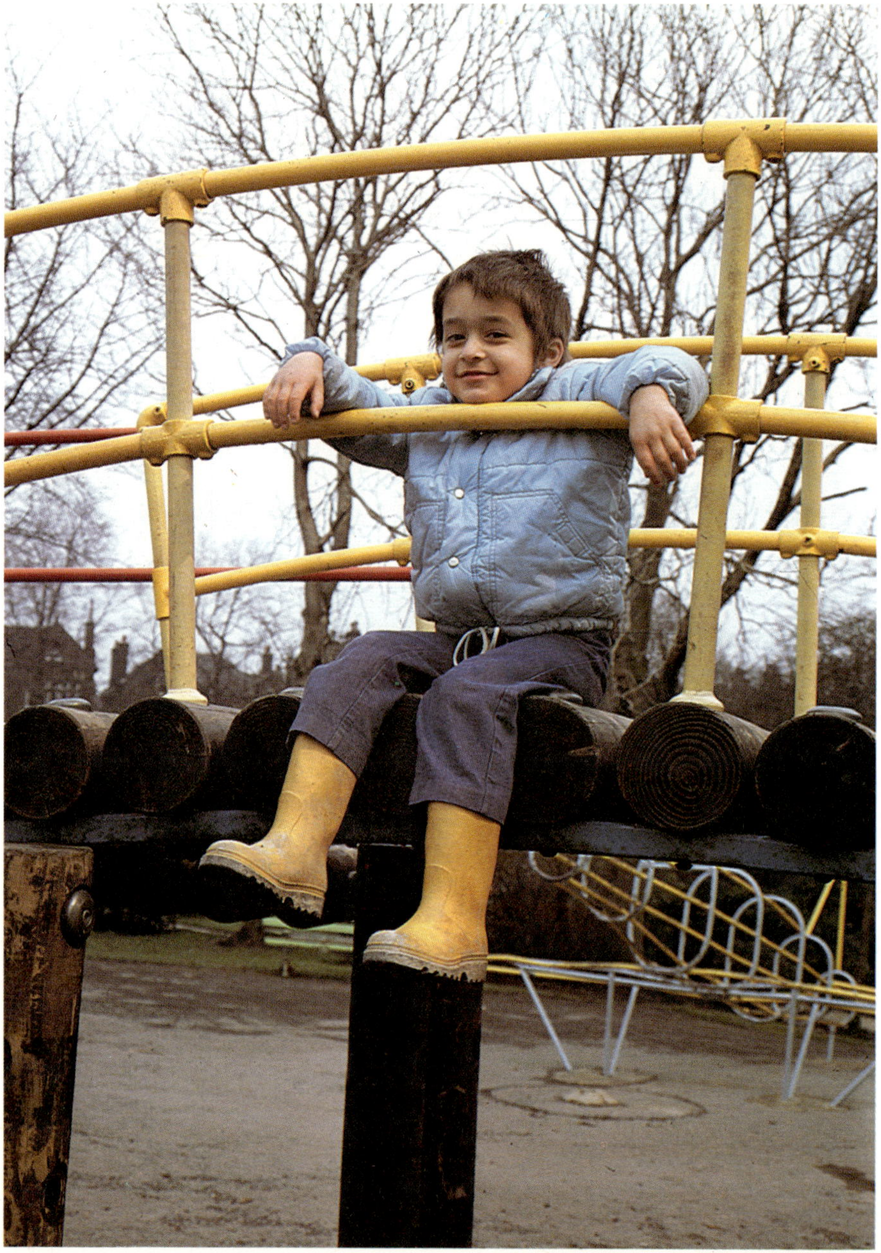

After focusing, check with your lens what depth of field you will get by reading across from the depth of field scale to the distance marks on the focusing ring. Depth of field depends on aperture – the lens on the **right** is set for f11, and the distances corresponding to the two f11 markings on the depth of field scale are about 2m and 10m, so everything in the scene between those two points will be in focus

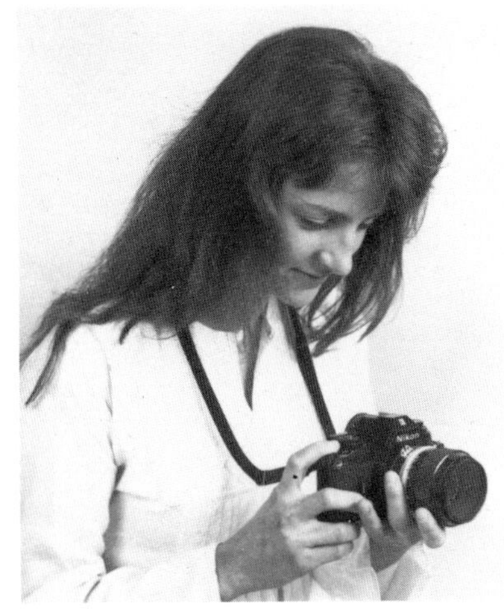

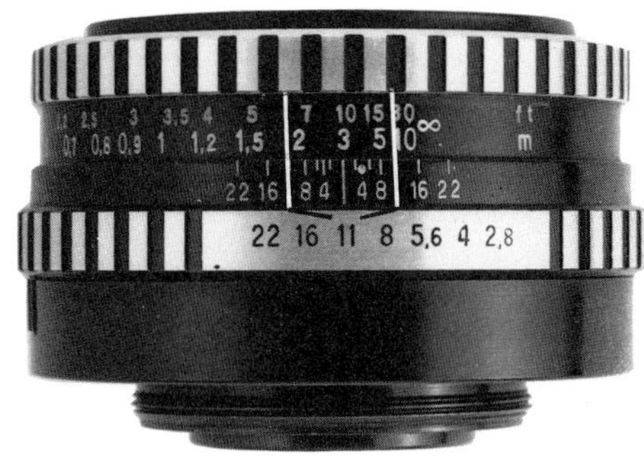

focusing: pressing this button enables you to see exactly what depth of field you are getting – and where it will be situated within the depth of the scene.

Closest focus distance   With a standard lens, the closest distance at which you can focus is usually around 450mm (18in) with some cameras not focusing closer than 600mm, and some focusing as close as 330mm. If you want to do really close work – such as duplicating slides or photographing insects – you need a different type of lens, or some lens accessories (see Chapter 7). It's one of the important advantages of SLRs that you can add these extras to the basic camera.

Autofocus lenses   A few cameras are available with zoom lenses (see page 81) into which an autofocus motor is built. At present they are big, heavy and expensive.

Flash

SLR cameras do not have built-in flash units so if you want to be ready to take flash pictures you must carry a separate unit around with you, and be nippy about connecting it to the camera. Flash units for SLRs are almost invariably electronic these days.

Using flash is made a bit easier if you buy one specially matched to your camera – a *dedicated* unit – which will set the correct shutter speed on the camera and signal in the viewfinder when it is ready to fire. Most camera manufacturers have a range of these dedicated units, and you can also buy independent brands.

The instructions with the flash unit will tell you what to set the aperture to. Most give you a choice so that you can trade off depth of field against flash range (that is, the greater the depth of field you choose, the smaller the distance to which you can light up subjects) and with some cameras, when used with their dedicated units, you can use automatic flash with any aperture. Other camera/flash units give you more help in setting the right aperture: setting an aperture on the flash unit may automatically set it on the camera; or the flash may adjust its output to allow for the aperture set (either manually or automatically) on the camera. Some cameras will signal when the aperture has been (manually) set to a size which wouldn't give proper flash exposure. For more details about separate flash, see Chapter 10.

Viewfinder information

In the days of manual-only cameras, you didn't need sophisticated information systems to tell you what was going on in the camera. You set apertures and speeds and switched on flash units yourself – you didn't need to be told again what it was you'd just done. The same is true, but for a different reason, with programme-only automatic cameras: the camera sets everything for you, and you can't do anything about it even if you disagree with its choices. So any information it gives you is superfluous – frustrating to an expert, and overwhelming to a simple picture-taker.

In the middle lie the automatics with some manual functions, or with manual over-ride systems. Here, it's vital to know what's going on, and what the camera has selected so that you can make your selections or take control completely. So the modern SLR needs to show quite a lot of information and the best place to display it is in the viewfinder, where you can take note of it as you are composing your shot.

Exposure   An indicator shows you what shutter speed the camera has selected when you have set the aperture on an aperture-priority camera; or the aperture when you have set the shutter speed on a shutter-priority camera. On some cameras, you may get indicators giving both exposure details. This is very useful on cameras having a programme mode – it tells you, for example, if the shutter speed is likely to be too slow for you to hold the camera steady (in which case, you'd have to switch to another mode). And with priority automatic cameras it reminds you of the settings you have selected so that you don't have to peer over the viewfinder at the scales on the camera and lens itself. In some cases, you can switch the exposure information off – useful, as you might find the information distracting on occasions.

What form does the indicator take? It varies – at its simplest, it is a meter needle; on the more 'electronic' cameras you are likely to get a moving point of light or a set of lit-up figures. Some examples are:
● **simple needle**   Usually used in semi-automatic cameras. All you have to do is to get the needle in a little frame or above a little circle by adjusting the shutter speed or aperture (or both). Needles are not always easy to see in poor light
● **light-emitting diode (LED)**   Three, or more, little lights arranged in a row down one side of the viewfinder. The middle light comes on if the exposure is correct: if you have set for over- or under-exposure, the upper or lower lights come on. Lights are easier to see in poor light conditions
● **digital read-out**   Here you actually see a number, corres-

ponding to the speed or aperture that the camera has set (and sometimes the other factor as well). The numbers can be formed in a variety of ways: LCD (liquid-crystal displays) are quite common.

A warning that your picture may be over- or under-exposed is valuable. Normally, you can tell this from the built-in exposure meter. But on a few cameras, the meter will gaily give you a reading which is not within the range of shutter speeds or apertures that the camera or lens is capable of! A better system is one with a special indicator: some cameras have a little light; others will even bleep at you.

Wrong exposure isn't the only problem: with aperture-priority cameras, you also have to watch out that the shutter speed selected by the camera – even though it might be within the camera's range – is not so slow that you can't take successful hand-held pictures. The slowest speed at which you can hold a camera steady (without using a tripod, stand or a handy wall top) depends on the focal length of the lens – see page 79 – and also on how good you are at holding a camera steady.

Flash   Cameras used with their dedicated flash units show you in the viewfinder when the flash is charged up – usually, the shutter speed indicator moves to the *flash synchronisation speed* of $\frac{1}{60}$ second or $\frac{1}{125}$ second.

Other indicators   Check what other indicators may be seen in the viewfinder – these may tell you:
● if the battery is okay
● if you have set to manual
● what frame number you're on (that is, how many pictures you've taken on that reel of film)
● if exposure compensation or memory control (see page 52) is being used.

Lenses

The big attraction of an SLR is that you can interchange lenses on the same camera 'body', which greatly increases the range and scope of your picture-taking.

The lenses on the first SLR cameras were attached to the body by a screw-thread fixing – and the thread was a standard one so that anybody's lenses would fit anyone else's camera body. But screw-mounts did have some disadvantages.

Fitting a screw mounting takes some time and care, and the thread on the body or the lens can become damaged if the two parts do not engage correctly. The distance between the lens and the film is altered if the lens is not screwed completely home, which might lead to difficulties in focusing. Finally, with automatic cameras, it's essential to be able to feed clear electrical signals back and forth between the lens and the electrical or electronic control systems in the camera body, and it is not easy to get good connections for these signals when you use a screw mount.

So most cameras these days employ a bayonet mounting. Changing lenses is much easier – just press the locking button, then give the lens a quarter-twist or so. Bayonet mounts are less susceptible to damage, and will always fit perfectly – so there is no problem with transmitting information between lens and camera.

Sadly, though, bayonet mounts are not standard – a Nikon lens, for example, won't fit on to a Canon body. Not only are there differences in bayonet design between brands but also sometimes between older lenses and the latest lenses within a brand, so when you buy a new camera, be sure to check whether your old lenses can still be used.

Although you do need to take care when buying lenses, the situation isn't totally chaotic. For example, one type of bayonet is common to Pentax, Ricoh and a few other brands. And many manufacturers make lenses or adaptors that will fit well-known cameras, so you are not limited to the camera manufacturer's lenses.

Standard lenses   Cameras are usually sold together with a 'standard' lens having a 50mm focal length and a maximum aperture size of f1.7 or f1.8. The most common alternative is a

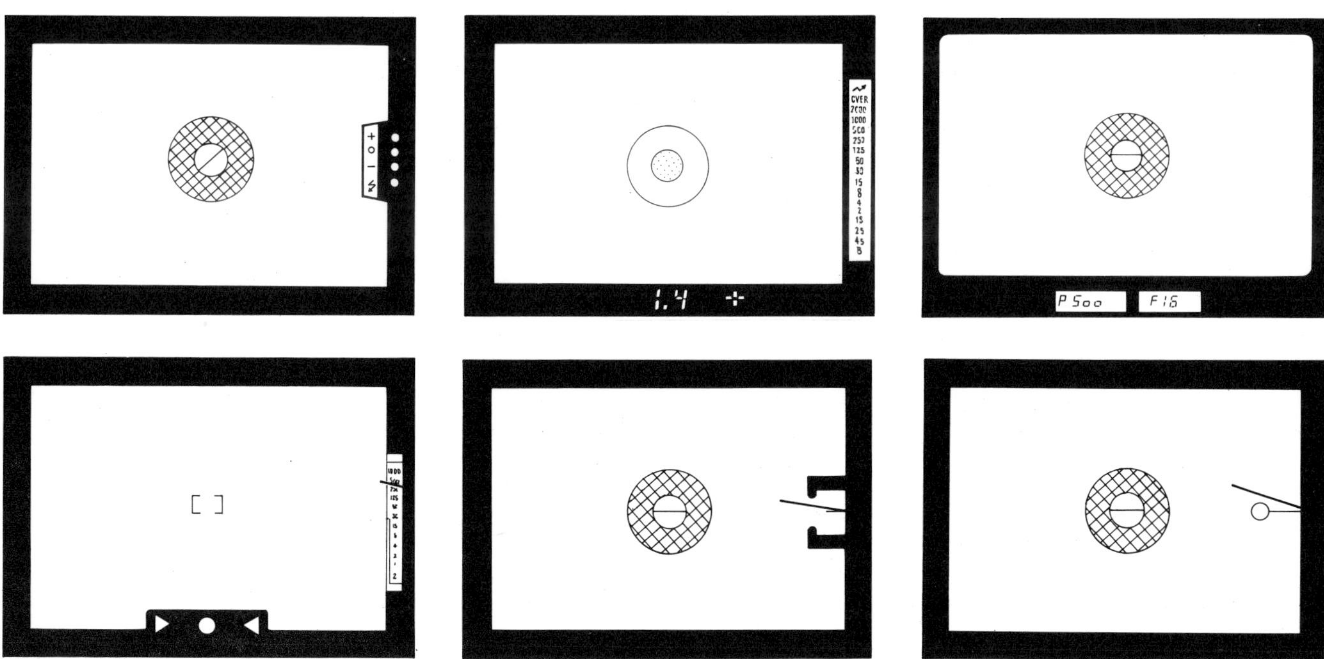

Different viewfinders use different methods – lights, needles, digital read-outs – for displaying information on focusing, aperture and shutter settings

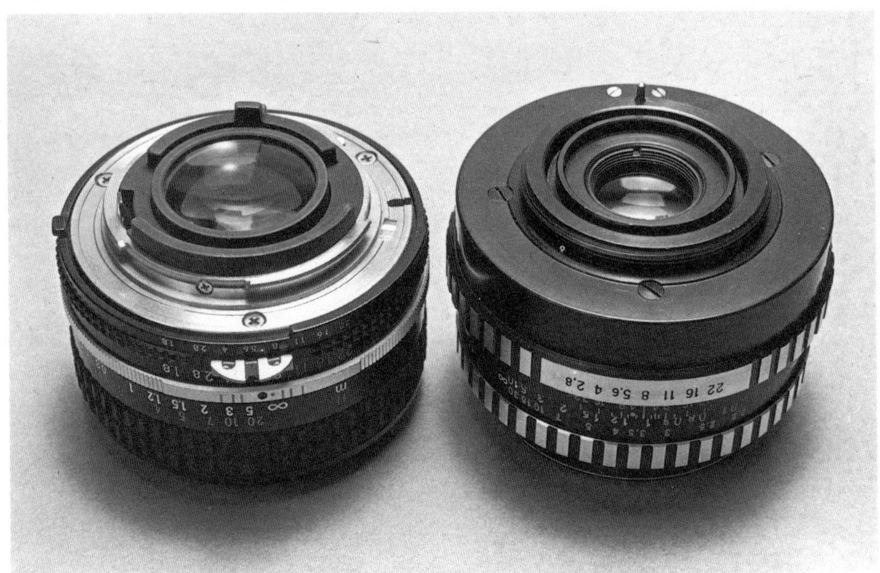

Left Lenses for SLR cameras may have either a bayonet mounting to attach it to the camera (**left** of the pair shown) or a screw mounting (**right** of the pair) which is trickier to fit

Right Loading an SLR camera is usually a little fiddly. You must pull the end of the film across the back of the camera, slot it into the take-up spool, and then wind on the film carefully, making sure the sprocket holes mesh properly with the cogs

lens with a maximum aperture of f1.4, which will add around 20 per cent to the price of the camera/lens combination and 50g or more to the weight. Though you get the advantage of an extra half a stop in the amount of light the lens lets through (and a slighter brighter image to focus on) this isn't very important because you rarely need to use the maximum aperture for taking a picture now that fast colour films are available and flash is so easy to use.

It is perfectly possible to buy your camera body and lens separately – useful if you decide you'd like something different from the usual lens on offer with the camera you are intending to buy.

Other lenses   The wide range of other types of lens which SLR cameras use is described in detail in Chapter 7.

Other features

SLR cameras frequently have a multitude of features, some of which are very important, some of which are of passing interest, and others which you will use only if you have very specialist interests. Here is a list of most of the more important.

Film loading   Most SLR cameras give you little help with film loading – you have to slot the end of the film into the take-up spool, and take care to ensure that the film is lying correctly and held securely before you close the back. View 'easy-loading' systems with some suspicion: some cameras which claim to have these are not much of an improvement over normal loading systems. With the best easy-loading systems, you simply put the cassette into place, pull out the film across the camera and close the back – the motor drive (see below) then automatically moves the film on until it is ready for the first exposure.

With normal loading systems, it is all too easy to fail to load the film properly: and you may not realise that the film is not advancing until you have 'taken' 36 pictures, and start to wind the film back. One reason for this is that the frame counter on most cameras starts clocking up pictures as soon as you close the back and press the shutter – irrespective of whether there's actually a film in the camera at all, let alone whether it is advancing properly. Some cameras have a special indicator to show that the film is moving; failing something like this, get into the habit of checking the rewind knob after loading a film – if the film is moving properly, this

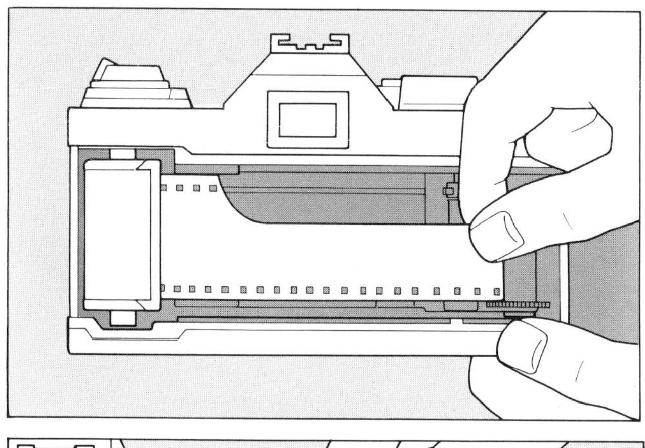

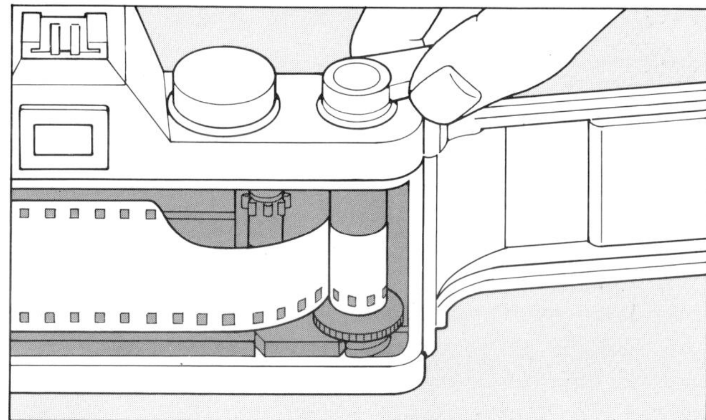

will turn as you operate the film advance lever. (But turn the rewind knob first, to take up any film slack inside the cassette.)

Film winding   Most SLRs are available with attachable motor winders to move the film on automatically as soon as a picture has been taken – you can usually take the next shot after about half a second. And for action pictures you can usually choose continuous shooting (at least, that is, for as long as you can afford the film).

Though motor wind is quite a useful convenience even for amateur photographers, it does add considerably to bulk and weight – a separate unit (as most of them are) adds nearly half as much again to the weight of an SLR. This is a considerable

inconvenience and means that, for most people, motor drive on an SLR probably isn't worth worrying about. In any case, the small added convenience of not having to wind the film on by hand is lost besides the many bits of fiddling with lenses, apertures and so that you're probably involved in if you are using the SLR to its full potential.

There are some cameras with built-in motor winder and these are generally lighter and more compact than the combinations.

Shutters   Most SLRs use **fabric blind** shutters. Operating the shutter release causes two blinds, with a slit in between them, to move horizontally past the film at a constant speed – the film is exposed as the slit travels across its surface. The shutter speed is not set by the speed that the blinds move but by the size of the slit. Some SLRs use blade-type shutters – a set of moving metal blades which operate in a vertical direction.

A fabric blind shutter moves rather more slowly than a metal-blade type, and this could lead to distortions when photographing objects moving at great speed – at a motor-race, for example, cars appear bigger or smaller according to the direction they are moving in. More importantly, you can synchronise for flash only at speeds of 1/60 second or slower with most focal-plane shutters; with metal-blade ones you can use the faster 1/125 second (or even perhaps 1/250 second) speed, which is particularly useful when taking flash pictures against the light. On the whole, though, these points are not too important – you should not make shutter type one of your priorities when selecting a camera.

Shutter speed range   Nearly all cameras are capable of shooting at speeds up to 1/1000 second, so that you can 'freeze' motion in action shots. The faster 1/2000 second is rarely necessary. If you want to take special effects – such as a drop of water splattering – you can always use an automatic electronic flash which, close up, can give speeds up to 1/100,000 second or faster.

At the slow end of the range you are likely to find more differences. For a start, the maximum length manufacturers quote for timed exposures varies a lot from camera to camera – from 1/4 second up to 20 seconds or more (though speeds of 1 or 2 seconds are most common). Secondly, whether the camera can actually use these slow exposures automatically depends on whether the exposure meter is able to take a reading in very dim light. This matters particularly if you are using a very fast film which, even in dim light, may allow an exposure time well within the bottom end of the shutter's range. But it still requires a meter capable of measuring in such dim light.

Cameras, even those without normal manual control, invariably have a B setting on the shutter speed dial — the shutter opens as you press the button and stays open for as long as you hold the button down, closing only when you release the shutter. Using the B setting you can make exposures of as long as you like. Of course, you won't get any help on long exposure times from the built-in meter (or from any exposure meter for that matter). You will have to guess at how long to leave the shutter open for, but fortunately it isn't necessary to be too accurate. And don't forget that a sturdy tripod is also essential.

Multiple exposures   In the days of the Brownie the biggest worries for amateur photographer was forgetting to wind-on after taking a picture—so you ended up with a ghostly picture of Aunt Agatha superimposed on the Houses of Parliament. Nowadays, there's no problem — after taking a picture the shutter is locked until you wind the film on. On the other hand, you may *want* to superimpose shots, for a special effect.

You can do this (except on some cameras with motor wind) by first pressing the rewind button—the button on the bottom of the camera that you press to enable you to rewind the film into the cassette after shooting the whole reel. This disconnects the film advance lever from the take-up spool so you can pretend to wind on the film as normal without actually doing so—in turn, this fools the shutter lock and allows you to take two pictures on the same frame. Check that the rewind button is reset after you use the advance lever, so you don't take more superimposed pictures than you intend to.

The problem is that the system may not be very precise, and operating the advance lever, even with the rewind button depressed, may move the film on very slightly — enough perhaps to ruin your double image. You may get better results by using the rewind knob first to take up any slack in the film, and then holding the knob as you operate the advance lever. Some cameras have a special multiple exposure button which should get round this problem — but even with these the film *may* move slightly between exposures.

Mechanical or electronic?   Until a few years ago, cameras were marvels of mechanical precision. They still are, but nowadays control and measurement of light rely more and more on electronic devices. Electronics usually have several advantages: they are more reliable than mechanical devices; they tend to be cheaper; and they allow much more scope for automation.

The main drawback with fully-electronic cameras is that when the batteries are flat the camera conks out! So a battery check light (see 'Viewfinder information') is essential — and always make sure you are carrying a spare set of batteries. With a few cameras you can take manual exposures on at least one setting without any battery — better than not being able to take pictures at all.

Film

SLR cameras can generally be set to take any of the normal 35mm films available — look for a film speed dial that can be set for any film from 25 ISO to 1600 ISO. This is adequate for the films currently available, but there are two reasons why a wider range could be an advantage: if you are using a film rated at either extreme of the camera's range, your ability to compensate for difficult-exposure shots may be restricted (see 'Exposure compensation'); and faster films may be available in the future.

Ease of use

You cannot expect an SLR camera to be very small. Even so, size has been decreasing over the years, especially since the advent of electronic control, and there are some models that are designed to be as small as possible. Smaller cameras are usually also lighter cameras — a trend which has been helped by the use of synthetic materials rather than metal for many of the components.

Compact SLRs are usually more convenient, especially for everyday use — even if they are definitely not pocket-size. However, a compact design is not always easy to handle when used with a large telephoto lens or a big zoom lens — the lens tends to throw the camera out of balance and can make focusing difficult. And some compact cameras achieve their small size by omitting some useful features. Remember also that the camera body is only the start of an SLR outfit, and its weight and bulk is often overwhelmed by that of the other gear you may want to carry around with it.

Some cameras come in two versions with a different body – one with a metallic finish and the other all-black (at about £10 dearer). The all-black version has no real advantage, except where the photographer wants to pass unnoticed (no, not for clandestine pictures of the Royals at play, but possibly for some types of wild-life photography).

In most aspects of ease of use, there is generally very little to choose between different models of camera – it's probably more a question of simply becoming practised with your camera's particular automation, and the over-ride systems. Other points to bear in mind include:
- **viewfinder information** To some extent, the more the better, but you may get confused if too much information is presented (so an on/off switch may be useful) and you want to be able to see everything even in poor light
- **film changing** A true easy-loading system is worth-while (but this may be possible only with the use of a motor winder, which will increase the bulk and weight of the outfit)
- **shutter release** Generally not so convenient on the front of the body as on the top
- **changing lenses** Bayonets are easier than screw fittings
- **using the viewfinder** Check that the image in the view-finder is reasonably bright. (This will depend to some extent on the lens, and its maximum aperture). Using a viewfinder is made much more difficult if you wear glasses. Some SLRs are easier than others to use in this case – but this is a personal point of view and something you will have to check out for yourself. It would probably be better to have the viewfinder fitted with a corrective lens, and lift up your glasses when taking a picture – this can be done for almost all cameras at a cost of about £4

- **ease of focusing** Check that it is easy to turn the focus ring, and that you can easily see in the viewfinder when you are in focus
- **ease of handling** This may be no problem with a standard lens, but more difficult when you fit a telephoto or large zoom lens: check that you can keep the camera steady. Take more care in checking out' ease of handling if you are left-handed, or cannot-view with your left eye.

Don't expect a complex camera like an SLR to be very robust – whatever you buy, treat it gently.

BUYING GUIDE

A single-lens reflex camera is not the best choice if you simply want to take snap-shots. True, the fully-automatic types are very easy to use and will give excellent results. But you're paying a lot more (and lugging around heavier and bulkier equipment) than you need to. As a rule of thumb, it's probably not worth considering an SLR unless you intend to make use of its most important feature – the ability to use two or three different types of lens. If you don't intend to do this, go for either a disc camera, or a fully-automatic non-reflex camera.

Convinced you want an SLR? Then certainly go for an automatic type – even the most dedicated photographer wants an easy life some of the time – but make sure it can be used in fully manual mode. Don't consider the camera in isolation – make sure that suitable lenses, flash units and accessories are available, and that these, *together* with the camera, make a good-value combination.

It doesn't matter too much what level of automation you go for – all other things being equal the more the better, (except, perhaps, for the multi-programme cameras). Remember to check a camera for ease of use before you buy.

CHAPTER SIX

INSTANT PICTURE CAMERAS

Instant picture cameras give you photos within minutes of taking them. That makes them indispensible on some occasions. But picture quality is not as good as on some other cameras

Instant picture cameras are just what they say. With any ordinary camera, you aim and shoot. But before you can see the results of what you have just taken, you wait until you have finished the whole reel of film, and then have to wait again while the reel is developed and printed by a processing laboratory. With an instant picture camera, you aim and shoot as usual. But then that very picture is ejected out from the camera. Within its layers is a complete processing laboratory, which sets to work developing and printing so that within minutes you have the finished print.

There's no doubt that instant picture cameras are fun and can be useful in a number of ways. At weddings and other functions (or simply, as the pictures opposite show, when granny comes to call) you can give the subjects of your shot a picture immediately to take away with them. Professionals use them to check that the composition of their shot is just what they want before they take the picture with ordinary film. Instant picture cameras make it easy to have second thoughts: if you don't like what you've taken, you can take it again, right there on the spot. Finally, watching a photograph develop before your very eyes is simply great fun.

However, the pictures you get are not as good as from ordinary cameras, and the price is about four times as much. Development isn't as instantaneous as you might think, and takes even longer if the film is cooler than about 15°C. The cameras are also much bulkier than other types, largely

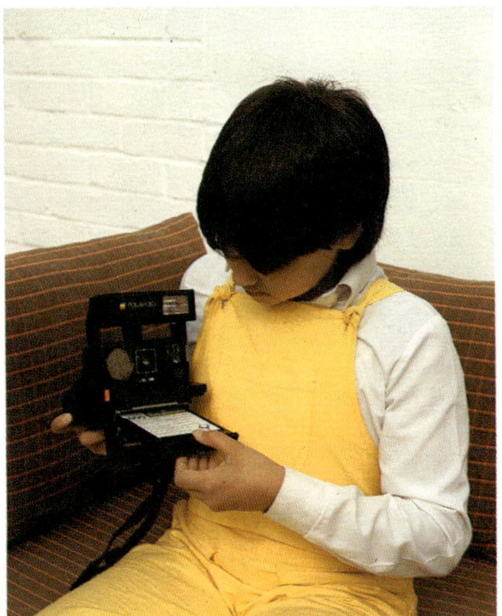
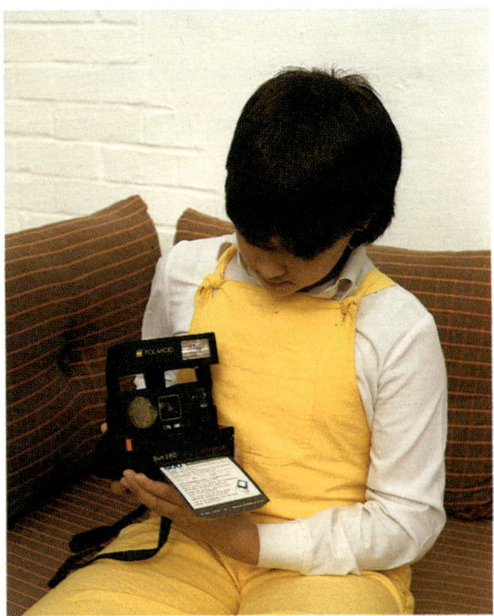

Using an instant picture camera. **From left to right** loading the film; ejecting the covering card; disposing of the card; taking the picture; watching the print ejecting

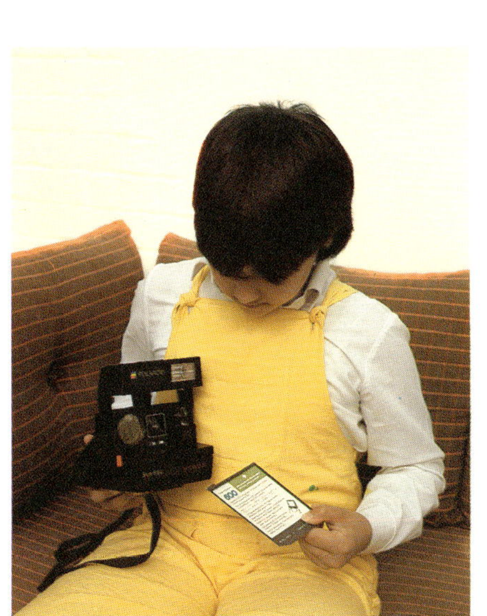

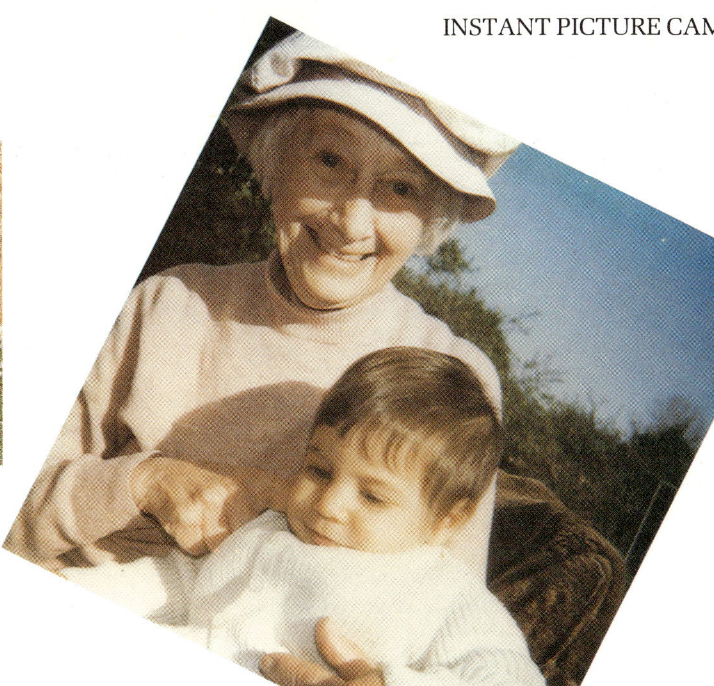

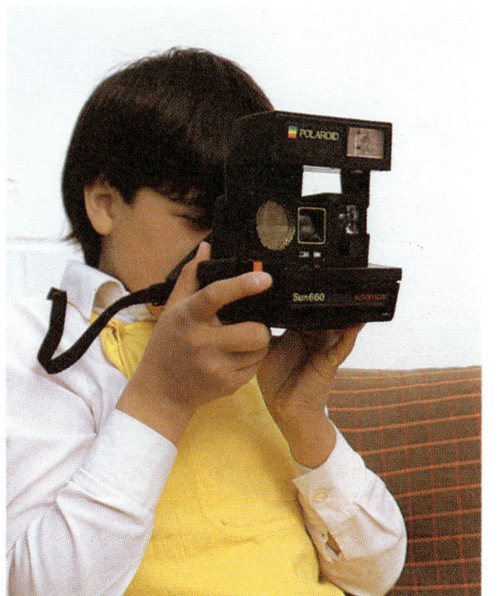

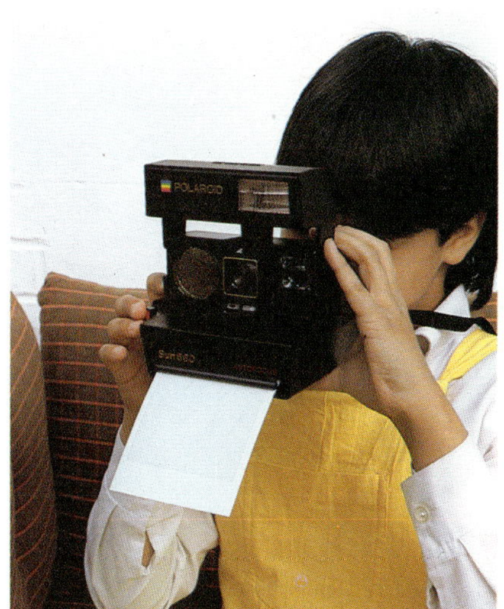

because they have to hold and expose full-size prints. Though most of the cameras fold to some extent for carrying (and therefore have to be unfolded again before you can take a picture) they are still rather large and mostly quite heavy. Cases are available as optional extras, but this doesn't make them much easier to carry around.

There are very few cameras on the market, and they are all made by either Polaroid (who were the originators of the process) or Kodak.

Exposure

All cameras have automatic exposure control – the shutter speed and the aperture size are regulated automatically so that just the right amount of light falls on to the film to give a picture that is correctly lit. The systems used are quite accurate.

A useful addition is an *exposure warning light* to tell you when the exposure time is so slow that you are likely to get blurred pictures (through not being able to hold the camera steady enough) unless you use a tripod. When *Which?* tested cameras in May 1984, they found that only the Kodak ones had exposure warnings, but they tended not to warn you until the exposure was already too slow.

Also useful is an exposure compensation control, usually called a *lighten/darken* knob, to adjust the exposure a little. These will help you take better pictures under some circumstances – see pages 52 and 53 for details of similar systems on SLR cameras – but you do need to practise before you know when and by how much to adjust exposure. (Instant picture cameras make gaining this sort of experience easy, because you can take a shot, study it within a few minutes and try again immediately – but experimenting is not cheap.)

Focusing

The cheaper cameras have *fixed focus* – everything from about 1m or so away should be acceptably sharp. Some cameras have a built-in close-up lens: for taking, say, a head and shoulders portrait, or perhaps a picture of a flower, you can move an extra lens into place, and this allows everything from about 1.2m (4ft) down to about 0.7m to be in focus.

The more expensive cameras use automatic focusing – one system for Kodak (now discontinued), another for Polaroid. Both work well, though both can be fooled by different types of shot – for example, the Polaroid ultra-sonic system will not work through glass. Watch out for autofocuses that can't be switched off: there may be occasions on which you want to decide which part of the picture should be in focus (assuming all of it can't be). When you switch off autofocus you may be left with what is effectively a fixed focus camera – in which case, find out how close it can focus, it may be no closer than about 1.8m (6ft). Or you may be left with a manual focus camera, in which you can alter the focusing until the image seen in the viewfinder is sharp.

Flash

All but the cheapest cameras include built-in flash. The flash fires with each picture unless you deliberately over-ride it – the exposure systems are designed to balance any daylight with light from the flash. This is known as 'fill-in' flash and should ensure that no details are lost in shadow, even in daylight, for subjects that are not too far away from the camera.

With electronic flash, you usually have to wait a few seconds for the flash to charge after turning it on, and between each flash picture. With some cameras, the flash is switched on automatically as you unfold the camera, and then stays on until you fold the camera up again. Assuming you have at least a few seconds' pause between pictures, this means that the flash is almost always ready for work. This is more convenient than the type where the flash switches on only when you lightly press the shutter button – you always have to wait a few seconds before you can take a picture.

The cheapest cameras use Flipflash or flash bar (see page 114). These cost quite a bit to run and, after about 50 flashes, you would have been better off paying the extra for a camera with built-in electronic flash. Plus, of course, it's more inconvenient to have to change separate flash bulbs, and you don't get the benefit of a permanent fill-in flash.

Viewfinder information

These cameras give very little information in the viewfinder. Generally, they are not of the single lens reflex type (you don't look through the same lens that the film looks through) and, in common with other non-reflex cameras, you tend to see *less* in the viewfinder than appears in the final print. You may also find that the viewfinder is aimed slightly off-centre.

These errors can spoil the composition of your pictures – so watch out for them and experiment until you can correct automatically for them. Only some viewfinders have a 'bright frame', to mark the outlines of the picture you are about to take.

Some viewfinders are a bit tricky to use, and you may find that you get best results by not placing your eye too close to the eyepiece.

Film

It's the film that makes instant picture cameras unique: there are different films for different brands and models of cameras, and in general you can use only one type of film with one type of camera.

Cameras intended for amateurs use a *dry process* film. The developing chemicals are locked into the film and are activated automatically when the exposed print is pushed out of the camera.

There are still some cameras, now used mainly by professionals, which take the original *peel-apart* film. This uses a separate negative and print which are brought together as a sandwich (with the developing chemicals forming the filling) on being ejected from the camera. Development takes a couple of minutes after which the print can be peeled away from the negative. You then throw away the negative and the remains of the developing chemicals; you wait another ten minutes or so for the print to dry off completely.

The main drawback of the peel-apart system is that the negative and remaining chemicals are messy to handle and can be poisonous, so you must be careful how you dispose of them. And the total developing time is quite long.

The Polaroid cameras available in mid-1984 took Polaroid 600 film; the Kodak cameras took Kodak Trimprint. Both come in packs containing ten prints. With Polaroid, the prints start appearing after about 30 seconds compared with about 50 seconds for Kodak; you have to wait a few more seconds before you know whether you have a successful picture. Development is almost finished after four minutes for Polaroid and eight for Kodak, although in both cases the prints continue to get darker for four minutes more. Development is faster in hot weather, but the films will not develop properly below about 15°C. If you want to take pictures on a cold day, immediately put the print in a warm place –

underneath your clothes next to your skin, say (not something you'd want to do on a winter skiing holiday).

The Polaroid prints are rather bulky to put in albums because there is a pod of developing chemicals left along one edge. With the Kodak Trimprint the backing can be peeled off safely about an hour after taking each picture. This leaves a print no thicker than one from an ordinary colour film.

Polaroid 600 prints are square – measuring about 78mm x 78mm on a rectangular backing of around 90mm x 110mm. Kodak prints are rectangular – which gives you more flexibility in composing pictures – measuring 92mm x 68mm, held on a 100mm x 110mm plastic backing.

You can, of course, still get the older films for use in older cameras (the Kodak PR-10 and the Polaroid SX-70 Time Zero, or peel-apart films for very old cameras) but you can't interchange new and old, with one exception – Kodak Trimprint can be used in the old Kodak cameras, but may give over-exposed prints unless you use the darken control each time.

Colours The colour rendering you get from instant picture film is often disappointing. There's no clear-cut winner between the two brands, but according to the latest *Which?* tests Kodak has the edge, especially for outdoor scenes where the Polaroid film tends to be too blue or too yellow. Though skin tones with Kodak are often rather pale, this is better than the Polaroid where they can be too red.

Very long and very short exposures can affect the colours of prints. Polaroid prints may tend to be rather bluish when used for exposures of several seconds (you can't take long exposures with Kodak cameras). On the other hand, for very short exposures (as you might have when automatic electronic flash units are taking very close-up pictures) Polaroid prints go slightly pinkish, and Kodak prints are not affected.

If you want to take instant pictures in the Tropics, beware. Kodak pictures taken in hot conditions tend to turn blue and too dark (use the lighten control, as the instructions tell you) whereas Polaroid prints are more acceptable. In very hot and steamy conditions, you must keep film packages sealed – and you may find only Kodak film remains useable even then. Keeping sealed films in a refrigerator or freezer (see page 100) will help.

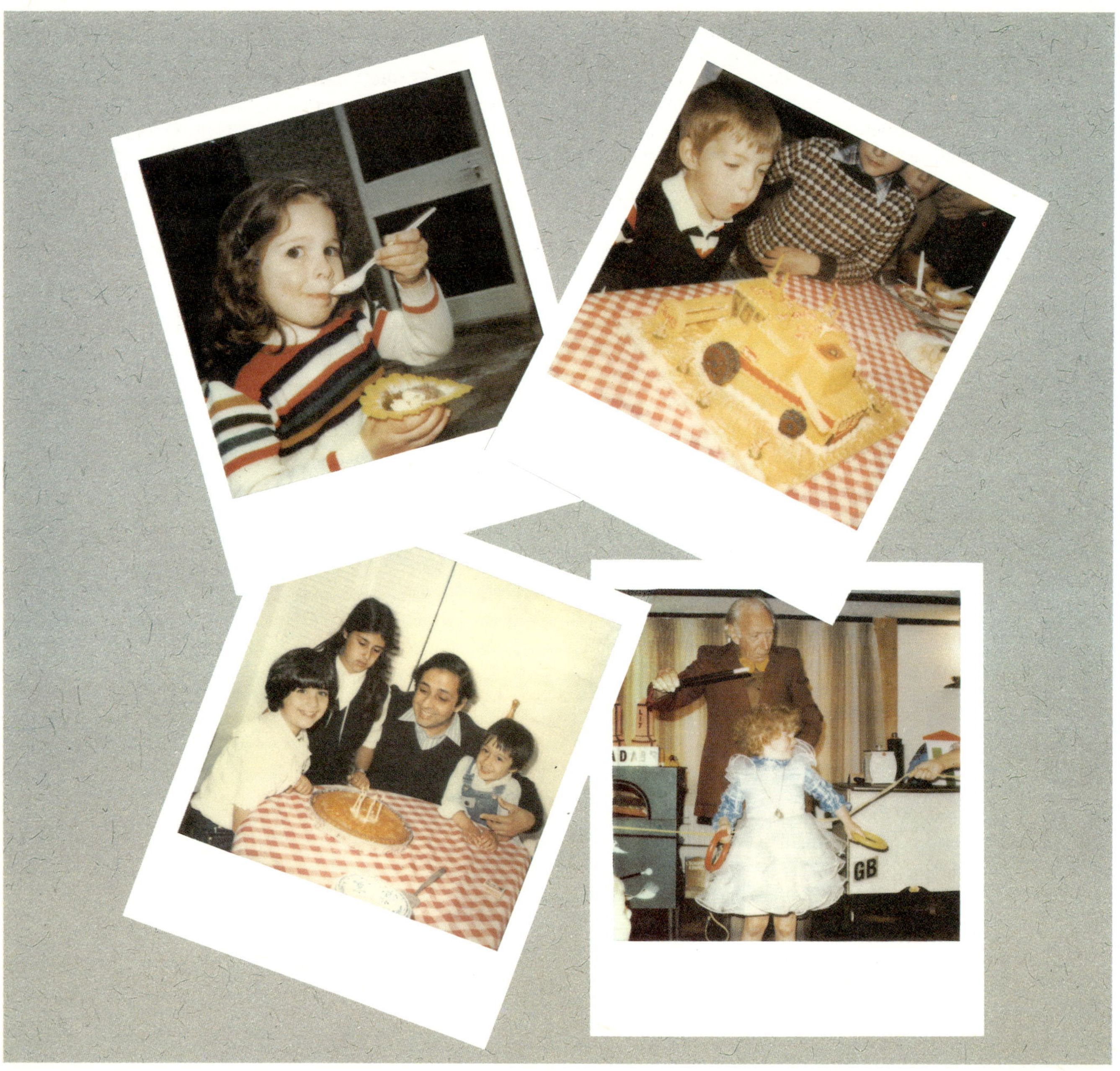

Most colour prints will eventually fade if left in strong daylight, and instant prints are no exception. Some photo processors will make copies of instant prints and it would be sensible to put one of these on display, keeping the original print in an album or tucked up in a drawer – remember that you have no negative from which to make copies in the future.

As copies are only about half the price of the original take care not to get carried away when shooting – don't take more pictures of a scene than you need for giving away at the time. You can also get enlargements of photos you particularly fancy, but sharpness will not be so good as with enlargements from a good 35mm negative.

BUYING GUIDE

Instant picture photography has its uses for special needs or for fun. But it is very expensive, the colours are often not very good, and the cameras are heavy or bulky to carry around. And now that ordinary print films can be processed on the same day, or even in a couple of hours, there is less need for instant photography than previously.

If you do want an instant picture camera, consider it as a second camera rather than your usual one, and certainly not for recording holiday scenery.

Immediate results from your party pictures is one of the advantages of instant picture cameras

CHAPTER SEVEN

LENSES

An SLR camera starts to make sense only when you use it with different lenses – which can change the whole view, perspective and range of your pictures

Changing from one type of lens to another can mean just the difference between being able to take a picture at all and finding something else to shoot. Or it can mean one of the most important ways in which you can influence how your picture is composed, and so how you can bring creativity into photography. Although the theory of lenses and their different effects is the same no matter what type of camera you have, it is almost exclusively with the SLR that you have any say in the type of lens fitted to your camera.

Lenses are usually described in terms of their *focal length*. Technically, this is the distance that the lens has to be positioned from the film, in order for subjects at infinity (in practice, over 20 metres away) to be in focus. It gives you some idea of the physical size of the lens unit – often, a lens with a long focal length is equally long; one with a short focal length is quite stubby – but it doesn't give you much idea of the sort of picture you will get with the different types.

A better description is in terms of the angle of view that the different types of lens give you. A **wide-angle** lens encompasses a wide angle of view: you can get a lot of the scene in front of you into the picture, but of course all the objects will appear relatively tiny. A narrow-angle lens is often called a **telephoto**, and it does act in the same way as a telescope: it makes objects a long way away appear very close, but at the expense of not including very much of the scene in the picture.

The 'standard' SLR lens has a focal length of about 50mm. There is a range of wide-angle lenses available, all the way down to the 'fish-eye' with a focal length of 8mm and an angle of view of 180°, and an even greater range of telephotos going up to the monster 1000mm with an angle of view of 2.5°. A good choice for a beginner would be a 28mm wide-angle and a 200mm telephoto in addition to the 50mm standard. (You may find a 200mm lens a bit unwieldy, in which case an alternative is a 135mm lens, though this of course has less 'telephoto' effect.) These three lenses will do for most of your needs, and they are different enough for your choice to have a real effect on your compositions (and for us to show you what those effects are).

The lenses described so far have a single angle of view, and are known as *fixed focal-length* lenses. An alternative is a lens with a *variable* angle of view and focal length: see page 81 for details of these **zoom** lenses.

What different lenses do

Different lenses affect the angle of view, and so how much of a scene you can get in the picture. But they also affect two other things:

● **depth of field**   This is the range of distances which remain in focus – see page 17. For a given aperture setting, or f-stop, wide-angle lenses have a greater depth of field. For example, with a 28mm lens at f8, and set for 4.5m (15ft) the depth of field is from infinity down to 2.3m (7½ft) – for most outdoor subjects in reasonable light, you need hardly change focus at all. Sometimes, though, you *want* a restricted depth of field (so that only the main subject is in focus, and all the remaining unwanted detail is left undistractingly fuzzy): a telephoto lens has a short depth of field and would help to give you this effect

● **perspective**   With close subjects, wide-angle lenses produce pictures which have a feeling of increased depth – that is, objects in the foreground tend to dominate the picture more than they would normally. So portrait pictures are out with wide-angle lenses – to get a large enough image of the face you would have to get so close that the nose would appear unduly prominent. On the other hand, a long telephoto lens squashes the perspective and produces pictures that appear to have very little depth in them.

There are some occasions on which you'll be forced to use one type of lens rather than another – when you can't get close enough to a scene you'll have to use a telephoto; when you can't get far enough away, you'll have to use a wide-angle. The fun comes when you can change *your* position relative to your subject, and could use any one of the lenses. Explaining what's possible, however, is no substitute for showing you; the photographs over the next five pages will give you an idea of how different lenses behave, and what is possible with each one.

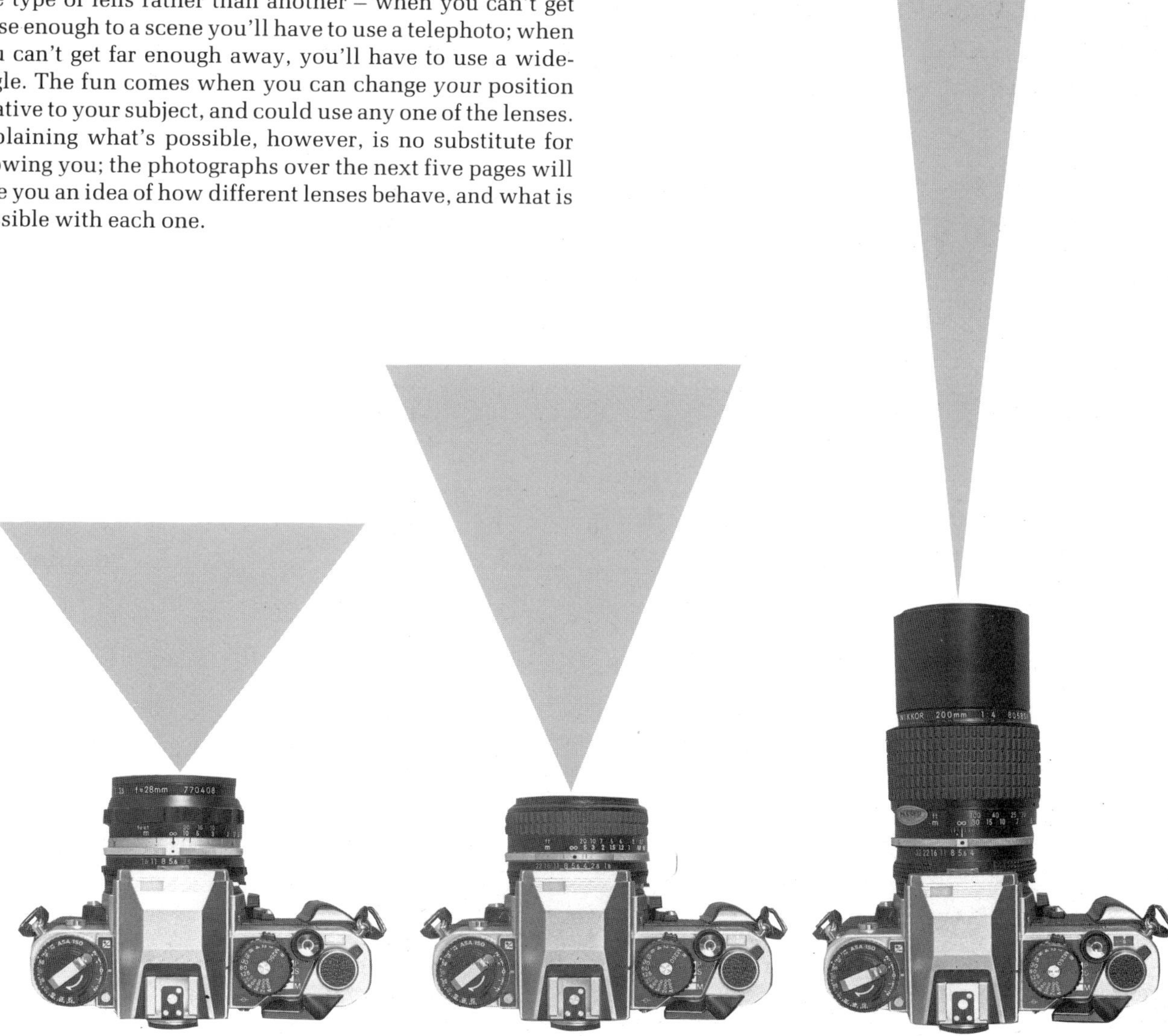

Lenses of different focal lengths give different angles of view.
From left to right 28mm; 50mm; 200mm

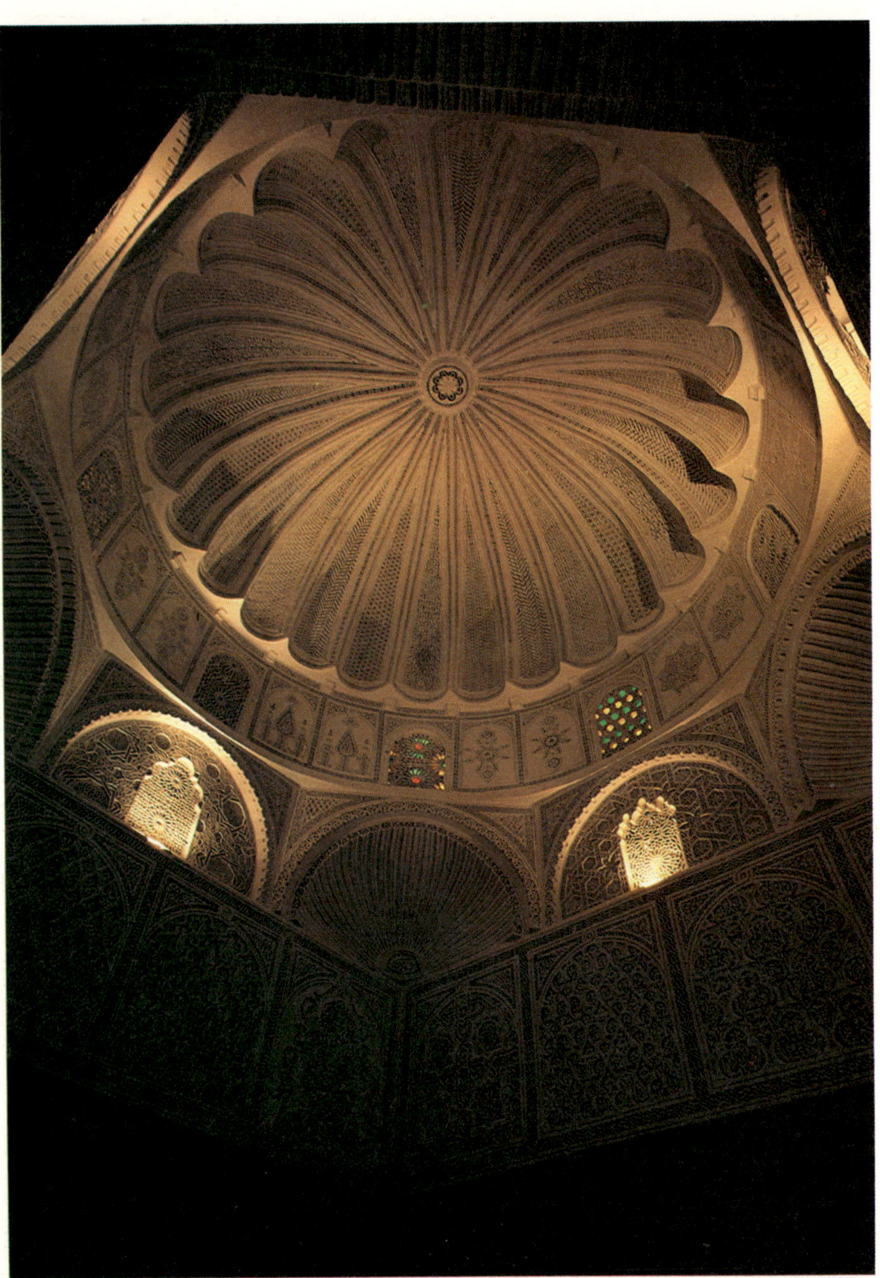

A 20mm lens allows you to make a little out of a lot: you can cram the whole of this dome into your picture without having to dig a hole in the floor to get a long distance away

A 1000mm lens lets you make a lot out of a little: the setting sun and the chapel on the hillside fill the picture, even though the intervening water prevents you from getting close to the scene

Lenses of different focal lengths are sometimes essential, simply so that you can get a picture of just the amount of the scene you want, as on the previous pages. But when you have the choice of both the type of lens you can use *and* where you can stand, you can exercise a great deal of control over the composition of your pictures. The three pictures on this page were all taken from the same spot using, **from top to bottom**, a 28mm, 50mm, and 200mm lens. The differences in the amount of the scene each shows, and the sizes of the subjects within it, are obvious...

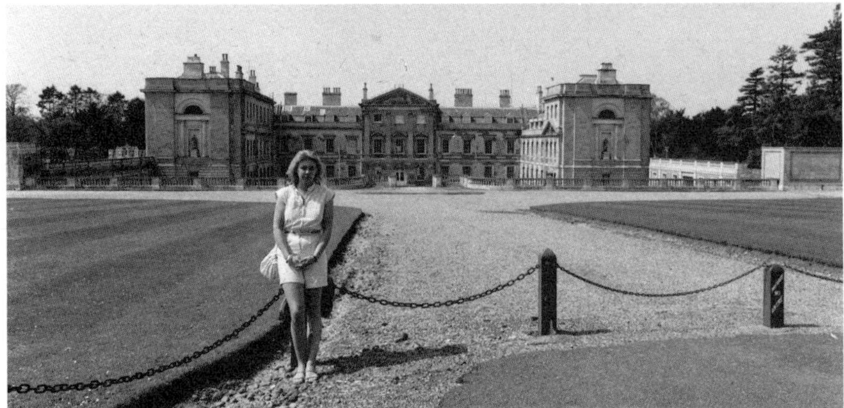

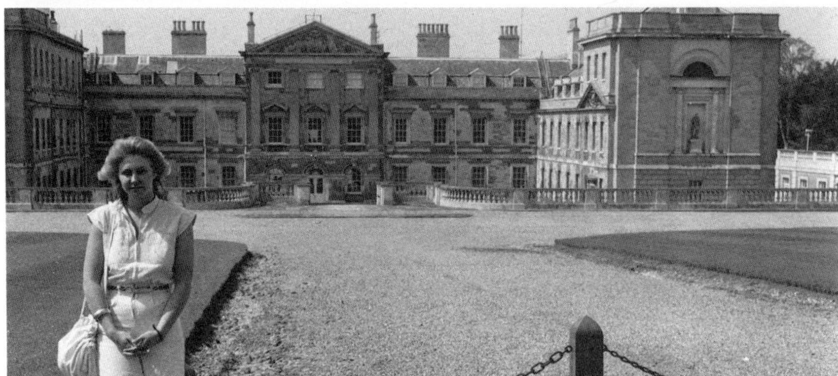

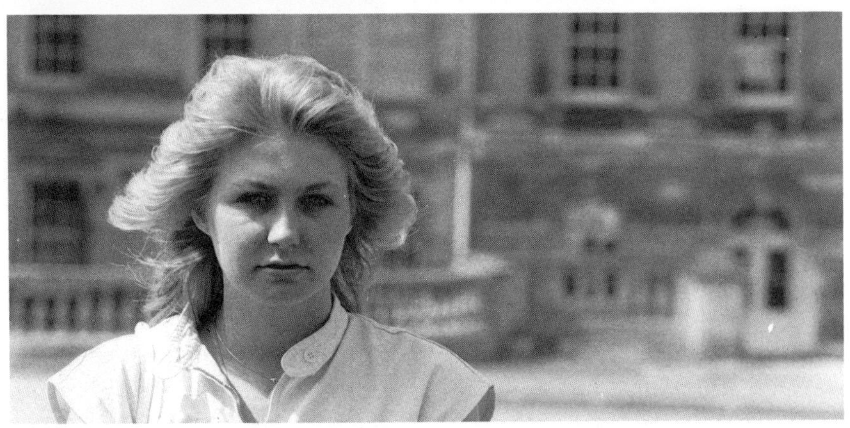

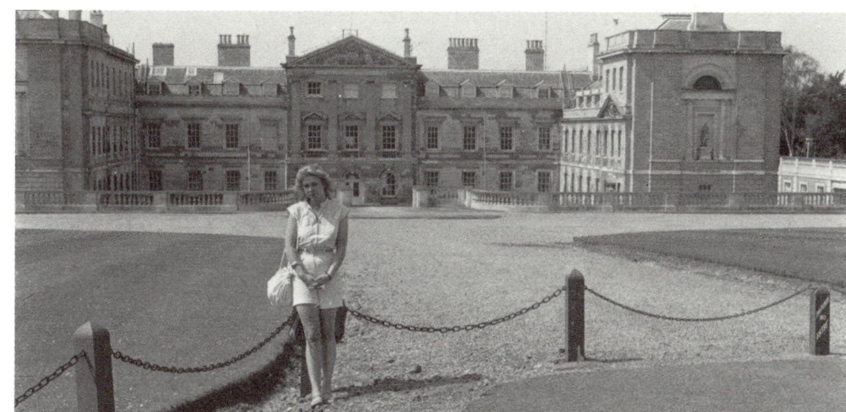

...these three pictures are all taken using the same 50mm lens, but getting gradually closer to the subjects. Compare them with those on the previous page: in each pair, the girl is the same size, but the relative size of the house behind her is dramatically different

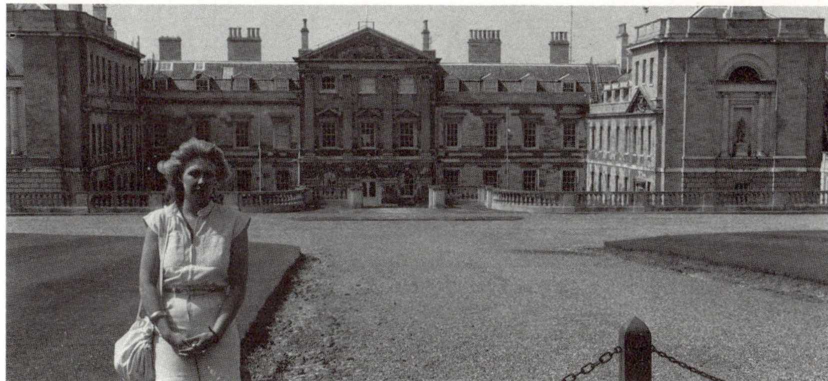

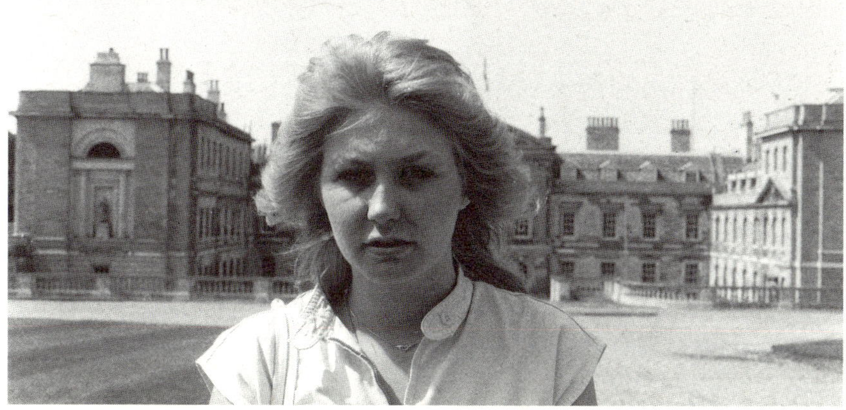

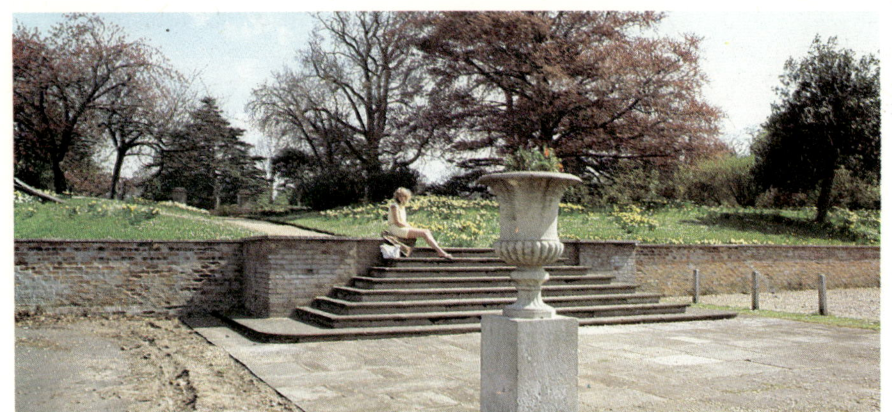

Using a different lens does *not*, in itself, change the perspective in your picture (though it can contribute to that effect by allowing you – even forcing you at times – to change your position relative to your subjects). These three pictures were taken from the same spot, again using 28mm, 50mm, and 200mm lenses. The **bottom** one is simply an enlargement of the centre portion of the **top** one, and we could have achieved the same effect by simply 'blowing up' the top picture – except that picture quality suffers when you start to make big enlargements

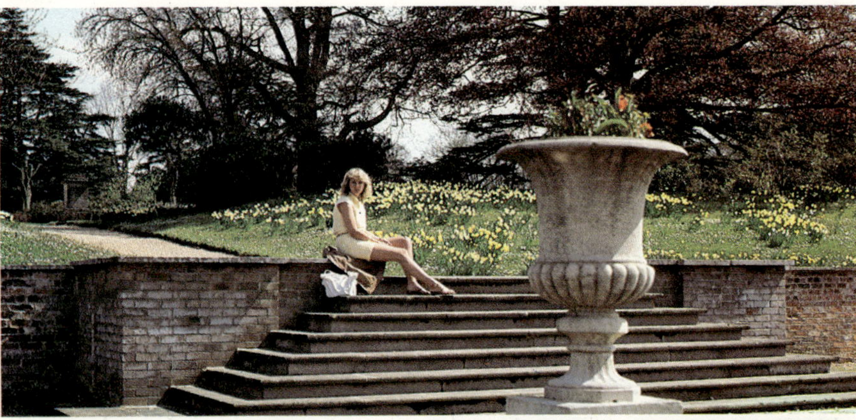

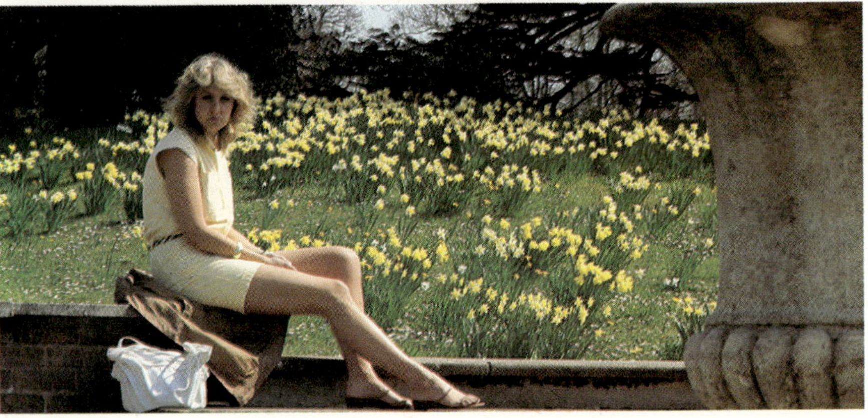

Practical points

Photography is a mixture of art and science. Choosing a lens that will give you the perfect composition is only the start – there are also some practical problems to overcome which will affect the photographs you can take.

Camera shake   A 200mm telephoto lens enlarges the image you would get from a standard lens by a factor of four – but the slightest movement is also magnified fourfold, so there is much more chance of camera shake making your pictures blurred. The answer is to use faster shutter speeds with the longer focal-length lenses.

As a rule of thumb, use a shutter speed that is faster than 1 over the focal length of the lens you are using. For example, with a 200mm lens use something faster than $\frac{1}{200}$ second, say $\frac{1}{250}$ second or faster. Using this rule gives you a slowest speed with a standard lens of $\frac{1}{60}$ second, and means that if you can use a wide-angle lens you should be safe with shutter speeds down to $\frac{1}{30}$ second. It also implies that the occasions on which you can use a telephoto lens over 200mm are limited – you'll need a fast film and good light to be able to use the necessary shutter speeds of $\frac{1}{500}$ second or faster. The problem is made worse by the fact that you can't use very large apertures (low f-numbers) with telephoto lenses – see below for why – as a means of compensating for the faster shutter speeds you need.

Of course, all this doesn't mean you *can't* take successful pictures at slower speeds – just that you're unlikely to be able to hold the camera steady enough without resting it on a tripod or the top of a wall or something.

Maximum and minimum apertures   The amount of light that any lens lets through on to a film depends on the focal length of that lens – for a given physical size of lens aperture the longer the focal length the less light gets through. It's impracticable to make lens units with a very large diameter, so this places a limit on the lowest f-number you can achieve – a limit that gets stricter the longer the focal length of the lens. So 200mm telephotos are normally restricted to an f-number no lower than f3.5; and longer telephotos to perhaps f5.6. Standard lenses of f1.8 (or even f1.4) and wide-angle lenses of f2.8 are common.

In most cases, a maximum aperture of even f5.6 is not really a great limitation – and the greater availability of fast films means that you can still take pictures in poor light with apertures of this size. (But bear in mind that smaller apertures make the image in the viewfinder less bright, which makes focusing more difficult.) You *can* get lenses with larger apertures than these if you really want to – but the addition of even half a stop to the aperture usually adds a lot to the price. As an extreme example, one model of 200mm lens costs over twice as much in its f2.8 version as in its f4 version. Take care when shopping around, and checking adverts in magazines and so on, that you really are comparing like with like as far as the f-number goes.

Minimum apertures can also vary from model to model. However, there are very few lenses offering anything poorer than f16 – though this *might* not be small enough if you wanted to use a very fast film in very bright conditions, you're unlikely to be faced with this situation often. If you do meet this problem, one way round it is to use a 'neutral density filter' over the lens to block out some of the light (see page 106).

Closest focusing distance   As you might imagine, the closest focusing distance (that is, how close you can get to the subject and still achieve sharp focus) varies with the type of lens – being greatest for telephotos and smallest for wide-angles. A reasonable figure for a 200mm lens would be about 2m (6½ft), for a 50mm lens about 0.45m (1½ft), and for a 28mm lens about 0.3m (1ft).

If you must focus closer than these distances, you'll need some sort of extension ring, bellows, close-up lens, or a lens with a **macro** capability – see pages 85 to 89.

Matching your camera   Remember (see page 61) that lenses of different brands are not normally interchangeable – that is, you can't use one brand of lens with another brand of camera. Sometimes there is no interchangeability even within a brand – an older-style lens may not fit the latest body of the same brand. In fact, the situation is a little more complex than this. For a start, a lens may be 'interchangeable' in the sense that it physically fits a particular camera body – but you may not be able to get all the automatic facilities (which require passing signals between lens and body) to work properly. This is something to watch out for when

A zoom lens allows you the equivalent angle of view of several fixed-focus lenses in one – though you would still need several zoom lenses to cover the range of lenses shown here and below. From the left in this row: 20mm; 24mm; 28mm; 35mm; 50mm

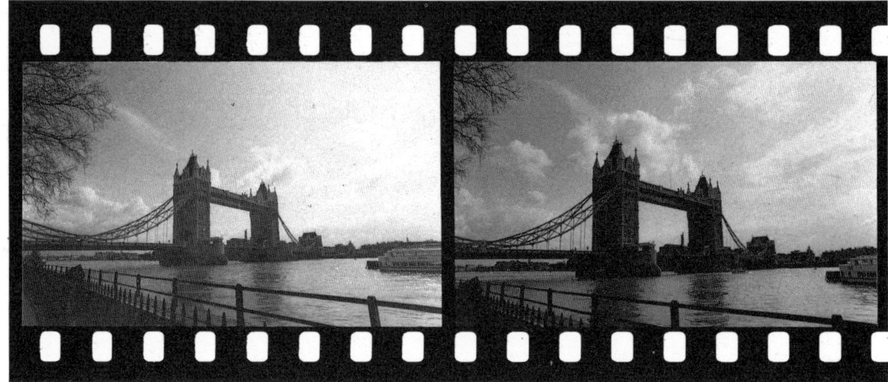

buying additional lenses – best to take your camera with you if shopping in person to make sure everything works. If you're shopping by post, make it clear what brand and model camera you're buying for, and that you will return the lens for a full refund (including postage charges) if they try to sell you something that isn't one-hundred per cent compatible.

Another source of confusion is that lenses do not necessarily have the same brand names as their corresponding cameras – so you can't just go on names. For example, Konica cameras use Hexanon lenses, and lenses for Olympus cameras are called Zuiko.

Finally, a lens from the camera manufacturer is not your only choice – many brands of lenses are available with alternative mounting connections to fit almost any camera. Usually you buy the version specially made for your camera, but a few manufacturers produce just one lens and you buy a special mounting adaptor to fit your particular camera.

Zoom lenses

If the best thing about an SLR is the *ability* to interchange lenses, then the worst thing about an SLR is *having* to interchange lenses – even with simple bayonet mount (see page 61) it's a fiddly job to remove one lens and fit another. And you've always got the wrong lens on at the crucial moment. *And* you lumber yourself with a load of equipment to carry around.

Each successive picture in these sequences is an enlargement of the central part of the picture before it. From the left in this row: 85mm; 135mm; 200mm; 300mm; 500mm

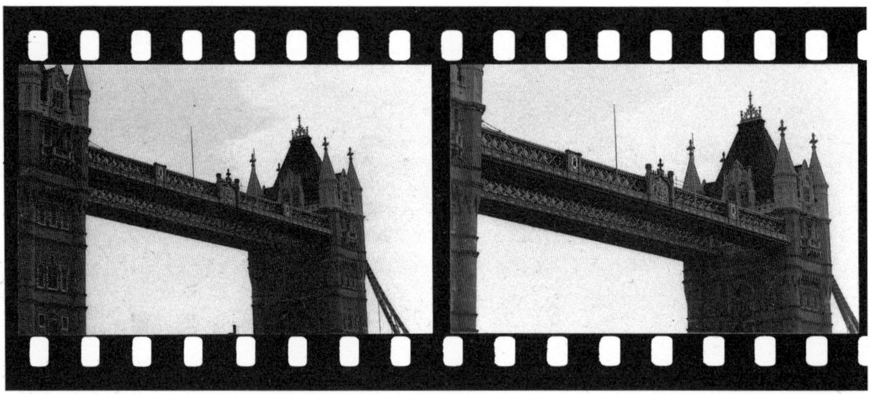

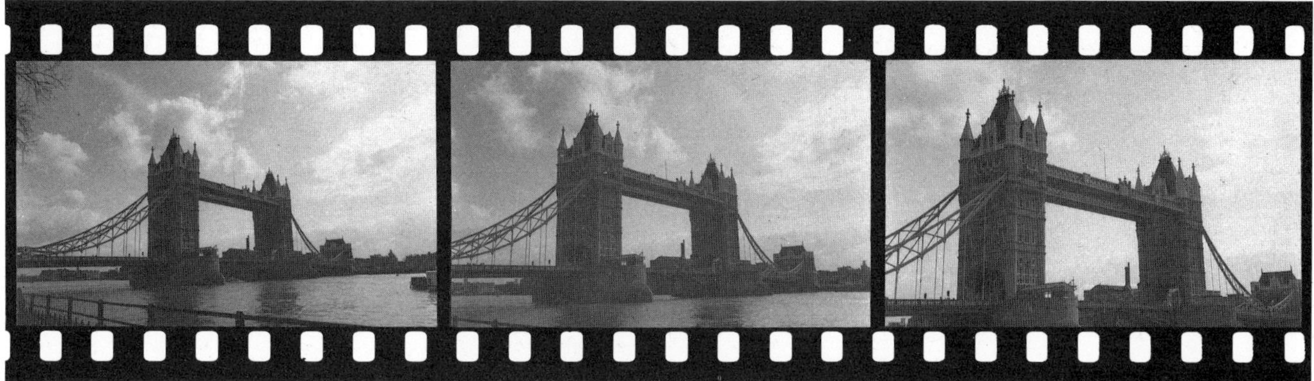

The zoom lens is several lenses in one, so it solves most of these problems. In fact, it's an infinite number of lenses in one – you can change it to any focal length you like between its minimum and maximum settings. There isn't one zoom lens that covers the *whole* focal length range, though, so you still have to choose, and you may still have to carry more than one lens around with you. The normal types available, and their focal length ranges are:

● **standard, 35mm to 70mm**   gives you a bit of leeway round the usual fixed-focus 50mm lens. It is useful for taking photos at, say, a wedding or other function – you can stay a little further back when you want candid shots, or expand your angle of view to take group pictures, without having to hold up the guests while you fiddle with different lenses. But the difference you get at either end of the scale, compared with what you get at 50mm, is not very great

● **wide-angle, 28mm to 50mm**   has no particular attraction for the amateur. If you just want wide-angle, you'd be better off buying a 28mm fixed lens – which would be cheaper and lighter than the zoom. If you must have a single lens for general use, a *28mm to 80mm*, or a *35mm to 105mm* would be better choices

● **short telephoto, 70mm to 150mm**   is quite a good choice in the telephoto department: it is relatively cheap and easy to handle. But its range at the top is a little bit restricted for many uses

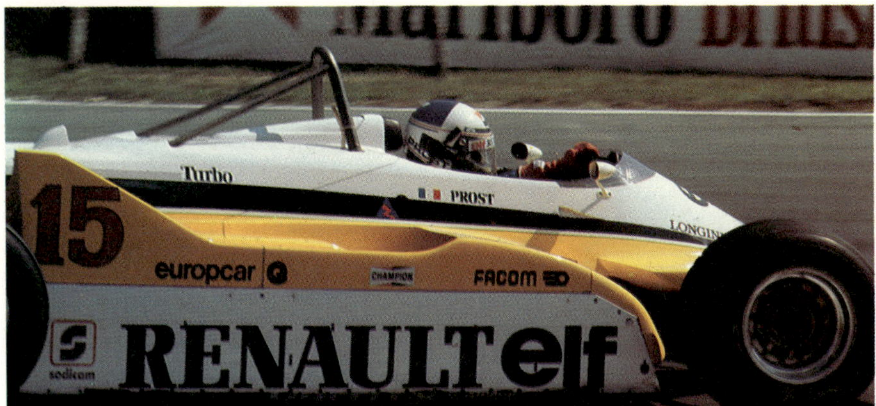

Left It's wise to keep some way back from racing cars on the track – a 300mm lens was used to allow the photographer to keep at a respectful distance and still produce this close-up of a car in action

Below A wide-angle lens is not normally a good choice for portraits – if you get close enough for your subject to fill the frame the perspective is quite distorted. But this distortion can sometimes enhance your pictures: here, a 20mm lens was used to emphasise the hands of the worker, and throw the back of the room into the distance

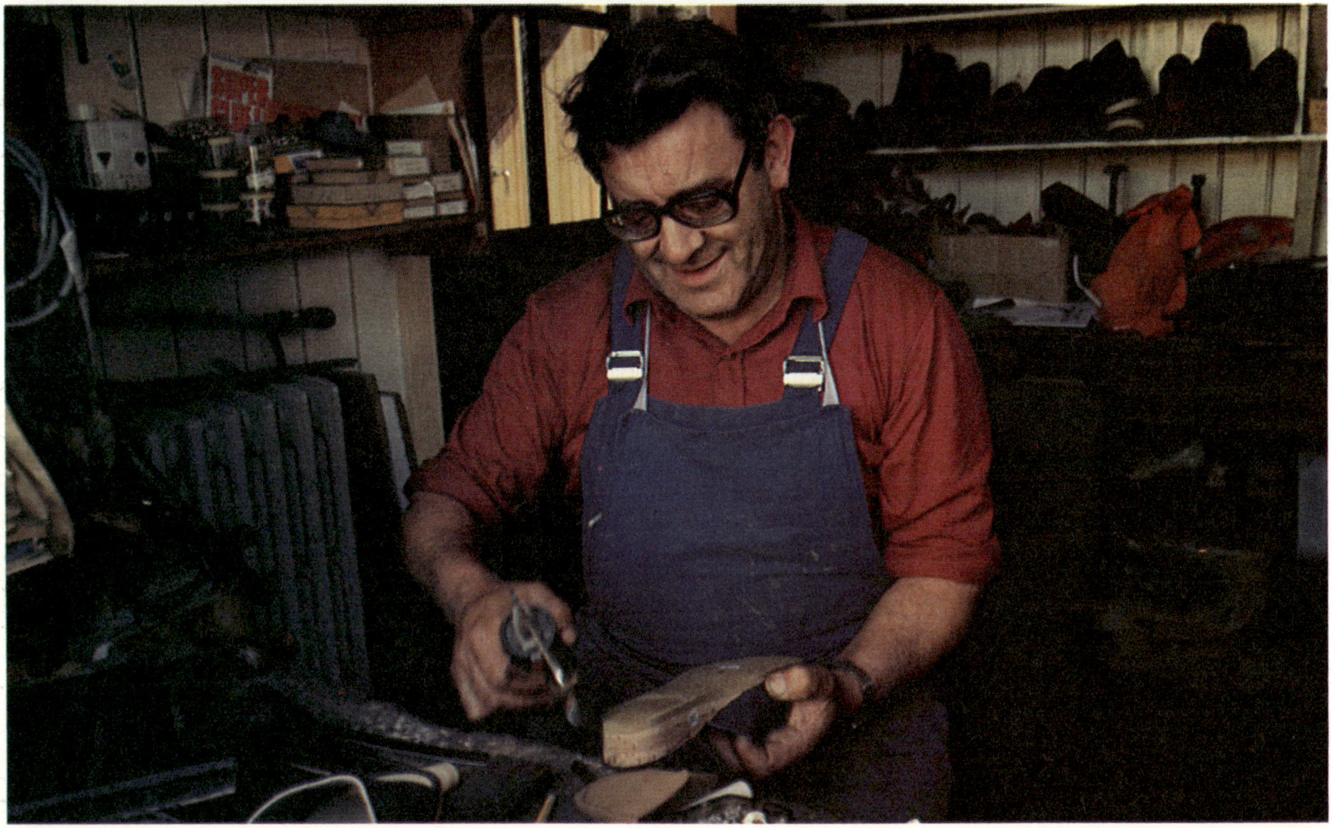

Right The classic lens for portraiture –
80mm – was used here: the subject fills the
frame, but perspective is not distorted and
the photographer can stand a little way back
and not intrude on the subject

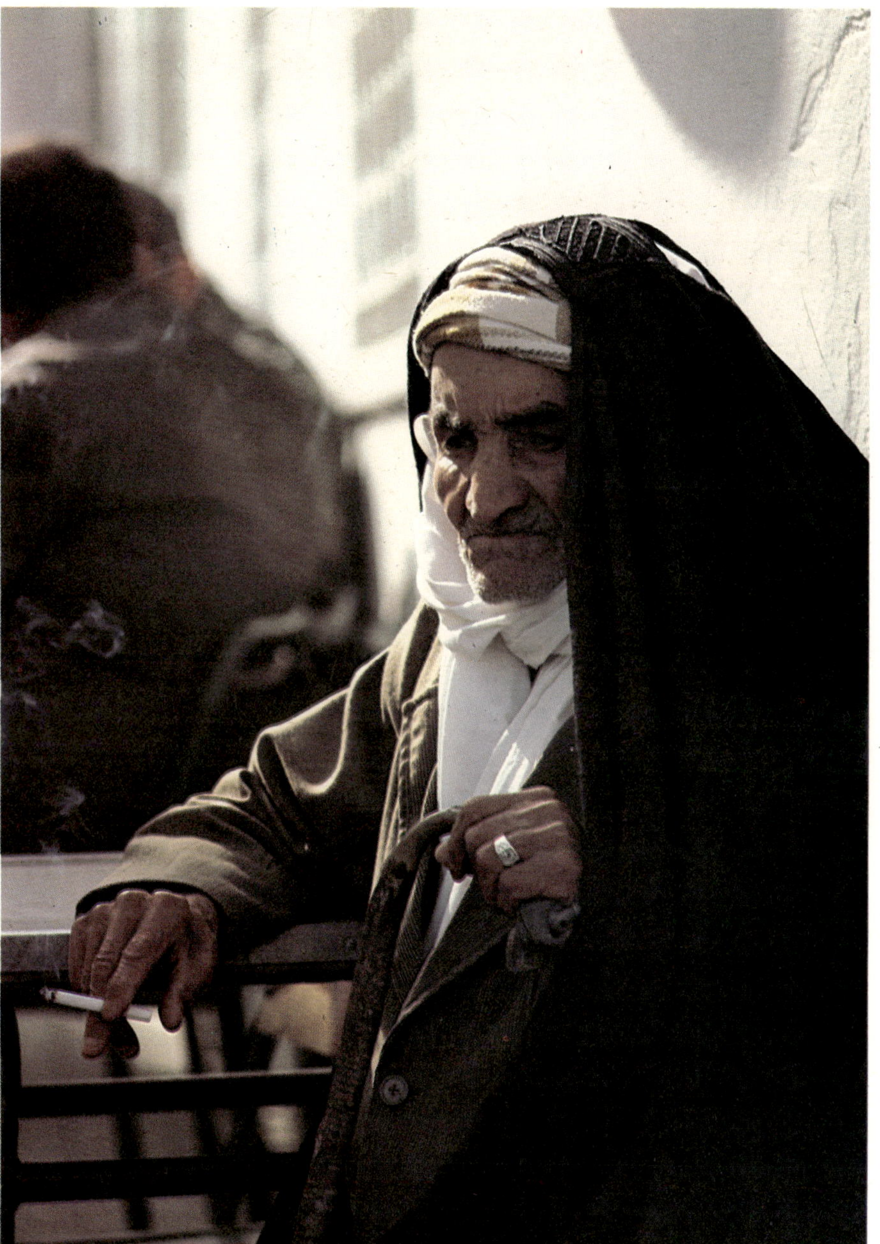

● **medium telephoto, 70mm to 210mm, or 80mm to 200mm** is probably the best-selling type. Though these lenses are rather expensive and a little cumbersome, they do give a wide range of focal lengths and cover the same ground as three important fixed lenses – the 80mm 'portrait' lens; the classic 135mm telephoto, and the more powerful 200mm telephoto – so they are a good choice.

Zoom or standard?

Serious photographers will argue the points for and against zoom lenses hotly. In the past zoom lenses did not give as good a picture as a fixed focal-length lens, but it is now possible to get zoom lenses of good quality and performance without having to pay the earth. So the main argument should be one of convenience.

Pros In favour of a zoom lens:
● you should not need so many lenses and you do not have to change lenses so often
● a single zoom lens is lighter and cheaper than the two or three lenses that it in practice replaces
● you can play around with the effect of different focal lengths easily, so the shots you take should be better composed.

Cons Against a zoom lens:
● a zoom lens is heavy and cumbersome – a 200mm zoom, for example, usually weighs about half as much again as a 200mm fixed lens
● you're stuck with the worst points of the longest focal length even if you rarely use this length – with an 80-200mm lens, for example, you have to put up with the equivalent of a 200mm lens (and more) on your camera even if most of the time you use only the 80mm-end of the focal length range. You are similarly restricted in maximum aperture: it's comparable to the smaller aperture you get on a 200mm lens, not the larger one that an 80mm lens can provide
● you still need more than one lens – to cover our Best Combination lenses (28mm, 50mm and 200mm) requires at least two lenses, and perhaps three – though of course a combination of zooms covers more than the same number of fixed lenses even if doesn't extend the range of focal lengths you can cover. 'Super-zooms', which cover a large focal length range (eg 35-200mm) are becoming available, but they are big and heavy
● the image you see in the viewfinder is less bright than for a fixed focal-length lens, and this makes the zoom lens less easy to focus.

Zoom in operation

One problem with zoom lenses is that you have another control to adjust while composing your picture – the one that alters the focal length. The complication is that by changing the focal length you can upset the focusing, so that as you zoom in and out, you also have to be correcting the focus.

Most lenses have a single control which you push or pull for zooming and twist for focusing – this **one-touch** operation is reasonably convenient to use. The alternative **two-touch** control has separate twist rings for focus and zoom, which you have to use one after the other (you can't have both hands on the lens, because you need one to hold the camera body) so it is slower in operation. There is now a one-touch lens with a switch to lock the focal length so that you can concentrate on the focusing. This also avoids the problem of some zoom lenses which 'zoom' by their own weight if pointed up or down at too steep an angle.

Tele-converter

A tele-converter is a small extra lens which you insert between the camera body and the main lens to increase its focal length. A x2 converter doubles the focal length (from 50mm to 100mm, for example); a x3 triples it (from 80mm to 240mm, perhaps). You can use a tele-converter with either fixed focus or with zoom lenses.

The main drawback of a teleconverter is that it reduces the maximum aperture of the main lens significantly – a x2 converter by two stops (down from f2.8 to f5.6, for example) and a x3 by three stops (f2.8 to f8). Another drawback is that the quality of the picture is poorer – focusing at the edges and corners deteriorates, and distortion and *vignetting* (a fault which shows up as the picture being darker at the edges and corners) are also more marked. These faults should not be too noticeable with a x2 converter, but it's probably best not to risk using a x3 converter.

Matched multiplier Until recently, tele-converters of one

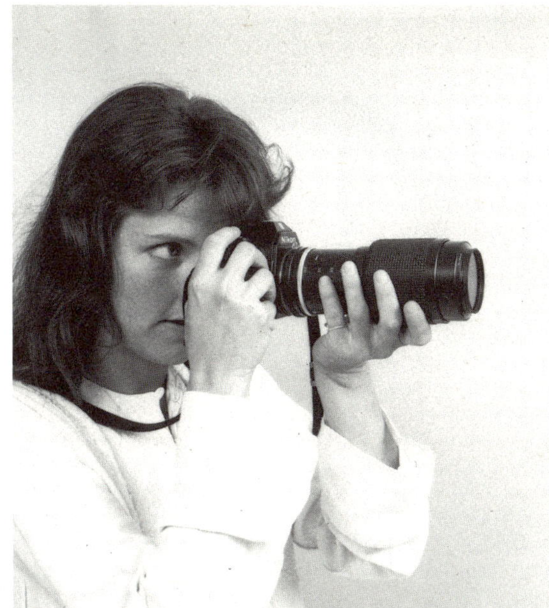

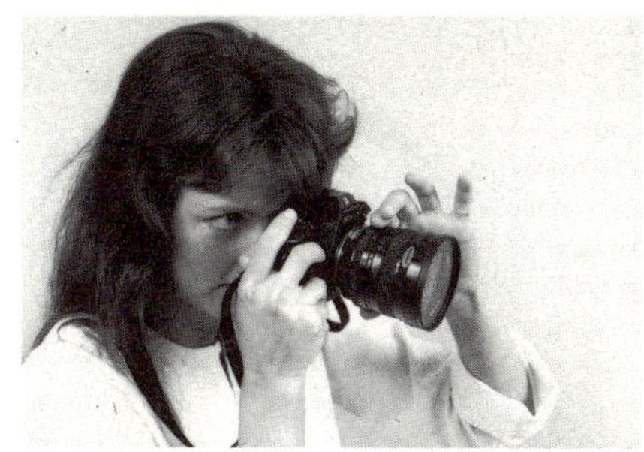

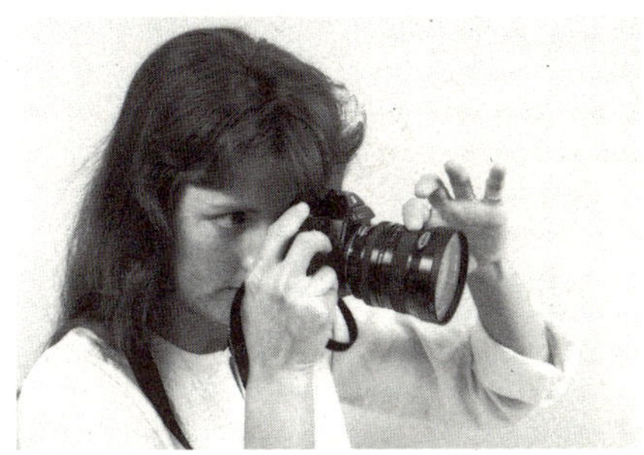

A *one-touch* zoom (**right**) allows you to alter focal length and focusing in one operation; with a *two-touch* zoom (**far right**) you must first alter the focal length and then, probably, correct the focusing

brand could be mounted on all lenses with the same mounting system. Now there are converters designed for only a single type of lens – *matched multipliers* – which aim to reduce faults and improve image quality; they are mostly intended for use with zoom lenses. A matched multiplier is better than a standard converter (though not perfect) and is worth buying if you do not want to spend a lot of money on a number of different lenses – it gives you an enormous range of focal lengths, with acceptable quality, for a reasonable price.

Macrophotography

True macrophotography is the art of photographing a (small) subject so that the size of its image on the negative is life-size or larger. Why make a fuss about the size? With ordinary lenses you could not hope to take a clear picture of a flower or an insect, or anything of that sort of size – the image on the negative would be very small and problems with grain using even a slow film (see page 91 for an explanation of this) mean that the picture would be very indistinct and lacking in detail. Getting close is not the answer, because there is a limit

to how close a close-up you can take and still keep in focus. So if you are interested in the prospect of photographing flies' eyes and bees' knees, consider the following options:
- a special macro lens with a focal length of about 50mm
- a macro lens with a focal length of 105mm or so
- a close-up lens
- extension tubes or bellows.

50mm macro   This costs more than an ordinary standard lens and its maximum aperture is less (probably f3.5). Some offer a true 1:1 *reproduction ratio* (the image on the negative is the same as in real life) but most give a smaller ratio. They can focus very close to objects – perhaps as close as 150mm (6in) and this helps you get close enough to photograph quite small objects satisfactorily even if the reproduction ratio is not as good as 1:1.

105mm macro   In effect a small telephoto lens, a macro with a focal length around 105mm costs even more than a standard macro, and its maximum aperture will be even smaller – perhaps around f4. Its main advantage is that, as

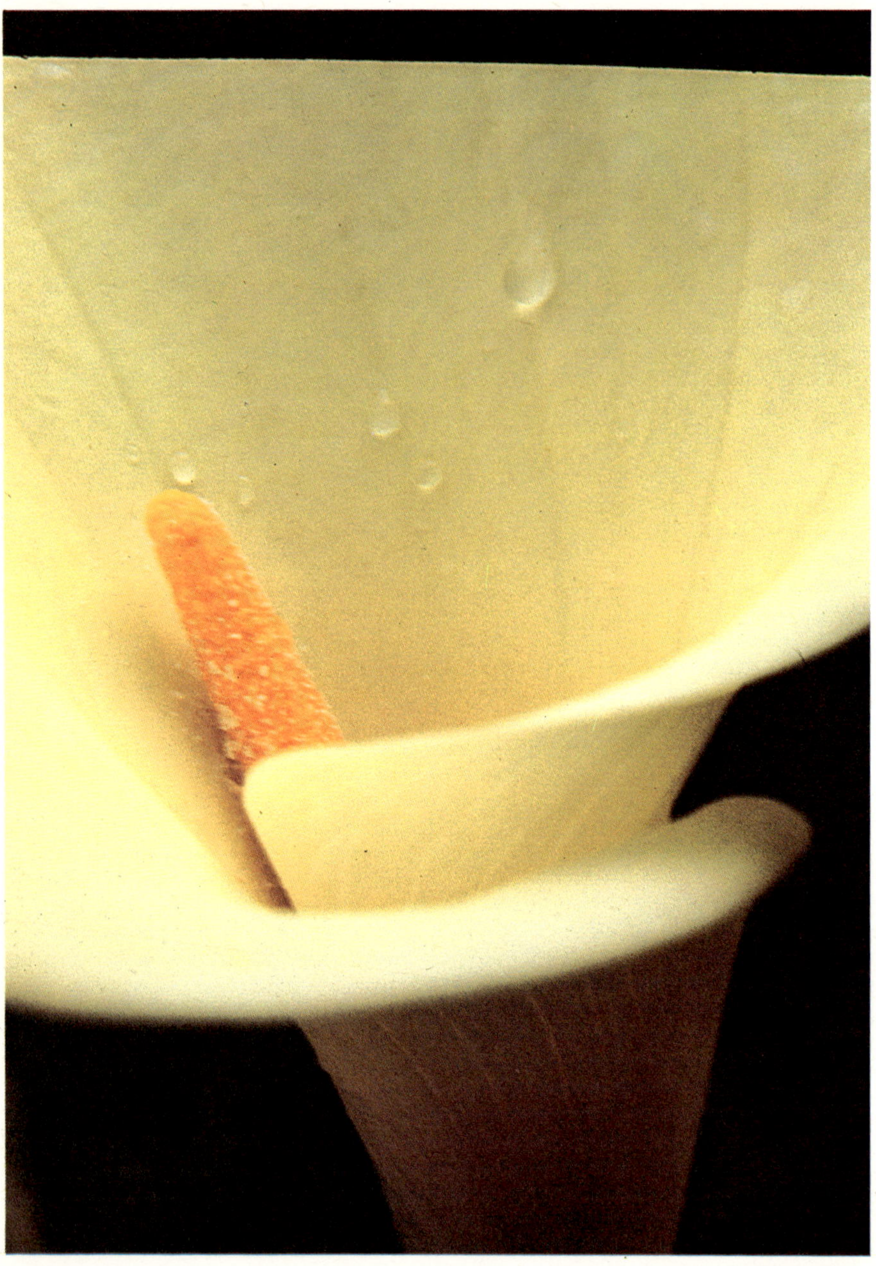

Left A macro lens is needed if you want to take clear close-ups of small objects like this flower

Right Perspective dictates that all parallel lines will appear to draw closer together the further they get from the camera's lens. This doesn't seem to matter with horizontal lines, such as roads and railways, but *converging verticals* can make pictures seem very strange – buildings, for example, look as though they are leaning over backwards. A special *perspective control lens* will correct for this – one was used to produce the picture **far right**

with all telephoto lenses, you can stay further back from your subject. This is clearly an advantage for a lot of macro work – flowers may stay put if you shove a camera close to them, but flies and bees are unlikely to. Staying back from your subject also makes it easier to light.

Both 50mm and 105mm macro lenses can also be used as 'ordinary' 50mm or 105mm lenses – they will focus on distant subjects and perform to the same standard. But the small maximum aperture and higher price mean they are not a good choice as your main lens unless your interest in photography is very specialised.

Close-up lens This is screwed to the front of almost any lens, whatever its focal length, and allows the camera to focus at a closer distance. They come in various 'powers' – 1, 2, 3, and 4 *diopters* are the most common. The higher the diopter number, the closer the lens can focus; you can use several lenses together if you want to focus closer than you can with a single lens. One drawback with a close-up lens is that it can reduce sharpness, but this is not likely to be noticeable if you use a small aperture (f8, f11 or smaller). It is an inexpensive, and for most people a reasonable, substitute for a true macro lens.

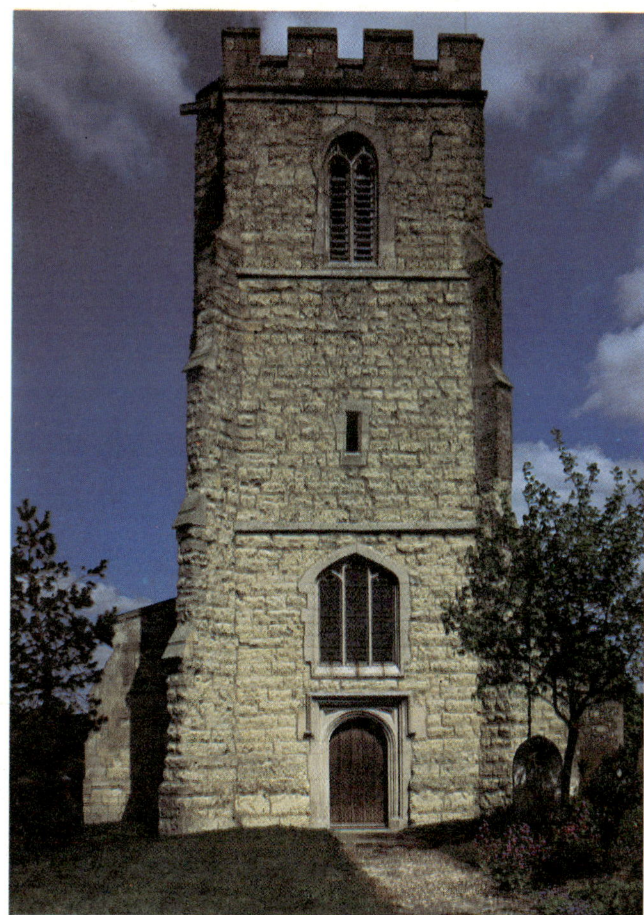

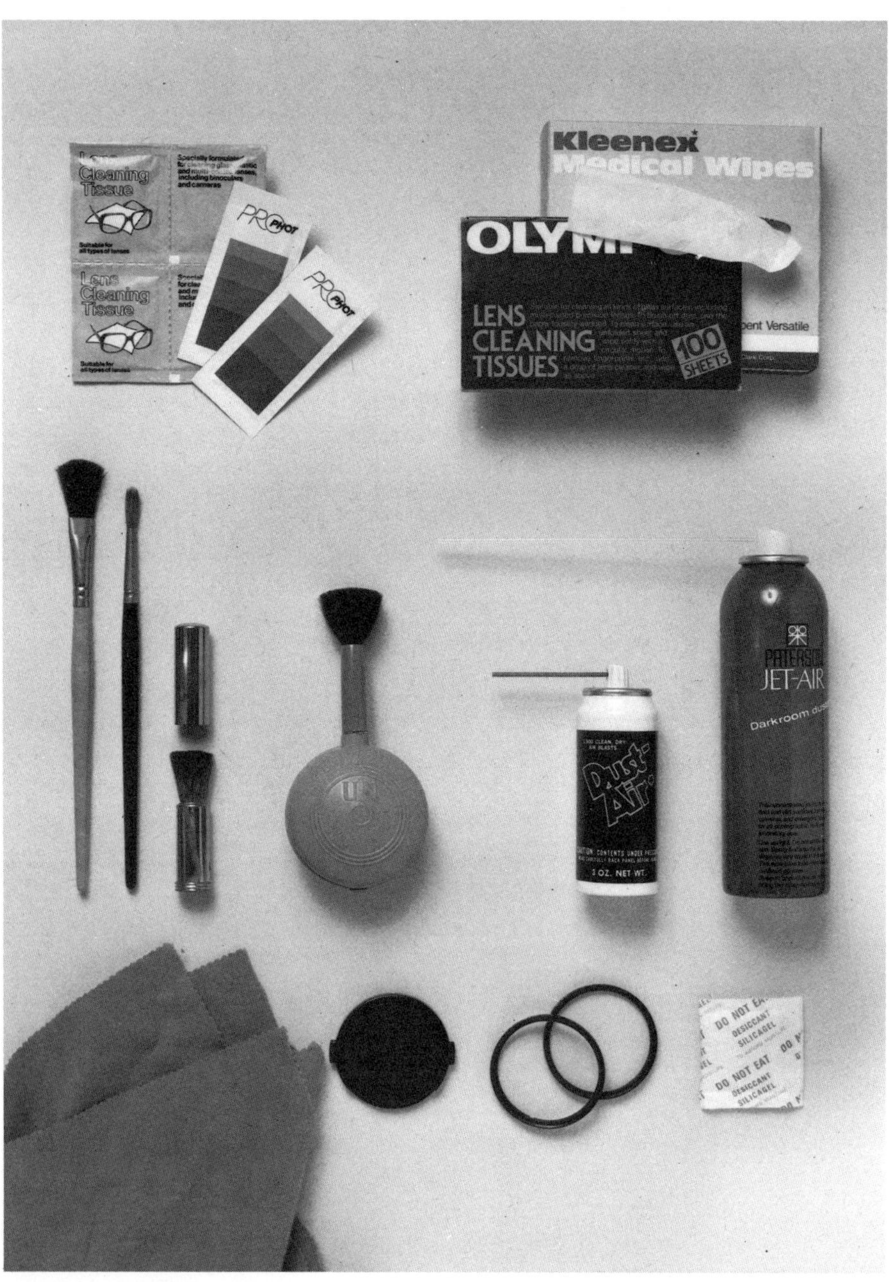

It's important to keep your lenses spotless if you want good pictures: there are lots of cleaning methods. **Top row** shows *cleaning tissues* – proprietary ones, some in waterproof sachets and pre-moistened with cleaning fluid; and medical wipes – which are good. **Middle row** shows soft *brushes* (which can't get rid of finger marks) and several *air blowers* (which get rid of dust, but not grease). **Bottom row** shows a *dry cloth* – it may cause scratching, and can create static which attracts more dust – and the two best methods of protection: a *lens cap* to keep your lens covered when not in use; and a *filter* (see Chapter 7) for protection during use. Also shown is a silica gel packet to help dry out condensation

Extension tubes and bellows   These allow much greater magnification than the other systems. All they do is increase the focal length of a lens by moving it further away from the film. An extension tube is the cheaper solution of the two, but it is less versatile because the reproduction ratio cannot be varied. The advantage of bellows is that they allow a continuous adjustment of the distance between the film and the lens, and so an infinitely-variable reproduction ratio.

Extension tubes and bellows can be used in conjunction with macro or close-up lenses.

BUYING GUIDE

Having a variety of lenses is essential if you intend to take photography seriously – and this almost certainly means your camera is the SLR type. But it is not necessary to splash out on a huge number of different types in order to extend the range of your picture-taking quite considerably. Two possible options for a beginner are:
● buy three **fixed focus** lenses – 28mm, 50mm (the type normally fitted to an SLR when you buy it) and 200mm, or possibly 135mm
● buy two **zoom** lenses – something like a 28mm to 80mm plus a 70mm to 210mm.

The zoom-lens solution is more versatile but bulkier and probably more expensive: it is likely to be the better route if you want to do a lot of photography of all kinds. Fixed-focus lenses will do you if you are less enthusiastic, or tend to take just one kind of picture at a time. If you choose zoom lenses you can save money by selecting them at the same time that you buy your SLR camera – that way you can buy the camera without the 50mm fixed-focus lens it usually comes with. In any case, don't consider the lenses in isolation make sure the whole of your SLR photo-outfit (lenses, camera body, flash and so on) is a sensible choice.

For more advanced photographers, or those with special needs, there are many other types of lenses that might appeal – a 70mm or 80mm for portraits; close-up adaptors or macro lenses, for example.

CHAPTER EIGHT

FILM

Photographic film is often taken for granted, but it is fundamental to picture-taking, and knowing which type to use and how to have it processed can have a large effect on the quality of your pictures

The basis of film is the small particles of light-sensitive material that are coated on to a flexible transparent base. When exposed to light, these particles form silver crystals which darken little by little until they become completely black. To see the effect of this chemical change, the film has to be 'processed' chemically. There are four types of film, each of which requires processing in a different way.

Even though most snap shots are now taken in colour, don't despise black and white film. It is particularly useful when you want to concentrate on the form of something without being distracted by colours; the results of processing are not so hit and miss (it is easy to process black and white film yourself); you can get highly sensitive black and white films, which allow you to take pictures in the dimmest of light, without the use of flash, which is not always a good idea (and in stately homes, cathedrals and so on, often banned).

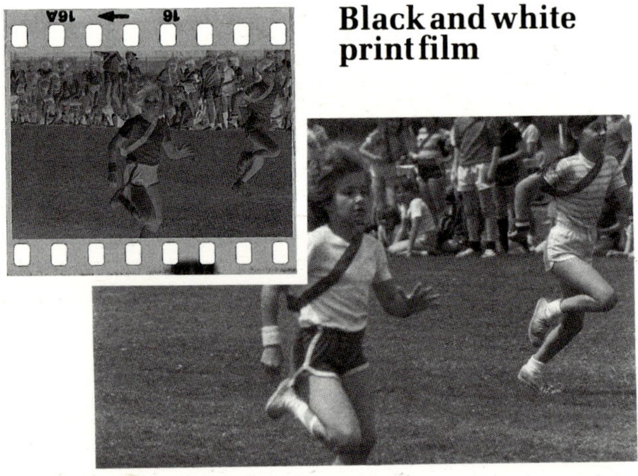

Black and white print film

This is covered with a single layer of light sensitive material. After being exposed to the light, it is 'developed' and produces a *negative* image – that is, the light parts of the original scene appear dark, and the dark parts light. The negative is then printed on to special paper which is itself sensitive to light on the same principle as film, and so a correct *positive* print is made.

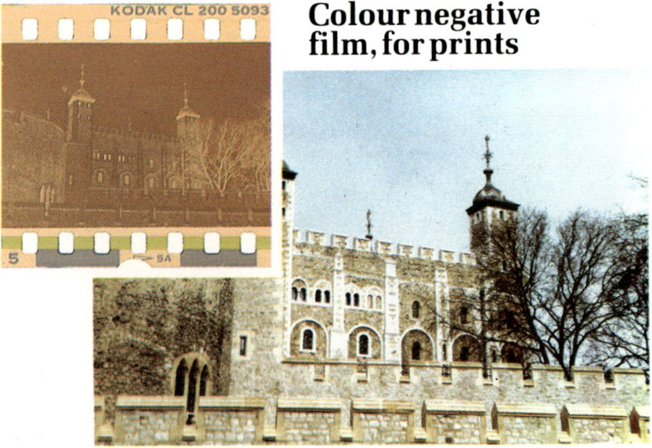

Colour negative film, for prints

Colour negative film is made up of three superimposed layers, each layer being sensitive to one of the three colours blue, yellow and red. Depending on the colour of the reflected light from each part of the scene, one or other of these layers (or more likely a combination of them) will be affected to some degree or another. Developing the film gives a negative not only in tone – so that the dark parts become light and so on – but also in colour – a light blue sky appears dark yellow, and green grass becomes magenta. When the negative is printed, the process repeats, so that the natural colours are formed.

Colour print films are the most popular type of film used by point-and-shoot photographers: for family albums, the addition of colour makes a great difference to the pictures you get; prints are easy to view; and these days they are not much more expensive than slides (see below) and can be cheaper than black and white. They are relatively easy to copy from, too – though this is not as cheap as getting the original prints made, or as cheap as getting duplicates at the same time the original film is developed. One of the main drawbacks is that you can't rely on getting good results from most of the firms who develop and print the pictures (see page 97 for more details).

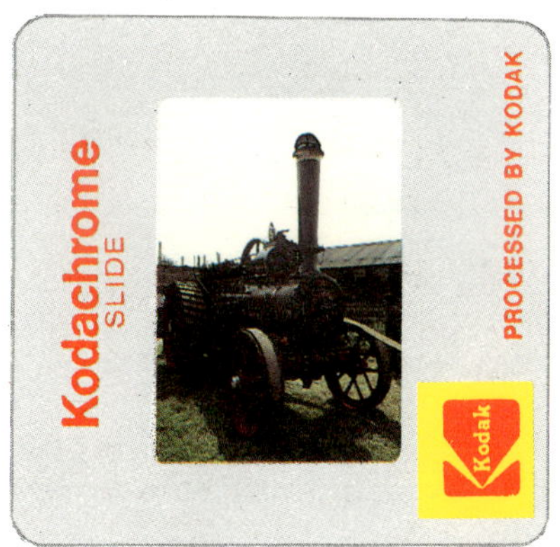

Colour reversal film, for slides

Colour reversal film does not produce a negative – as the film is exposed the colours and tones appear the 'right' way round immediately (though you can't see the result until the the film has been developed). Slides, or transparencies, differ from prints because you look at the light that is *transmitted through* them, not the light that is *reflected from* them. You can shine this light through the slide using a small hand-held viewer or, more likely, a larger *projector* which throws an image of the transparency on to a screen or wall.

Slides work out slightly cheaper than prints, and the processing is likely to be better. But digging out a viewer or projector in order to look at the picture is a bit of a bore; in any case, people like to seem to handle snap shots and pore over them at their leisure. Slides are more expensive to have copied – whether you have this done later or at the time of original processing. (Slides can be copied either as slides or prints, by the way.)

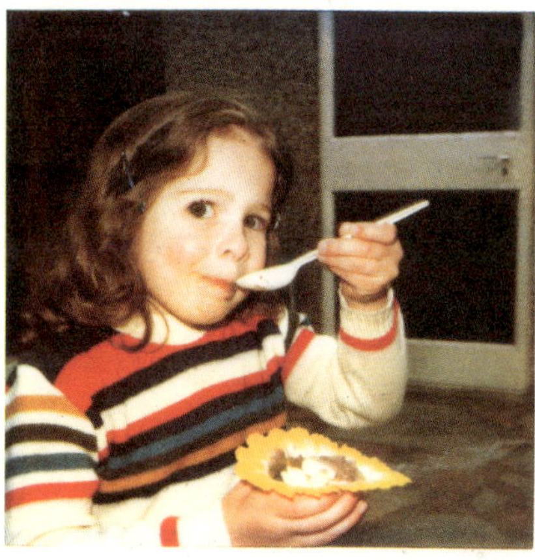

Instant picture film for prints

Film for instant picture cameras is rather different from the other types mentioned here. The most important difference, of course, is that picture is processed straight after you shoot it, so you can see the finished picture within seconds. Instant picture film is described in more detail in Chapter 6.

Film speed and grain

All films react to light when it reaches them, but not all do so with the same rapidity. A film that reacts quickly to light is called *fast*; one that is slow to change is *slow*. The 'speed' of a film is another factor, along with aperture size and shutter speed, that will affect whether the picture is properly exposed: doubling the speed of a film has the same effect on exposure as increasing the shutter speed or the aperture setting by one 'stop'.

So fast films seem to be a good thing – they allow you to take pictures in dull light (especially important with 110 and disc

Not the most scintillating of holiday snap-shots, but a good subject for illustrating *grain* in photographs. With 50 ISO film (**right**) the picture is well-defined, but with 400 ISO film (**far right**) grain is apparent – the surface looks rough and the writing is more difficult to make out. But both pictures have been enlarged enormously: far more than you would normally do so

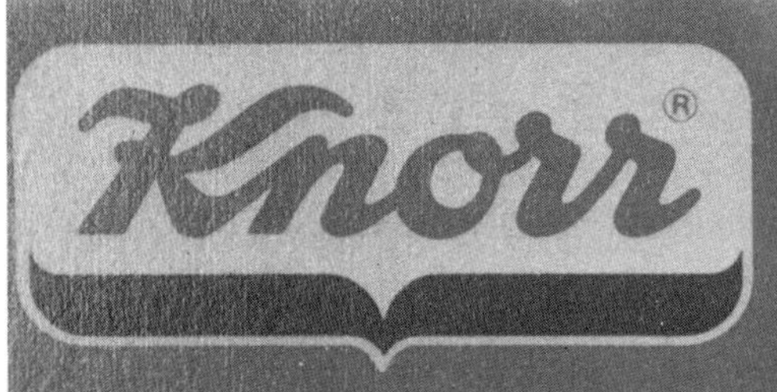

cameras); they increase flash range (again, important with the simpler types of camera); and they allow you to use larger apertures which reduce the need for precise focusing, or faster shutter speeds which reduce the risk of camera shake blurring your pictures.

But as usual, there is a drawback. Faster films are faster partly because they are made up of rather larger particles of light-sensitive materials, and this reduces the fineness with which the image can be made – to reproduce detail in a picture, the 'grain size' (that is the size of these particles) must be significantly smaller than the size the detail becomes on the film. The effect of increasing grain size is to reduce the amount of fine detail that is visible, giving a slightly unsharp effect to the picture – roughly similar to (but totally different from) the effect of an out-of-focus picture.

There is another problem with a large-grain film, though this is not apparent until you enlarge the original image. Then the individual grains that make up the picture become visible themselves – as if the picture had been printed on some rough surface. Of course, this effect is present whatever the grain size, but with fine-grain film you don't notice it unless you are making *very* large enlargements of a picture.

If the original film negative is large to begin with (and so the image thrown on to it by the lens is large) then for a given grain size finer detail can be resolved. At the same time, to make large prints does not require a great enlargement ratio – so the grain is much less visible as well. On the other hand, if the negative is small, fine detail is lost at the outset, and it doesn't take much enlargement before the picture appears grainy. That is one reason why 110 cameras give relatively poor pictures even with standard film – their negative size is much smaller than for a 35mm camera, so detail is lost and to make reasonable-sized prints requires a relatively great enlargement, so that grain becomes more apparent. Disc

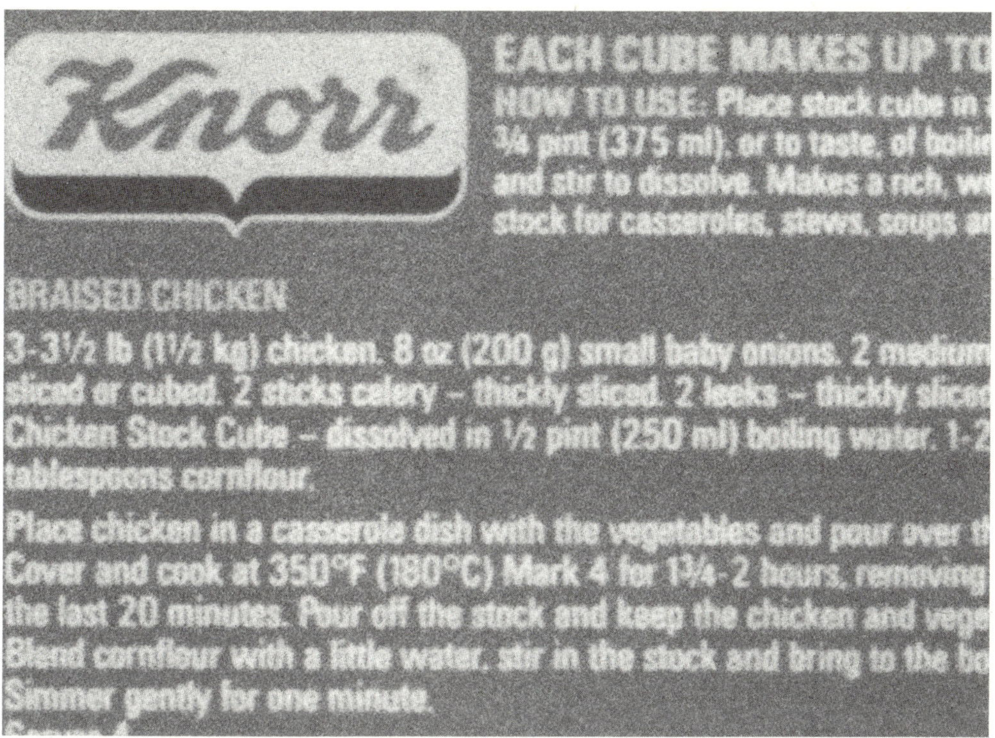

cameras suffer from the same problem – in fact, they use a relatively fine-grain film, but the negative is so small and requires such a lot of enlargement that grain is still visible, and pictures do not appear very sharp.

For the same reasons professional photographers often use cameras that take film much larger than 35mm – it preserves fine detail and allows much greater enlargement. Many of the photographs in this book had to be taken using a 35mm camera, because we wanted to show you the effects *you* could get by using such a camera, but where we could, we used a camera taking film 60mm x 60mm – nearly five times as big an area as with the 35mm format – to get better quality.

There are three main ways in which film speeds are expressed. You will often see *ASA* (American Standards Association) figures quoted – these range from ASA 25 (very slow) to ASA 3200 (extremely fast). A doubling of the ASA number implies a doubling of film speed – that is, the faster film requires half as much light for the same exposure. Speeds are also sometimes expressed in *DIN* (the German standards organisation, Deutsche Industries Norme) figures, ranging from DIN 15 to DIN 36: the figures are based on a logarithmic scale, so that a difference of 3 DIN is a doubling or halving of speed. You can't convert easily between the two systems, but it's worth noting that 64 ASA is 19 DIN; 100 ASA is 21 DIN; and 400 ASA is 27 DIN.

The main system now used is the *ISO* (International Standards Organisation) one. A full ISO speed designation is simply the ASA and DIN figures together – for example, 400/27° ISO. But on many film packages you may see just the first part of the number quoted – 400 ISO, say. In effect the ISO rating is just the ASA rating under a different name.

Films divide into three broad speed categories – slow, standard and fast. Examples of the three types, and their pros and cons, are shown overleaf.

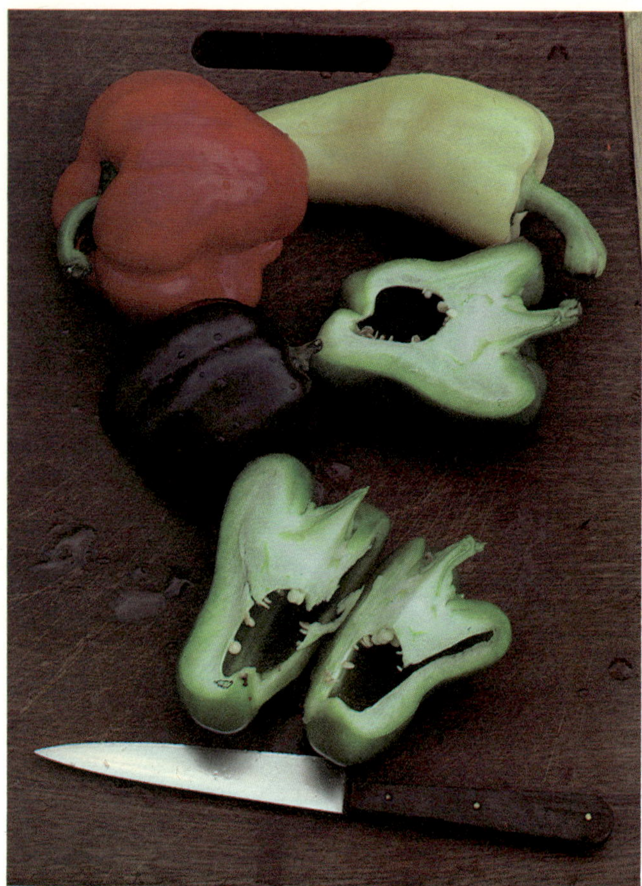

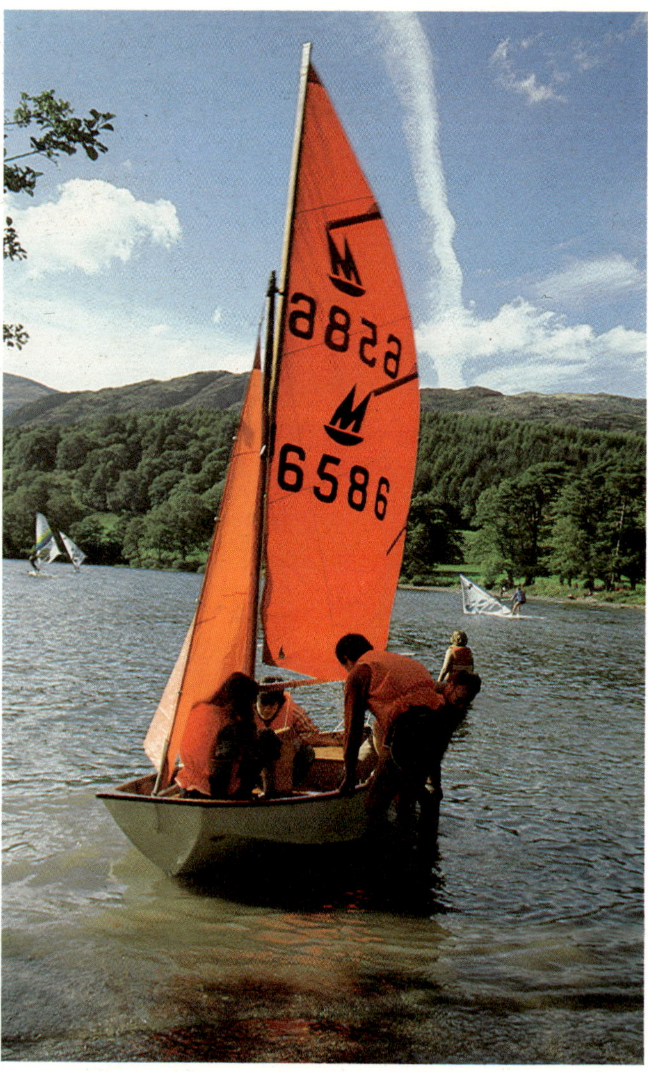

Slow films (25 to 64 ISO)   These give fine pictures with plenty of detail and contrast, and the ability to handle a great deal of enlargement. You can use them when you are able to get away with slow shutter speeds and/or large apertures – in good lighting conditions or where you can use powerful flash, and on motionless subjects.

Slow films are rather specialised, and are not likely to be used much by amateurs. If you do use one, remember that with the slow shutter speeds you are likely to need it is essential to mount the camera on a tripod or stand: there is no point in using a film capable of showing very fine detail if the camera is allowed to move and blur the picture.

Standard films (100 to 200 ISO)   These offer a good compromise between speed and grain, and allow a reasonable latitude in both exposure time and aperture. Quite reasonable enlargements are possible without the grain being too apparent. Use them for all your holiday snaps in good weather – and in poor light, too, if your camera can cope.

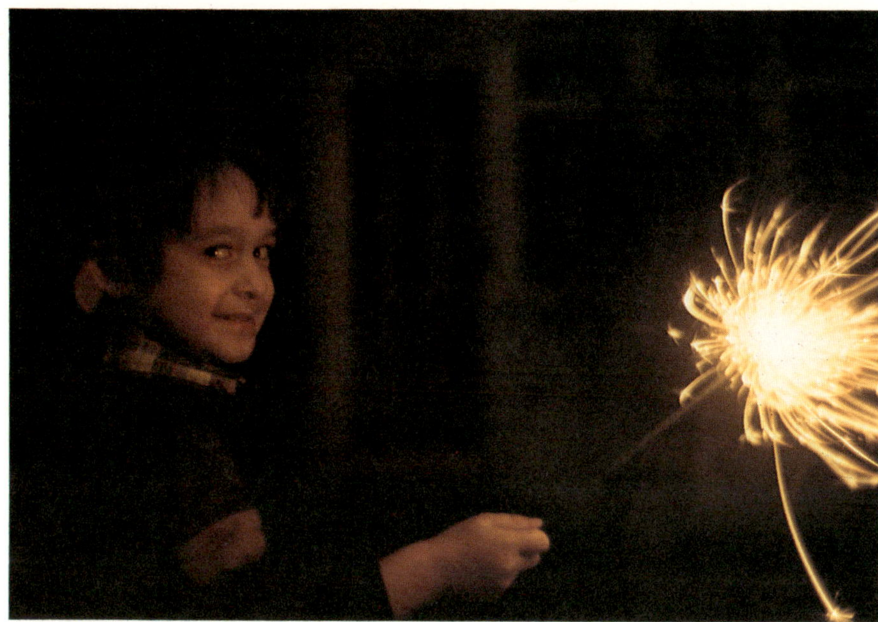

Fast films   Faster films are becoming more popular, and clearly have their advantages if you want to take pictures at night or indoors, especially if your camera is not a very sophisticated model.

However, even a 400 ISO slide film may be too fast for some non-reflex cameras if used in very bright conditions – beaches in the sun, or sunny snow scenes, for example. But usually you will be able to switch to a fast enough shutter speed and small enough aperture to allow proper exposure. This should even help your pictures turn out better – unless you are after a special effect, such as restricted depth of field or blur in moving objects – by ensuring more of the scene is in focus, and reducing the chances of camera shake blurring the picture. (A very small aperture, however, is not recommended because image quality often deteriorates.) There is not likely to be a problem with 400 ISO *print* film, whatever camera you use, because print film is quite tolerant of over-exposure.

The new films of 1000 ISO may well be more of a problem if your camera does not have a speed setting of $\frac{1}{1000}$ second or faster, and an aperture of smaller than f16. And most non-reflex cameras do not have settings for 1000 ISO. Again, though, with print film you need not worry over much because you can over-expose by three 'stops' or so without losing very much detail from your picture. But with slide film a neutral density filter (see page 106) becomes essential to reduce the light level and so prevent the film from being over-exposed. In general, these films are useful only when light is very low (dark interiors, deep shadows, night photos) and when the subject demands very short exposure times, as with sports snapshots.

So a moderately fast film is rarely a drawback from the speed point of view (at least with an SLR camera). But is the grain and detail a problem in reality? With a disc camera, it would certainly be so – even standard disc prints appear fairly grainy. And 110 prints would suffer quite badly, too. But with a 35mm camera – either non-reflex or SLR – the differences in sharpness and graininess are not likely to be detectable unless you go in for huge enlargements. Even the photographs on pages 92 and 93 had to be enlarged 15 times before we could show you clearly the difference in graininess between the slower and the faster films.

Black and white films   Black and white films are available in the same speeds as colour films, though the designations standard and fast may be applied to different ISO ratings.

There are also what are billed as *variable speed* films – on the same film, you can take photos using speeds from 125 to 1600 ISO. In practice, these are simply 400 ISO films with a high exposure latitude so that even if you greatly over- or under-expose the film, you will still be able to obtain an acceptable picture.

Uprating

With print film you can effectively alter the exposure at the processing stage. You can take advantage of this if you want to shoot pictures when your camera tells you they would be under-exposed – in very low light, or poor light combined with fast movement when you cannot use a slow shutter speed. Take the pictures anyway, and ask the processor when the pictures are developed to 'push-process' them – that is, give them extra developing time.

To make this rather more accurate, so that you can tell the processor just how much extra development to give the film (and so that you know there will be a good chance of the pictures coming out properly) tell the camera a fib by adjusting the film speed dial up a couple of stops – if you're using a 400 ISO film, for example, set the film speed to 800 or even 1600. Then use your camera as you would normally – that is, adjust the controls so that the camera says you will be getting a correctly exposed picture (though you know it will be under-exposed). Tell the processor whether the film is under-exposed by one or two stops so that they can make the proper amount of correction to the developing time.

A few words of warning, though. You cannot necessarily push every film in this way: check with the film's instructions. The image quality you get won't be quite as good. You must make sure the processors realise the film has to be pushed, and that they will do this (you will probably need to go to a processor working mainly for professionals, and that will work out more expensive than using the large processing firms). And, of course, all the shots on the reel of film will be pushed by the same amount, so you can't use this technique on just part of a reel (unless, of course, the pictures are so important to you that you don't mind possibly ruining the rest of the exposures).

Print film processing

Developing and printing – processing – a colour film is the most crucial stage of producing a picture and one that is, sadly, almost completely out of most people's hands. Particularly from the point of view of colour balance, difference in processing far outweigh differences in films and cameras and, to some extent, differences in your photo techniques too.

Aside from doing it yourself (which, for colour, is not the easiest of jobs) there are a number of ways of getting your film processed, including taking it to a local independent chemist, high-street chemist or photographic shop, or posting it to a film laboratory. If you take it to a shop, you'll usually collect from there; if you post it – perhaps using a coupon, or a special envelope that has come with a magazine or been pushed through your door – the film will be posted back to you with envelopes to use the next time.

But, whatever method you use, your pictures will end up at a laboratory. What you may not realise is that despite the confusing array of different names, there are only a handful of major processing firms. Most do their business under a wide variety of different names – often charging different prices for the same results, and handling films from all sources: big-name chemists, magazine film services, and envelopes-through-doors indiscriminately.

The bad news is that quality can vary a lot – just look at the pictures on page 98 to see how differently processors can treat pictures taken in identical conditions. The even worse news is that you cannot be certain that you'll get consistently good quality from one processor – though on the basis of *Which?* tests, you stand a better chance with some.

It pays not to be in too much of a hurry. The new 'mini-labs' or 'micro-labs' process films on their premises in only a couple of hours. However, they usually charge more than other processors and quality is not likely to be as good – to get consistent quality, you need very expensive computer-controlled machinery.

Prices   Check carefully on the offers you see (and, especially in the summer months, it's difficult to avoid being bombarded with 'special' offers). You may get a free film – but this is not worth so much if the film is a brand you don't like or, worse, a format that doesn't fit your camera (though

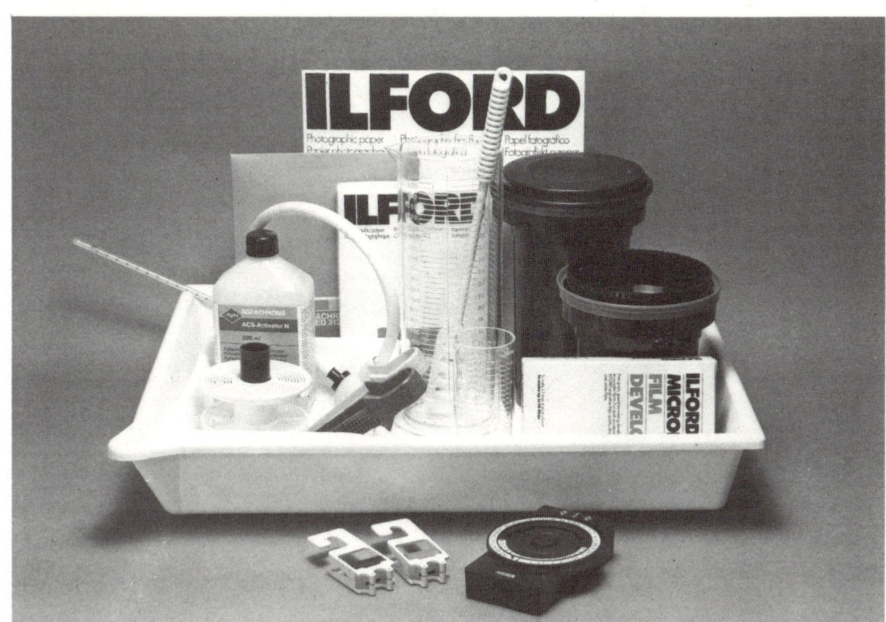

Developing your own photographs – particularly black and white ones – is not difficult. You require only a little equipment to get you started, as shown here, and it is not very expensive. Although you need a light-tight area to work in, you can adapt a bathroom to form a make-shift darkroom

this is unlikely). Some firms quote an attractive price per print, but hide a large extra price for developing. Don't forget extras for postage and packing, and check what happens about pictures that don't come out – if you have paid in advance, you may be given a credit voucher which is not as good as cold, hard cash. Or you may get nothing at all back – even if a whole film does not come out. On the other hand, if you pay after getting your prints back it will probably cost you more per print.

Some firms have a very attractive price to start with, but the envelope sent back with your prints quotes a higher price for the next batch. It is worth keeping all the special offer coupons and envelopes you can lay your hands on (though if there is an expiry date on the offer, throw it out when it is no longer valid) and compare prices when you have a film to send off.

Print size, finish and packaging   The usual print **sizes** are either 90mm (3½in) high for 'standard' prints, or 100mm (4in) for large prints. Width is about 130mm (5in) but this varies with the type of camera.

You usually get a satin-type **finish** on prints – it gives less trouble from reflections and fingerprints than the alternative gloss finish (which not all processors do) but the picture may appear less bright. Check, too, whether the corners of the prints will be rounded off if this matters to you.

Some processors put the **date** on the back of each print, which can be very useful. But (apart from disc films) prints are rarely numbered, so it can be a bit of a trial sorting out which negative belongs with which print if you want to order reprints.

Negatives should be protected in cellophane sleeves – but this is something not all processors do.

Reprints   Nearly all firms will make extra prints from negatives and may send you a special form or envelope to make ordering easier. However, reprints can't be dealt with by automatic machinery and so cost getting on for twice as much as the original print. Some firms offer to make two prints to start with from each negative, for a flat fee. This is convenient, and works out cheaper if you are sure you will want one extra print from more than about ten of the pictures

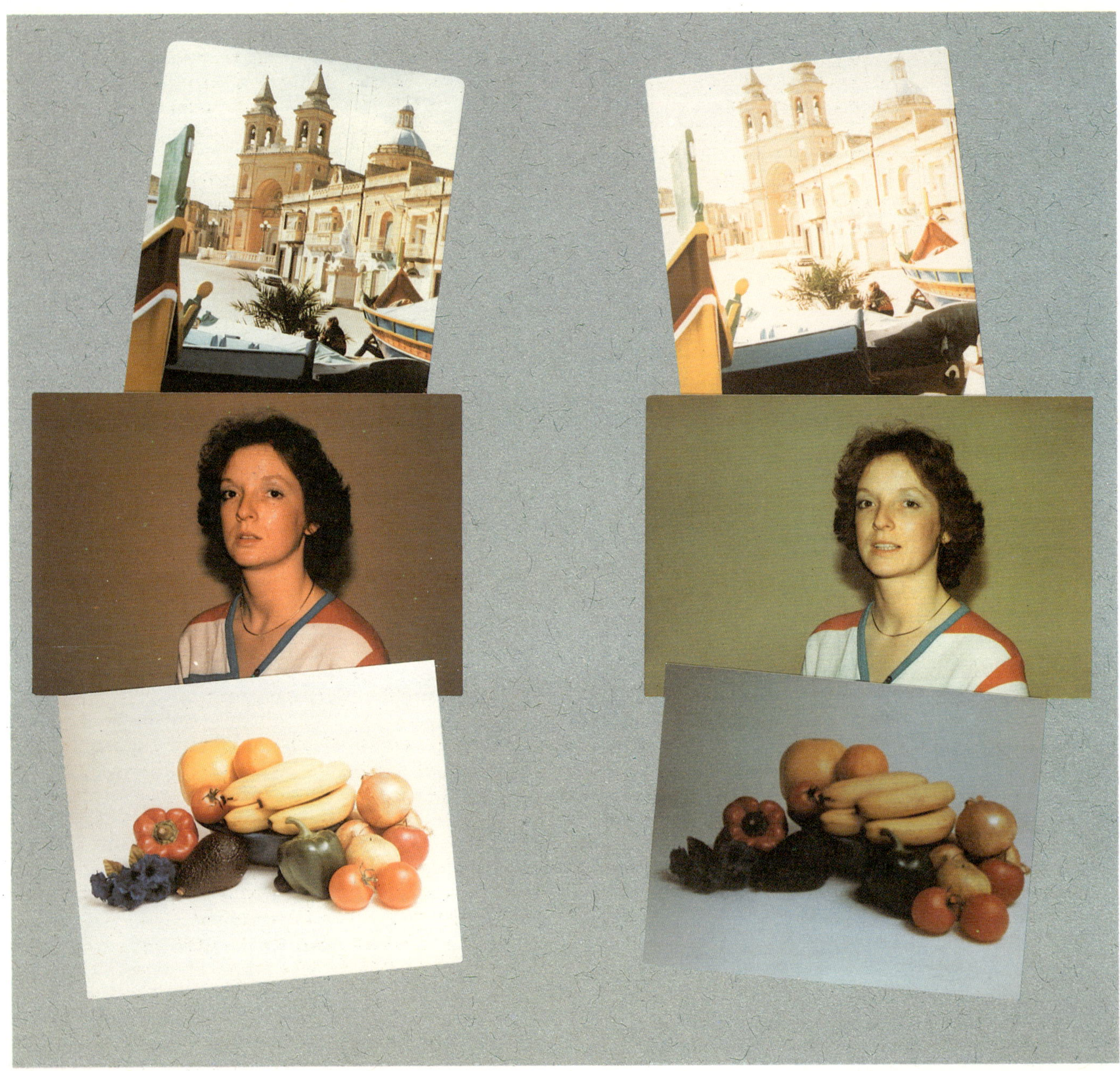

on a roll. Alternatively, *you* could take extra shots of scenes you think you'll want copies of. Again, if you can gauge it right, this is cheaper than the other options – it also means you can have as many copies of one print as you care to shoot; each a little bit different if you like. (Note that taking multiple shots is particularly worth while with *slide* film, where duplicates are very expensive to have made.)

Some firms offer a *print from print* service, which saves you looking for the right negative (assuming you haven't lost it anyway). Sharpness may not be so good as a print from a negative, but you should be more certain of getting the same colours (which may or may not be a good thing: see below).

Colour balance   This is the most obvious fault to occur during print-film processing. Films are processed in large, automatic machines very quickly. The computer controls average out the colours so that they match a typical scene – but the machines are not very clever and can easily be fooled if your picture is not typical. In theory, processors have (human) checkers to spot pictures that have fooled the computer and to send them back for reprinting, but this is rather a hit and miss affair. It's not realistic to insist that mass processors turn out perfectly colour-balanced pictures all the time. This can be done for almost any negative if you take it to a processor who will do the job by hand – but it is likely to cost several *pounds* a print, compared with the few *pence* that a mass-producer charges. However, do not hesitate to send back any print (together with the negative) to the processor if you think the balance could be improved and ask for a free reprint – and send it back again if it is still not right. Repeat prints will nearly always be given without any arguments – the Code of Practice for the Photographic Industry obliges the processor either to replace the photographs or to explain why the original cannot be improved upon, or to give credit. If you are still not satisfied with the processor, you can resort to the concilliation and arbitration procedure set out in the code.

Exposure   Negatives which are under-exposed by the camera produce prints that lack contrast and give dull-looking pictures. Over-exposed negatives will usually print well, but you may lose detail in light areas. In these cases, you can't expect to get a good print – though it should be as good as the negative.

If your picture includes both very light and very dark areas – for example a flash photograph of someone quite close and nothing in the background – the printing machine (which tries to average everything) may try to make a print in which all the details of your subject's face are lost. Here, you should be able to get a better print.

Other faults   You may get white specks on your prints, often caused by dust and dirt in the laboratory, or by splashes from chemicals. Other faults include slightly blurred prints. Check for bad cut-off, too – so that black edges aren't left around each print, the printing machines are set up to take in slightly less than the whole area of each negative. How accurately this is controlled varies from firm to firm. Camera makers know this, and know how infuriating it is to lose part of a picture off the edge. So, particularly with the simpler cameras, they arrange for the viewfinder to show much *less* than appears on the negative, and usually no matter how badly the printer is set up, you'll get at least as much of the picture as you saw at the time of shooting. But if you habitually lose part of your prints, make amends by allowing more leeway when you take the picture.

Checking for faults   Faults aren't *always* due to the processor, of course, so before being too rude it's worth making your own checks. Look at the negative – hold it by the edges only, and examine it carefully with a strong magnifying glass:
● specks that appear on the print but not on the negative are certainly a printing fault (remember that white spots will appear as dark specks on the negative)
● look for detail and sharpness: if they aren't there in the negative, you can't blame the print
● if you have lost an important edge of your picture, see if it is present in the negative: if it is, you can certainly ask for a reprint; if it isn't, the fault lies with you or the camera. Remember that you can't normally expect a print to include

material at the *very* edges of the negative – so if this is your complaint, don't expect a free reprint. You may have to take you negative to a specialist firm who will print it (not cheaply) by hand.

Once you have decided there *are* faults on the print that are due to the processor, send the negative and print back and insist on a reprint. But make it very clear what your complaint is.

Keeping your memories

If you have colour prints out on display you probably know that the colours fade – in a matter of months if the sun shines directly on them. This isn't due to the film, of course, but it can depend on the printing paper used. Worse, colour prints can deteriorate even when kept in the dark – in an album, for example. One problem is that the deterioration is slow, so it's difficult to remember what the pictures looked like originally – memories fade along with the photographs.

You can try getting new prints made from the negatives. Negatives too fade and may change colour after five to ten years of storage, but such changes may be correctable in the printing process (darker, over-exposed negatives should last longer than under-exposed ones).

Colour slides will also deteriorate with time, even if not projected. Resistance to ageing varies from brand to brand – but most films have not been around long enough for anyone to know with certainty how long they will last. However, it is known that Kodachrome colours are very durable, probably lasting over 50 years. Other slide films will probably not last as well, and you may notice changes after 10 to 15 years.

You can slow down this depressing-sounding deterioration in your photographic memories by keeping the photographs as cool and as dry as possible – every 5°C drop in temperature halves the rate of deterioration. So ideally you should put your pictures in sealed containers and keep them in the fridge or freezer. To avoid the risk of condensation, try to seal the container in cool dry conditions and let them warm up again before opening them later. With prints, you only have to store the negatives so you still have some pictures to show around; with slides that you want to view frequently, it would be worth getting duplicates made. (Or take two pictures every time you have something important in the viewfinder.)

If you want to put photographs on display in a place where you know fast-fading is likely to be a problem, you could get *Cibachrome* prints made from 35mm slides – the colours are very resistant to fading, but the process is expensive.

Looking after films

Taking care of the processed pictures is important, but looking after films so that they give you good results to start with is also worth doing.

It's clearly safest to use (that is expose *and* develop) films by the **use-by date** stamped on the carton. In practice, though, you can still get away with using black and white film (and to a lesser degree colour film) up to a year after this date. Once a film has been exposed, put it back in its protective wrapping and store it in a dry place.

Films are sensitive to **humidity**, **high temperatures**, and **chemical fumes**. Don't leave films lying in rooms where the temperature is above 21°C – in an overheated car or in the sun on a beach, for example. It wouldn't be a bad idea to put any unexposed film in a fridge (or freezer) either, especially if you intend to keep it for some time. But be sure to let it warm up again before unsealing the packet, or you could get problems with condensation. You should store exposed films away from petrol fumes, and fumes from dry cleaning solvents, naphthalene (moth balls), glue or other volatile solvents – the best idea is to pack them straight off to the processors as soon as they've been exposed, if you can.

Films are also sensitive to **x-rays**. But you need not worry unduly that the machines used for security checks at airports will damage films – the dose isn't normally high enough. To be on the safe side, though, pass films over by hand to the security officers, or pack them in your checked luggage.

Colour balance and slide films

Every light source produces light with a dominant colour. Electric light bulbs give a somewhat yellow light; the sun gives a much bluer light. Your eyes spontaneously correct these yellow or blue reflections, but a film does not. This doesn't cause any problems with black and white films – the difference in the colours appears as shades of grey, which the eye doesn't readily perceive. Nor is it too much of a problem with colour print films, because colour balance can be given some correction during processing.

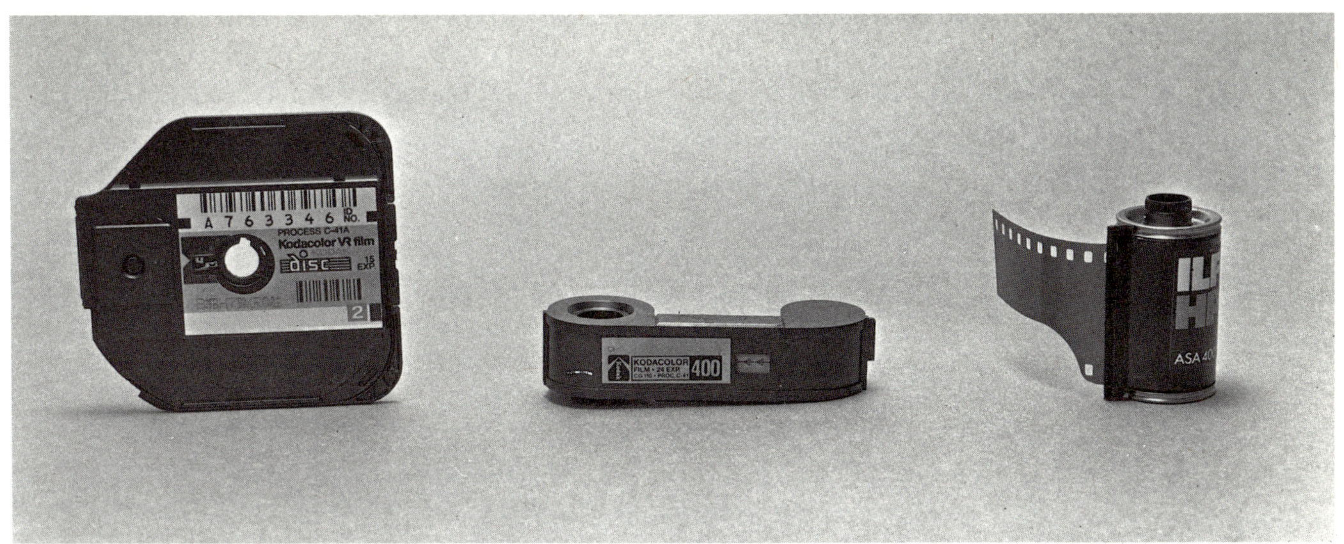

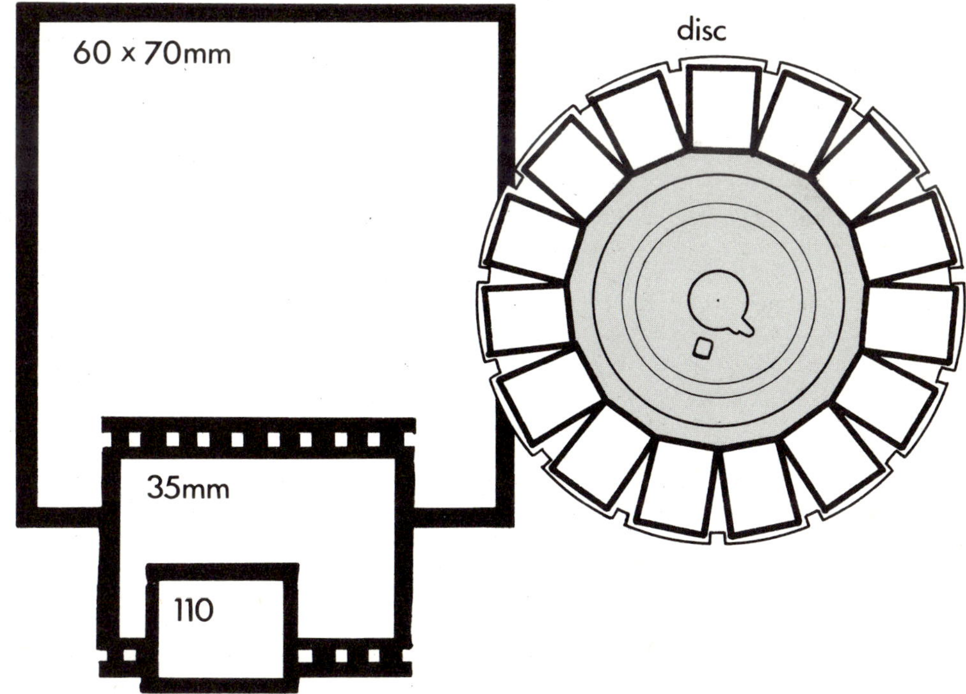

Above Different types of camera use different types of film – from the left are film packs for a disc camera, 110 camera, and 35mm (either an SLR or a non-reflex)

Right Different films produce different-sized negatives. The smaller the negative, the smaller the camera can be – but the greater the degree of enlargement that is needed to make a certain-sized print. In turn, big enlargements lead to loss of quality. Shown here are the actual negative sizes for 35mm and 110 film, and for disc (disc negatives are attached to a 'plate', and they are left on this plate after developing for easy storage). For comparison, a 'professional' format negative is shown – this is much bigger than the other three, so big enlargements can be made

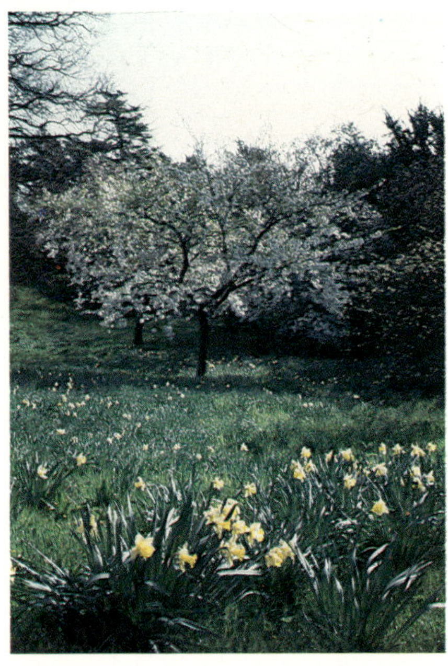

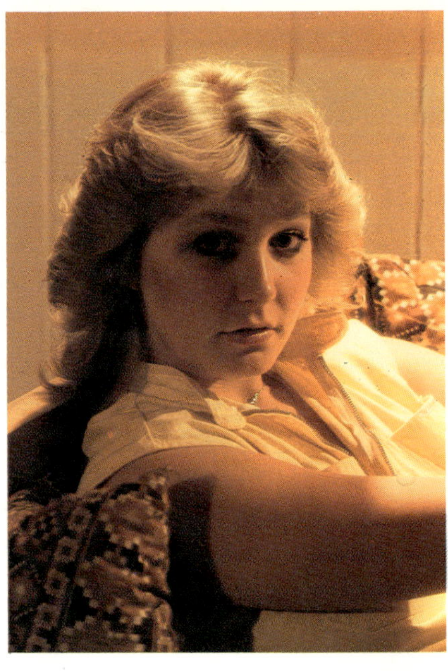

Daylight film. **Left** in daylight: the colours appear natural. **Right** under artificial light: gives pictures an orange hue

Artificial light film. **Left** under artificial light: the colours appear natural.**Right** in daylight: gives blue pictures

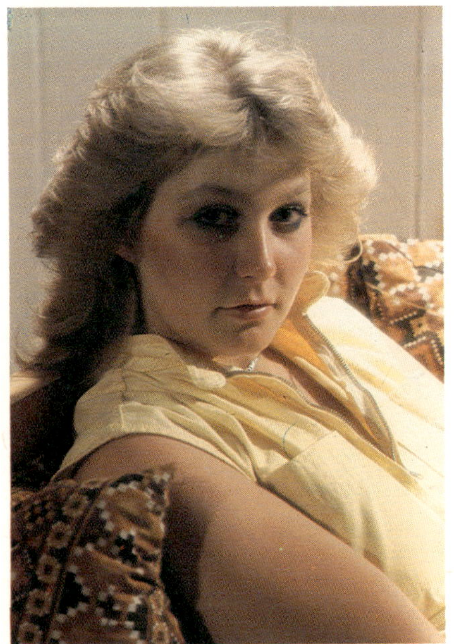

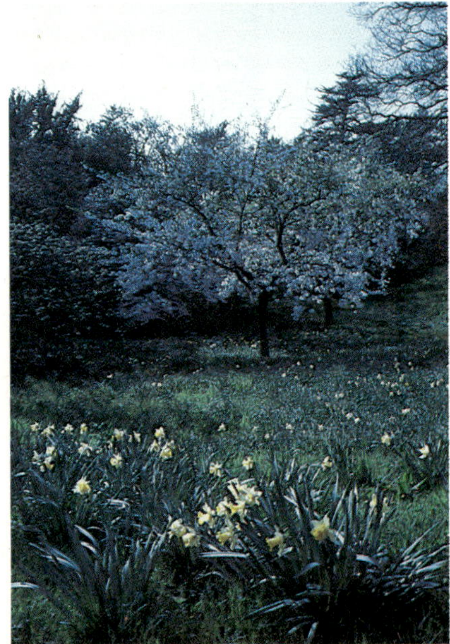

But it is something that has to be watched with slide film – so you get films that are made specially for daylight, and films that are made for artificial light. If you use the wrong film you'll get some very strange colour effects: see pictures opposite. (But note that you can alter the colour balance by using a colour filter: see page 106.)

Electronic flash counts as daylight, and so do ordinary blue flash bulbs. But you can get plain flash bulbs that are suitable for use with artificial light films; and if you use tungsten lights in a studio, these count as artificial lights too (provided they are proper studio lamps, and not domestic lamps which are far too yellow). Try to avoid mixing tungsten light with electronic flash in the same picture.

Another problem is that towards sunrise and sunset, even daylight behaves a little like artificial light, giving slides a yellow look – again, a colour filter will correct for this.

BUYING GUIDE

As this chapter has shown, there is more to film than perhaps you realised. Most of your needs, though, will be met with a standard-speed print or slide film, or perhaps a film of 400 ISO if your camera can cope.

If you want prints, then more important than your choice of film is your choice of processor. *Which?* tests film processors (most recently in August 1983) but even following their advice you may get prints which are better or worse than average.

Don't hesitate to send poor pictures back to be re-printed – but check first to make sure that the faults are likely to be due to poor processing.

CHAPTER NINE

FILTERS

Camera filters perform one of two jobs. The subtle one is to enhance your picture a little, and flatter the important parts. The other is to transform your picture so that it resembles nothing like reality

There's something about professional photographs that many amateur photographers can't understand. How are the skies so well picked-out? How are all the blooms and hazes removed? What makes the sky so dark, or the sea so transparent? And that's only in ordinary pictures – special effects are even more mystifying. How has modest public lighting been transformed into scintillating stars? How can the subject appear several times in the same picture?

It's not likely to be due to magic, but to the effects of different *filters* – glass or plastic screens, usually coloured, placed over the camera lens. Filters have become very fashionable in recent years – used judiciously they can enhance your photographs, and even produce stunning original effects, without a lot of effort or expense. Whatever you want to do, you're almost bound to find a filter that will do it for you.

Types of filter

You can divide filters into broad groups for:
- **'fine-tuning' colour films**   probably the most useful group
- **colour correction of colour films**   if you've got the wrong type for your light source
- **simple effects**   usually used with colour films for the more subtle special effects
- **black and white films**   for enhancing the effect of monochrome prints
- **special effects**   make your pictures look totally unreal: use with care.

All these types of filters are discussed in this chapter – but only examples are given because there is a huge range to choose from. In general it's only with an SLR camera that you would use filters: for one thing, it is almost essential to have the through-the-lens viewing capability an SLR gives you so that you have some idea of what a particular filter is doing for your picture.

Fine-tuning filters

Most of these affect the look of your pictures only slightly, but that little bit can be enough to turn a good shot into a stunner. There are various types in this category of which at least one is an essential part of a good camera outfit.

UV (ultra-violet)   Unlike the human eye, photographic film is sensitive to ultra-violet rays. These cause an undesirable haze on both colour and black and white photos which a UV filter will get rid of. UV rays are particularly strong at high altitudes – so you should always use a UV filter when shooting above 1,500 metres (5,000ft) or so. At lower altitudes it isn't so essential, but it's still a good idea to keep one permanently fitted to your camera to keep your lens protected – it's cheaper to replace a scratched filter than a scratched lens.

It's rarely a hindrance to keep a UV filter on your lens because it doesn't normally affect the quality of your pictures in any way (apart from removing unwanted haze). The exception is when you're taking pictures with the camera pointing towards the light – then a UV filter can create 'flares' (bright marks on the picture).

Skylight   This also absorbs UV rays. At the same time it is slightly pink, and this reduces bluish shadows which are often present on colour pictures and which give a rather cold look to your photos. Otherwise your pictures are not

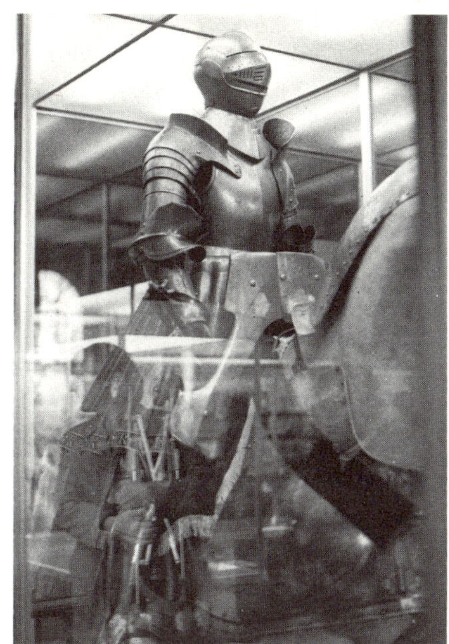

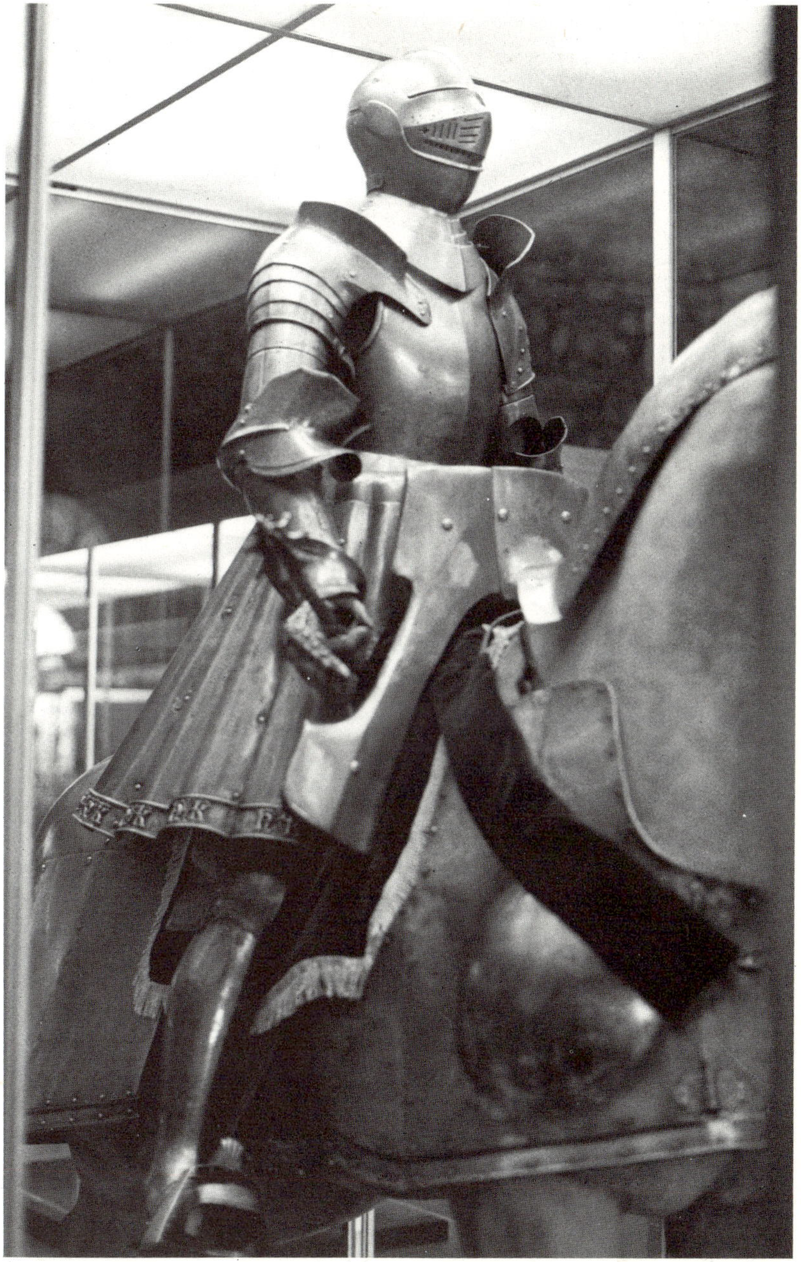

Glass cases often create unwanted reflections on photographs (**above**). These can often be removed almost entirely (**right**) by using a polarising filter correctly orientated

affected, so this is another filter that you could leave over your lens permanently (and probably a slightly better choice than the UV filter).

Polarising   These filters cut out light reflected from non-metallic surfaces such as glass or water. As a result, the sea can appear more transparent, or reflections from windows can be removed. The sky appears darker and bluer, because the haze resulting from the reflection of light from dust and other particles in the air is neutralised by the filter. In short, it acts much like the effect you get when wearing polarising sunglasses.

There's no special device in a polarising filter that tells it which reflections are wanted and which it should remove – it will cut out any reflections if it's rotated into the right orientation. So a polarising filter is fitted with a special mount that allows you to turn it round to get rid of just the reflections you *don't* want to appear in your picture.

Neutral density (grey)   This cuts down the amount of light reaching the film, as the 'grey' name suggests; the 'neutral' tag implies that it doesn't affect colour balance in any way.

Much of the time you're probably struggling to get light that is bright enough, without having to worry about how to cut it down, so neutral density filters are not very important. One of their uses, though, is when the camera is loaded with a very fast film, and you want to take a shot in full sunshine, work with wide aperture to produce a limited depth of field, or use a slow shutter speed to achieve an effect of movement – without a filter to cut down the light, you may find such pictures are over-exposed.

You can get different 'strengths' of neutral density filter – the higher the ND number, or filter factor (see page 112) the less light will be let through. The most commonly-used filters have ND numbers of 0.3, 0.6 and 0.9, which achieve the same effect as stopping down by one, two, or three stops. Or to put it another way, if you want to take a certain photo, but find (by using the information in your viewfinder) that you'd be two stops over-exposed using the shutter speed and aperture setting you want, you could put an ND 0.6 filter in front of the lens, and get a properly-exposed picture. If you're shooting with an SLR camera, the information in the viewfinder will confirm that you are now set for proper exposure.

You can, if you wish, use several ND filters together – just add up their ND numbers to find what their total effect will be. Unfortunately, despite their name, most neutral density filters have some effect on colour, so it is better to avoid using them if you can.

Colour correction filters
Colour slide films are made for use with a particular light source – a daylight film for outdoors, or with most forms of flash; and an artificial light film for use indoors with tungsten lighting. If you use the wrong film with the wrong light source, you'll get pictures with very strange colours. But if you don't want to change films, you can always correct for these colour effects with a filter. There are at least twenty different types, but only two are widely used:
- **orange 85B conversion filter**   This allows you to use a film intended for artificial light out of doors – the orange filter absorbs the bluish tone that you would otherwise get
- **blue 80A conversion filter**   This produces exactly the opposite effect, and allows you to use a daylight film by artificial light – the blue eliminates the yellowish cast.

Filters for simple effects
It's often the simple effects that are the most rewarding, and some of the best special-effect filters only slightly alter their pictures. Perhaps most useful is a **diffusion**, or **haze**, filter which gives pictures a soft, fuzzy texture, usually associated with a romantic feeling. With a **vignetting** filter, the centre of the picture is sharp, but it becomes more and more fuzzy towards the edges and corners.

Both vignetting and diffusion filters are available in neutral colours, or in pastel shades, and there are also variations which differ in the strength of their effect.

Diffusion effects are simple to achieve by using a thin layer of petroleum jelly, such as Vaseline; smooth this over a UV or skylight filter rather than directly on to the lens. You can increase or reduce the soft-focus effect by using more or less Vaseline, and get the same results as with a commercial vignetting filter by graduating the thickness of the layer from the centre to the edges.

An even simpler trick is just to stretch part of an old pair of tights over the lens: you can even get coloured effects by using coloured tights.

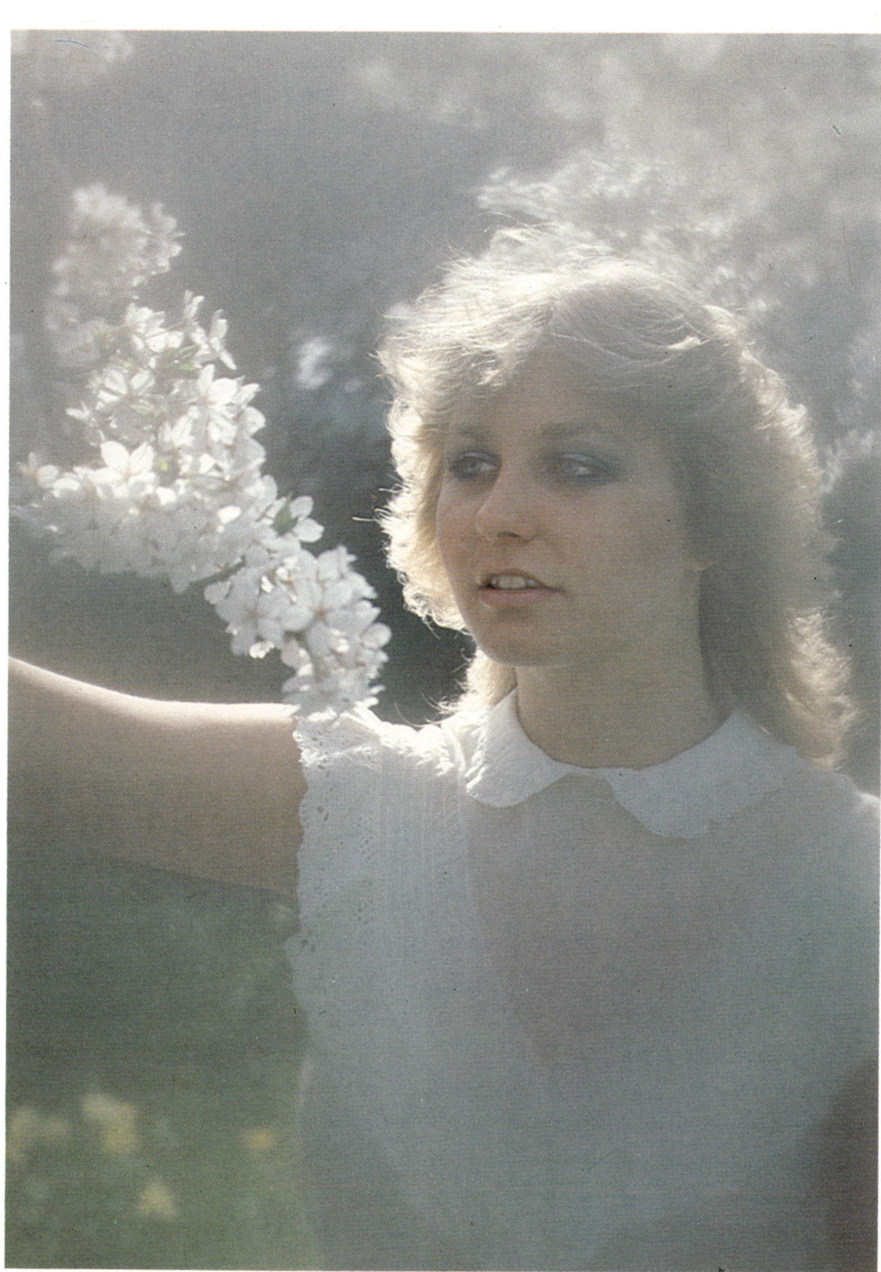

A diffusion filter gives your pictures a soft, romantic look

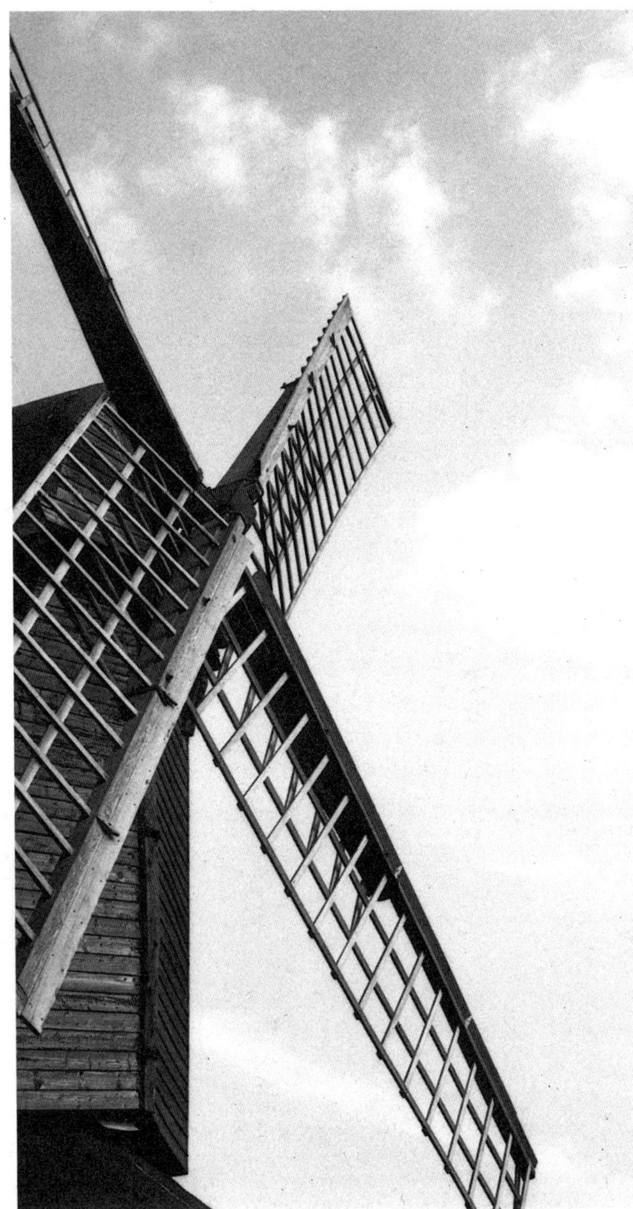

No filter

Filters for black and white films

Black and white photography is no poor relation of colour, but a special art in itself. Without the distractions of different colours, it's the shapes, and the contrasts in the different tones of grey that produce the results. You can enhance these very important shapes by, surprisingly, using different *colour* filters.

Black and white pictures render colours as different tones of grey. By using various colour filters, you can change the colours that the film sees, and so change the grey tones on the picture – this in turn changes the contrasts in the picture and gives it an entirely different look.

The Table opposite sets out the effects of the most commonly used black and white filters. This is included for completeness – but really, you are now stepping into the realms of serious hobby photography: the effects of these filters on black and white photos could be lost unless you either did your own processing (not too difficult a job, but beyond the scope of this book) or had them hand-processed by specialist laboratories (which would rapidly become very expensive).

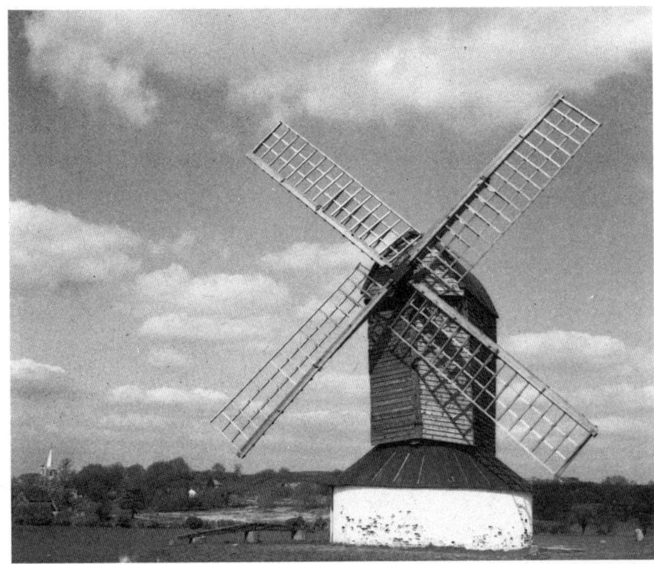

Yellow filter

Filters for black and white films

Filter colour	Filter factor [1]	Effect
Light yellow	1.5	Blue slightly darker, yellow lighter, red and green a little lighter. Tone rendering matches sensitivity of human eye. Useful for landscapes with cloudy sky and shots of snow with sun
Mid yellow	1.5 - 2	Blue darker, stronger effect than with light yellow. For photos of paintings
Deep yellow	2 - 3	Effect even more marked than with lighter yellow filters. In mountain country, blue sky turns black, especially if light level is low
Greenish yellow	1.5 - 2	Close to mid-yellow, fine rendering of green tones, very good for landscape, better rendering of skin than with yellow filter. (It's best not to use any filters for human skin)
Orange	3 - 5	Effect even more dramatic than with deep yellow filter. Blue sky becomes black, green and red are lighter. Suitable for red or yellow flowers taken against the sky, for dramatic architectural photos and for all the subjects listed above
Red	6 - 10	Effect even more pronounced than with orange filter. Scene appears as if moon-lit. Haze on horizon disappears, human complexion and particularly lips are too light, green is much lighter and blue becomes black. For dramatised landscapes
Blue	1.5	For portraits with artificial lighting. Lips are darker, eyes lighter, things like freckles are emphasised. Can accentuate the impression of haze

[1] see page 112

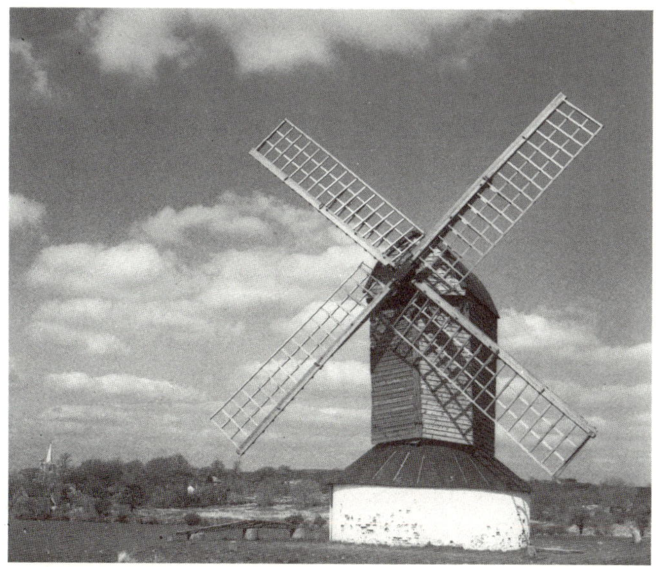

Orange filter

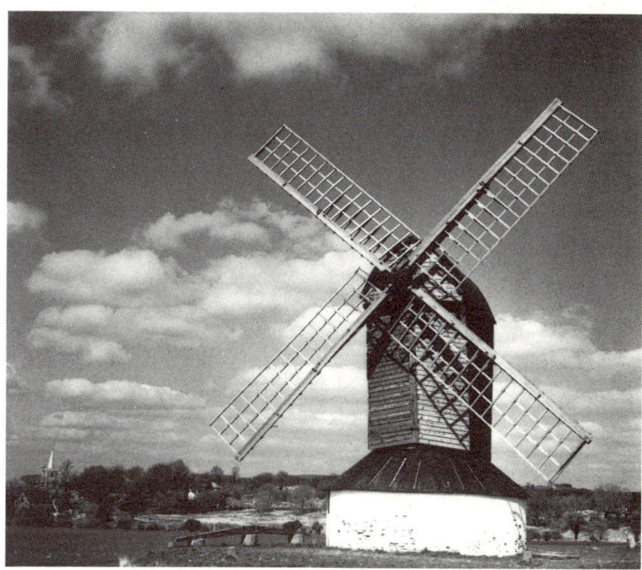

Red filter

Special effect filters

You'll either love the effects these give, or hate them: if it's love, be sure not to over-use them. The types described here are just examples of the range of special effects filters available.

Starburst   Transforms an ordinary light source – a candle, street lamp, or the sun, into a pointed star. You can buy filters with two, four, eight, or more starburst beams.

Multi-image (prismatic)   These multiply the image two, three or more times in the same picture.

Half-lens   Gives you a different focus point on both halves of the picture so, for example, you can have both very close-to objects and very far-away objects in focus at the same time.

Graduated (split-image)   Each half of the filter is a different colour. You can revolve them so that the split appears horizontally, vertically or diagonally. Because the filter is not in focus, the picture will gradually shade from the one colour-cast to the other; there won't be a stark line at the boundary between the two colours.

These filters are also available in a single colour which shades off gradually – these alllow you to darken part of the picture, such as the sky, or to reduce contrasts.

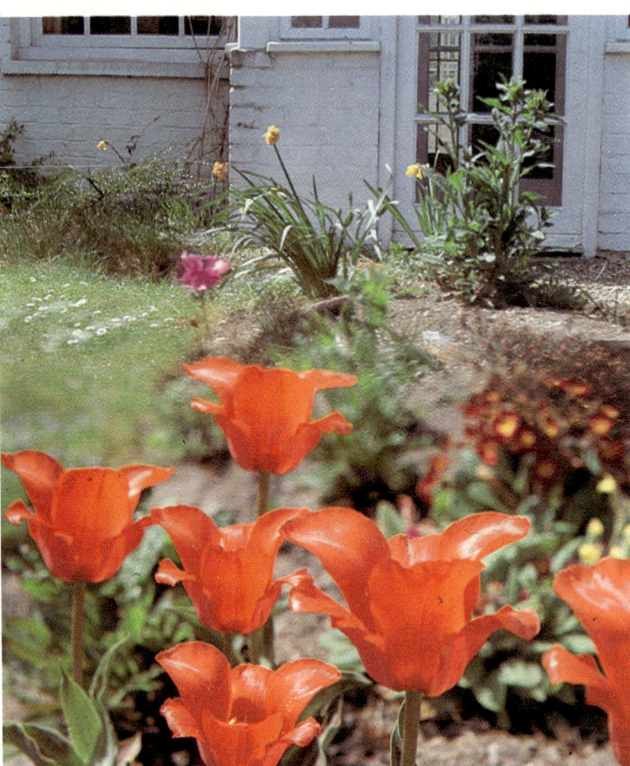

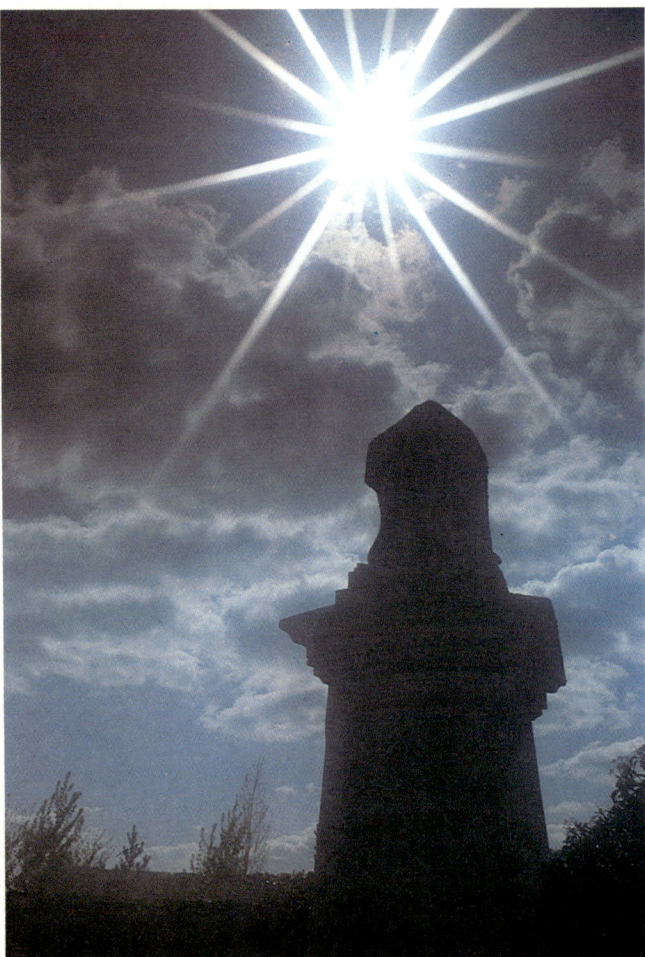

Three special effects filters: **far left** half-lens; **left** starburst; **right** graduated

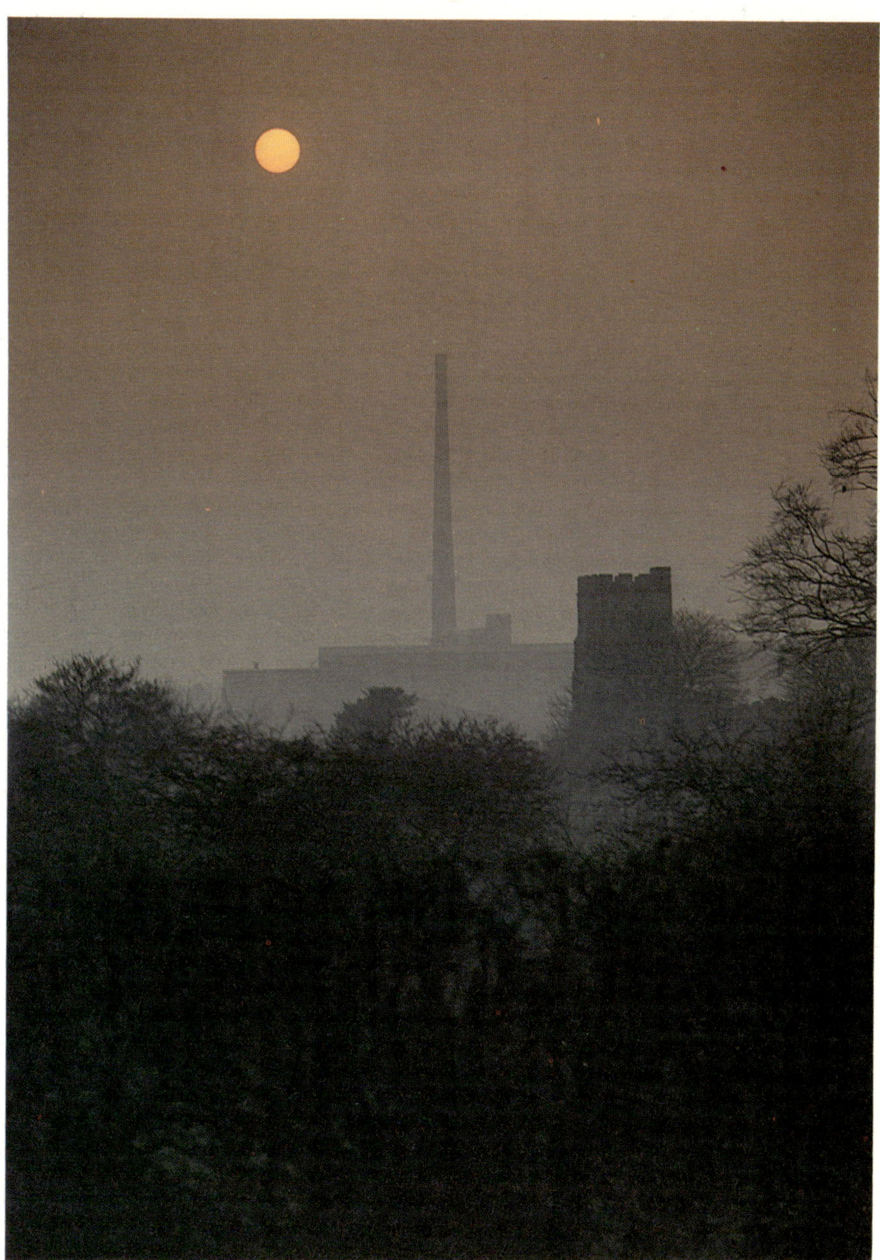

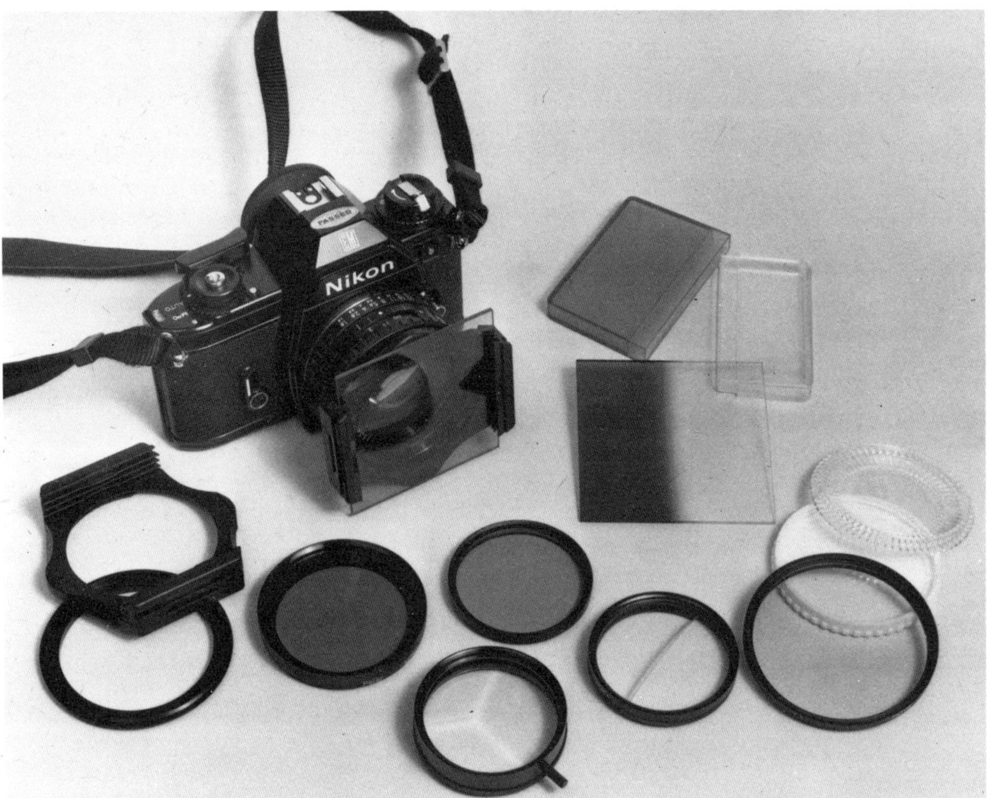

Filters come in various diameters to fit different-sized lenses. If you make a lot of use of filters, it's a good idea to fit a filter holder to your camera lens that you can slide filters into

Filters in practice

There are a number of points you should bear in mind when you are using filters.

Filter factors   Most filters absorb some light, so when you use them, you have to increase the exposure (with either a slower shutter speed or a bigger lens aperture). In general this is either taken care of automatically (with auto exposure cameras) or you can see the actual effects of the filter on exposure settings through the lens (with manual SLRs). There are very few modern cameras which both can use filters and wouldn't allow easy correction of exposure.

But if you have a camera like this, or if you want to take flash photos with a camera that does not have through-the-lens flash metering, you will need to know exactly how much light the filter is cutting out so that you can correct the shutter speed or aperture accordingly.

This is generally indicated on the filter by the *filter factor* number. For example, a filter factor of 2 means that the filter absorbs half the light, so you would have to increase the aperture by one stop (eg from f5.6 to f4) or halve the shutter speed (eg from $\frac{1}{125}$ sec to $\frac{1}{60}$ sec). Filter factors of 4, 8, 16 and 32 mean you have to increase the aperture by 2, 3, 4, or 5 stops respectively.

Fitting   Most filters simply screw on to the front of the lens. This is a good solution for UV and skylight filters, which can be left in place permanently. For more specific filters this is less suitable – screwing filters on and off is time-consuming, and if you have different lenses you would probably find yourself needing filters of different diameters for each one.

Instead, you screw on to each lens a *filter holder*, and into this you can insert both circular and rectangular filters of varying sizes. These holders have another advantage: you can slide just part of the filter into place, or vary the position of the filter across the lens. In this way you could, for example, position a split-image filter with the line of separation coinciding with the horizon, so that the sky comes out in one colour and the land in front of it another.

Using Filters need some trial and error before you become adept at using them. Buy only one filter at a time and take the time and trouble to experiment with it and study carefully the possibilities it offers. Even with an SLR camera, the image you see through the viewfinder may not exactly match with the results you actually get.

The effect of some filters (diffusion, for example) is heightened when you are working against the light or with large apertures or long focal lengths. On the other hand, the effect of graduated filters is increased with small apertures or short focal lengths.

Some special effects filters (graduated filter, for example) can upset a meter's weighting (see page 52) and so give you an erroneous exposure reading or setting. Only trial and error will help you over this problem.

Processing Developing and printing laboratories automatically 'correct' colours when processing print films. As a result, you run the risk of losing any artistic colour effect you've tried to get with special effect filters. Enclose a note with your films explaining what filters you have used where, and what effect you expect on the finished print. It would be better to restrict this sort of work to slides, or to films you process yourself.

BUYING GUIDE

If you have an SLR camera, a skylight or UV filter is an almost essential accessory. Other types of filter range from being useful to merely fun, and what (if anything) you should buy depends a lot on the type of photography you do and the quality of the results you expect.

A filter won't work magic on your pictures: to get the best results it is essential to spend some time learning what it will do and how to use it properly.

CHAPTER TEN

FLASH

The ready availability of flash lighting has helped to revolutionise amateur photography. Pictures indoors and in bad light are now no more trouble to take than those in clear sunlight

To obtain a good picture you need light. The more elementary the camera, the more light you need. With a simple pocket camera, for instance, your photos are likely to be very dull or under-exposed in dull weather. And even with the best of cameras, taking pictures indoors with just the normal lighting available is not easy. Flash is a portable source of intense light that overcomes this problem, allowing you to take good pictures indoors with little problem, and to compensate to some extent for failing light outdoors.

And like all aspects of photography, it has its artistic side – lighting is the whole essence of a picture, and altering the way that the lighting is arranged and controlled completely changes the nature of the composition. Flash can give you that control over the lighting.

Types of flash

There are two main types of flash unit – **flash bulbs** and **electronic flash**. With some cameras you don't have a choice – the very simplest cameras all use bulbs; and SLRs almost always use electronic units. Where you do have the choice, the main trade-off is between initial cost and running costs – electronic flash is more expensive to buy, but each flash costs less than a penny; with bulbs the initial investment is practically nil, but each flash costs 15p or more.

Flash units can also be divided into those that are **built-in** to the camera (as on many non-reflex cameras, for example) and those that are **separate** (which is all you can get for SLRs). In general, this chapter is about the separate units, though details of techniques apply also to built-in units.

Flash bulbs   The principle of bulb flash is very simple: the bulb contains a phosphorous capsule (like the head of an

ordinary match) and a piece of the metal zirconium (or an alloy of magnesium and aluminium). A battery passes current through a strip of wire, like that used in a light bulb or electric fire, which heats the phosphorous capsule, which in turn sets fire to the zirconium, which gives off a very bright light. Some bulbs don't need batteries: the flash is fired by mechanical action. It takes longer to read about than to happen: the whole operation takes only about $\frac{1}{30}$ second. There are various sorts of bulb flash – *flash cubes*, *Topflash* or *Flipflash*, *flashbar*. These are used in various sorts of simple and instant picture cameras – see those chapters for details.

Electronic flash   Electronic flash produces an intense brief flash caused by the discharge of an inert gas contained in a little quartz tube. The discharge is caused by passing a powerful electrical charge through the tube – a charge which is stored in a 'capacitor'. In turn, the capacitor is charged up either directly from the *mains*; from a rechargeable nickel-cadmium (*ni-cad*) battery; from disposable *alkaline batteries*; or (with a built-in flash only) from a long-lasting *lithium battery*. Unlike bulbs, where you can take pictures quickly one after another, with electronic flash you have to wait for the capacitor to recharge between pictures – this *recycling time* varies from under two seconds with lithium batteries to about four to eight seconds with fresh alkaline batteries, and much longer with weak batteries (but it can be under a second with 'thyristor flash', see page 120). If you can curb your impatience to take a picture it is best to wait as long as possible between flash shots: the more fully-charged the flash is, the more intense the light from it will be.

For amateur use, the main method of charging is dispos-

Carefully-placed flash lighting helps turn this shot of mother and baby into something special

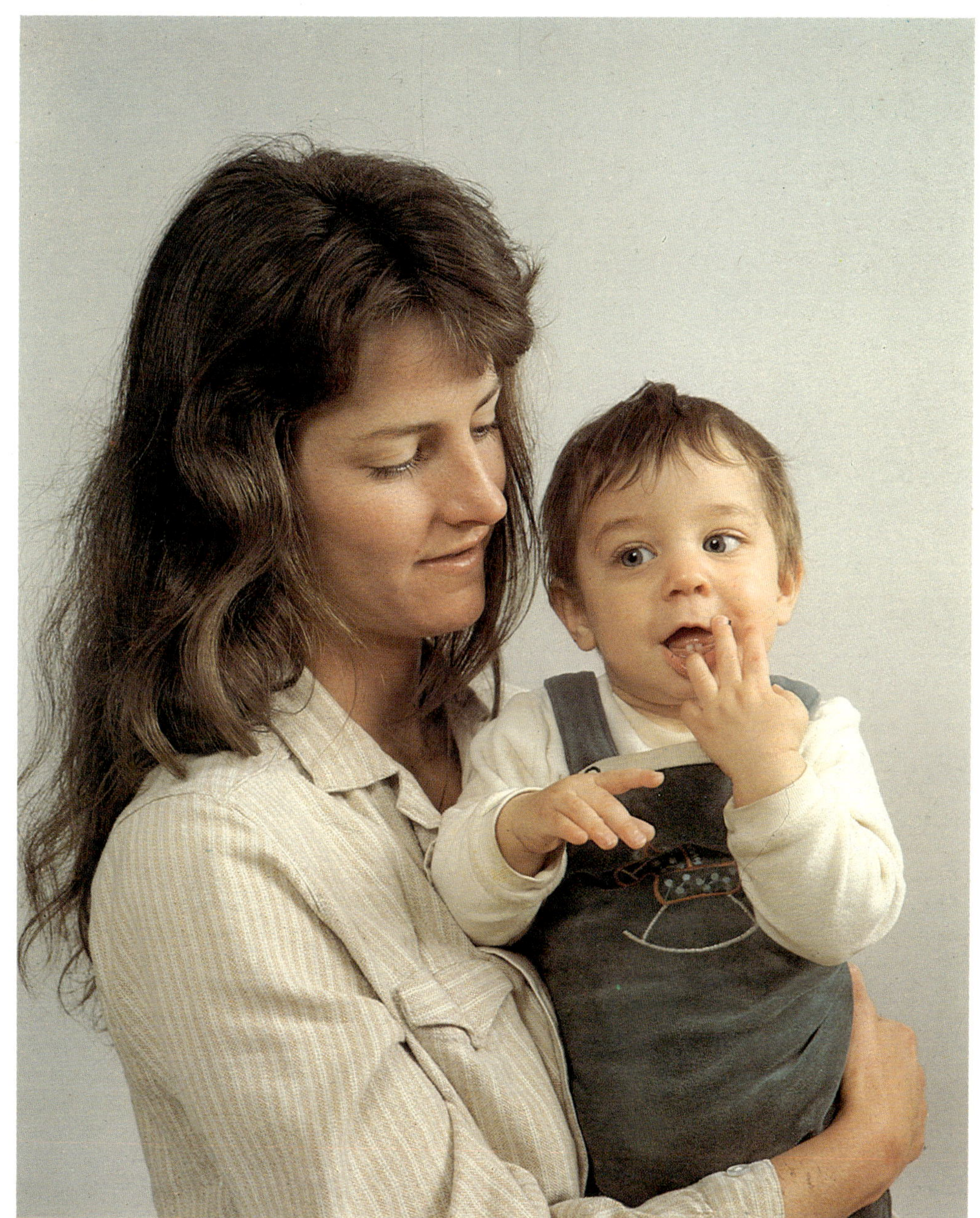

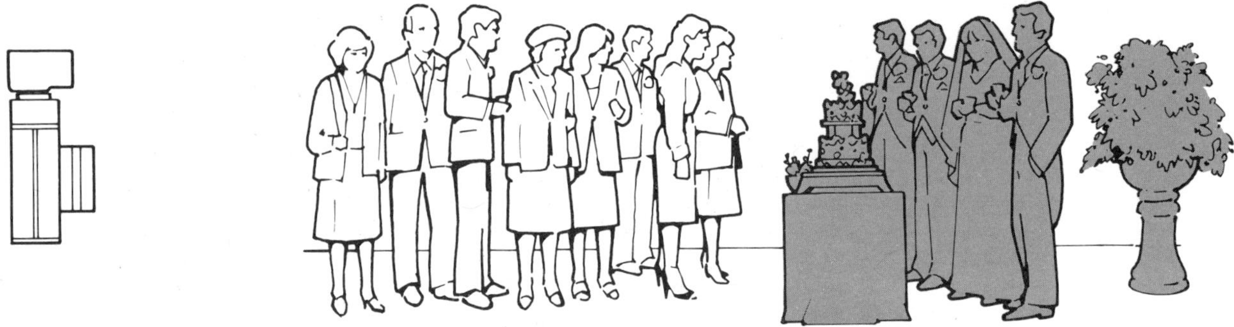

The built-in flash units on many disc, 110, and 35mm non-reflex cameras have a flash range restricted to three or four metres (10ft to 13ft) with 100 ISO film. And you can't achieve even this range unless

you use an aperture of about f5.6 (which in turn restricts the depth of field of your shot quite significantly)

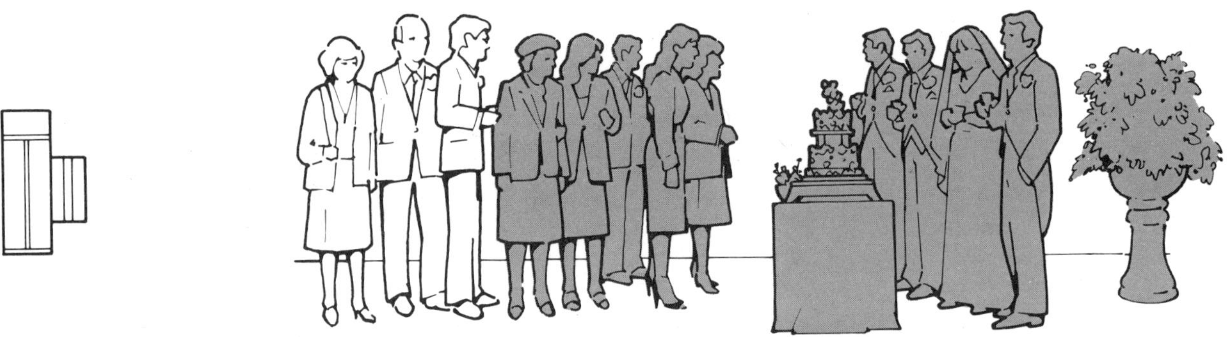

If you wanted to use a smaller aperture to get a better depth of field, the flash range would be less – f8, for example, would give you a range of about 2.5m

able alkaline batteries. Two advantages of these are that you don't have to fiddle about with re-charging, and they can be used anywhere. Though, obviously, there is a limit to the number of pictures you can take with a set of batteries most units give several hundred flashes a set so the chances of running out of flash are low, especially if you always carry a spare set of batteries with you.

Mains and ni-cads are hardly ever used by amateurs. Mains is cheap to run; gives quick recharging (so you aren't hanging around between shots); and can always be relied on to charge fully. *But* you need a power supply wherever you go. Ni-cads work out cheaper than disposable batteries, can be used anywhere and fresh ones have a very short recycling time. *But* once they are 'run down' they must be recharged from the mains, which takes 10 to 12 hours. It's important to keep ni-cads on charge while you're not using them partly because this increases their life (for the same reason, they ought to be frequently *dis*charged, too); partly because then

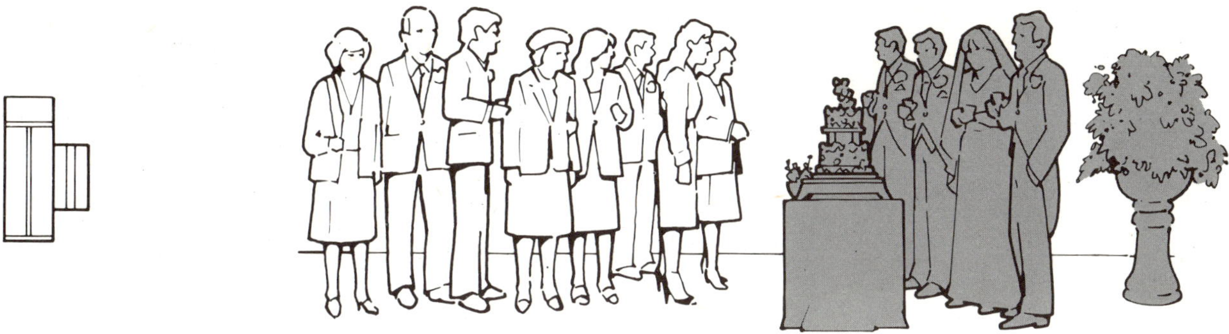

Even with a very low-intensity flash, the lighting will still be adequate up to 4m *if* you can select an aperture as large as f2.8. An aperture two stops smaller (f5.6) halves the range to 2m, but you can double it back to 4m if you use a film four times as fast (400 ISO). Using a faster film may be the only way to get satisfactory results from a very modest built-in flash unit

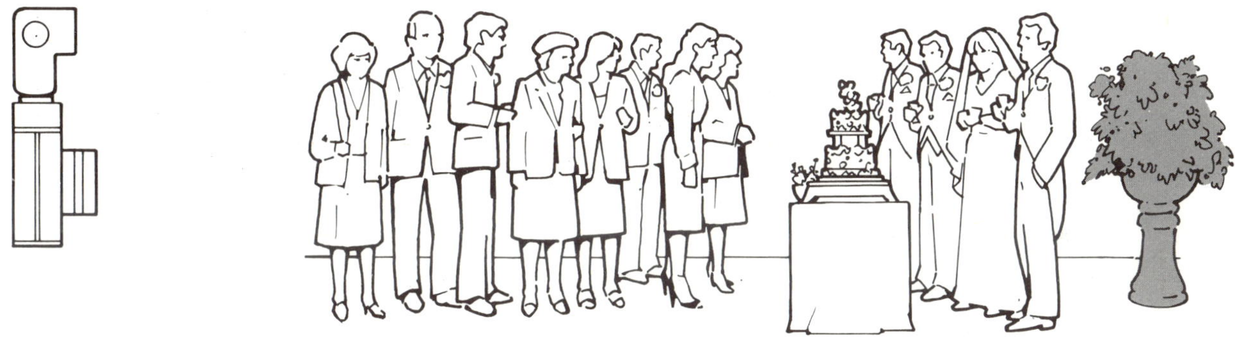

A powerful flash unit increases flash range – to, say, 12m at f2.8. Or allows you to use a smaller aperture if you don't need all this range – f8 still gives you a range of 4m. You don't get this sort of power from a built-in unit: a separate electronic flash is needed

you'll be certain that they are ready for action whenever you want them. As with disposable batteries, when ni-cads run down the recycling time is slower, so you might have to wait up to 30 seconds or more between pictures.

Exposure and flash range

Taking flash pictures that will turn out properly exposed can be more difficult than for pictures using only natural light. The main problem is that exposure is very uneven: the flash light is very intense, but its brightness tails off sharply the further you get from the unit – so objects close to the flash will tend to be over-exposed; those further away could be under-exposed. So there is a limited depth within which objects will be successfully lit by flash – this is the *flash range*. The more powerful a flash unit, the greater its flash range. However the range depends not only on the intensity of the flash discharge, but also on the aperture size and the speed of the film (see Chapter 8) being used: see the drawings above.

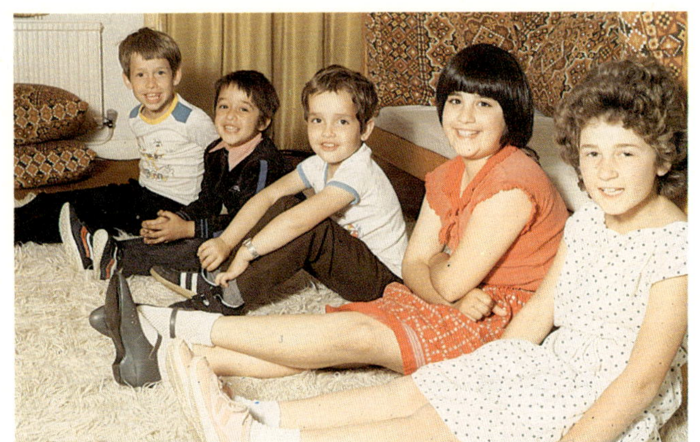 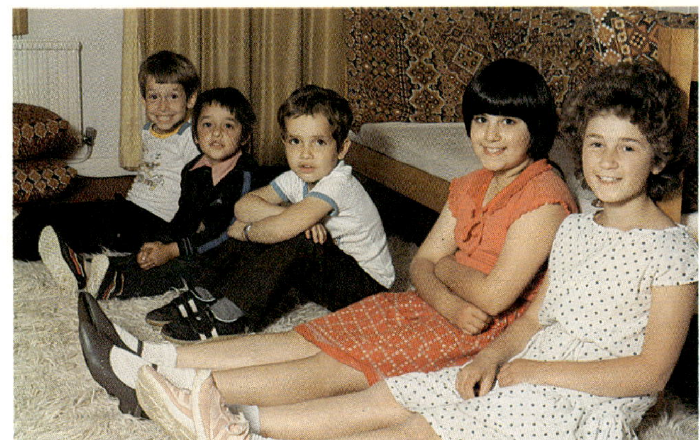

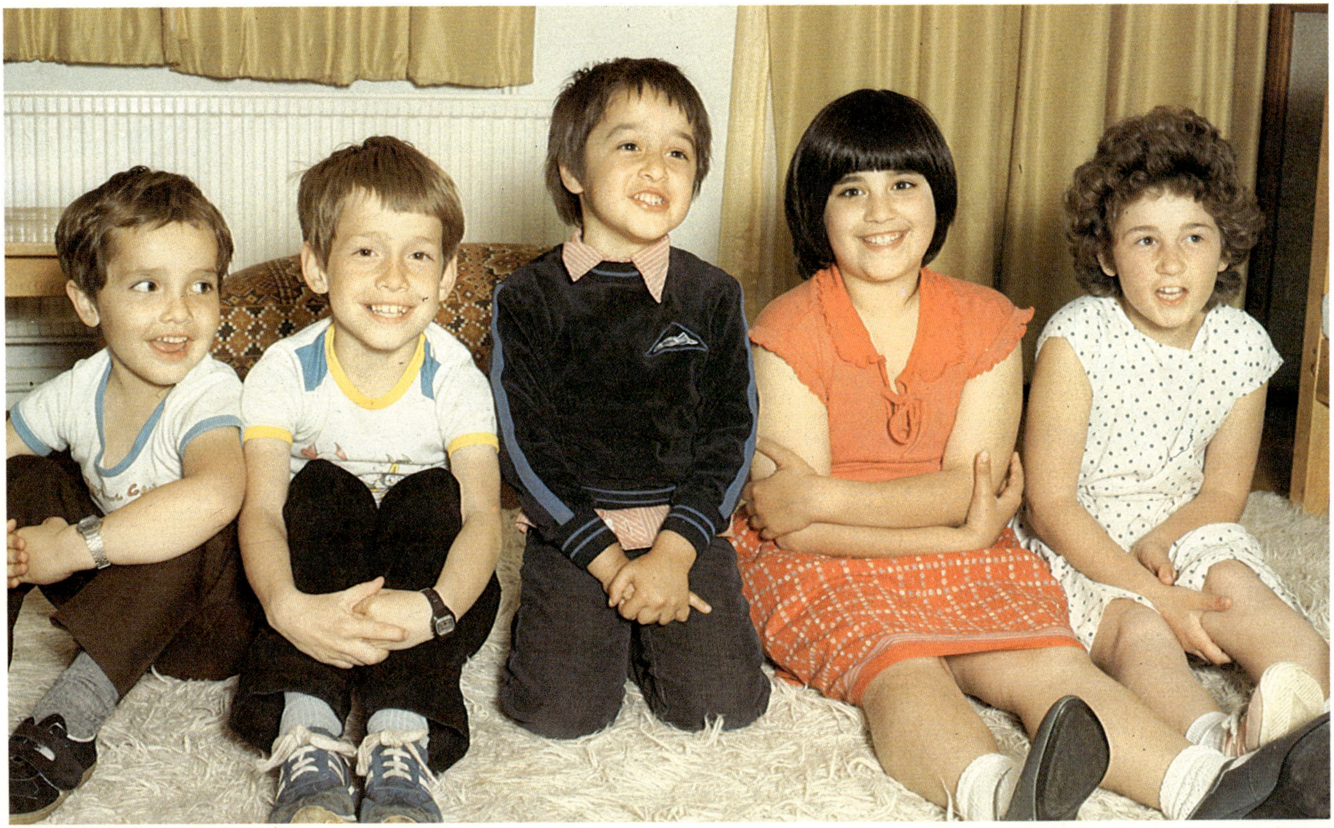

Left Flash will light up subjects at different distances from the camera by different amounts – either the nearest child is over-exposed, or the one furthest away is under-exposed. For an evenly-exposed picture (**below left**) keep your subjects all at roughly the same distance from the camera

Below Direct flash can give rise to *red-eye* – red spots in the pupils. Avoid it by keeping room lights on and not having your subjects staring directly into the camera

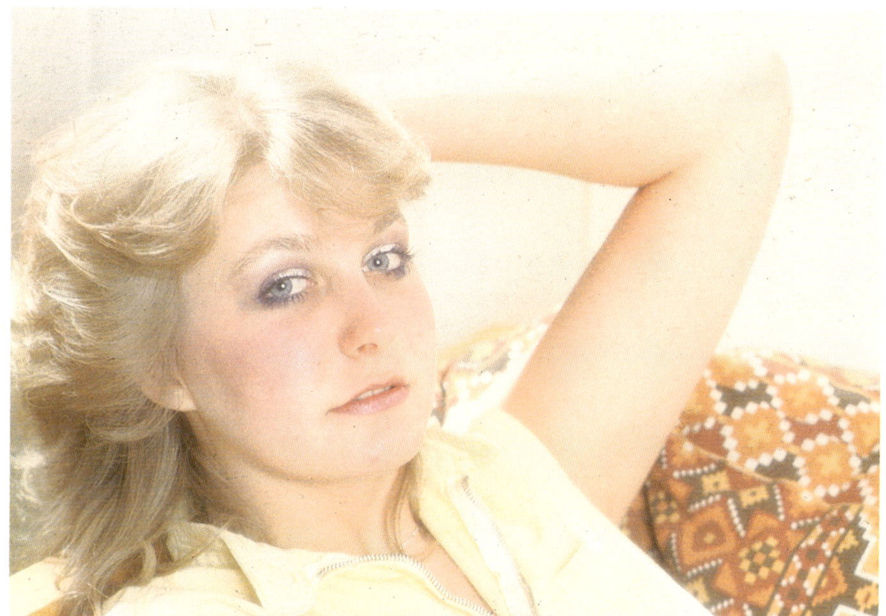

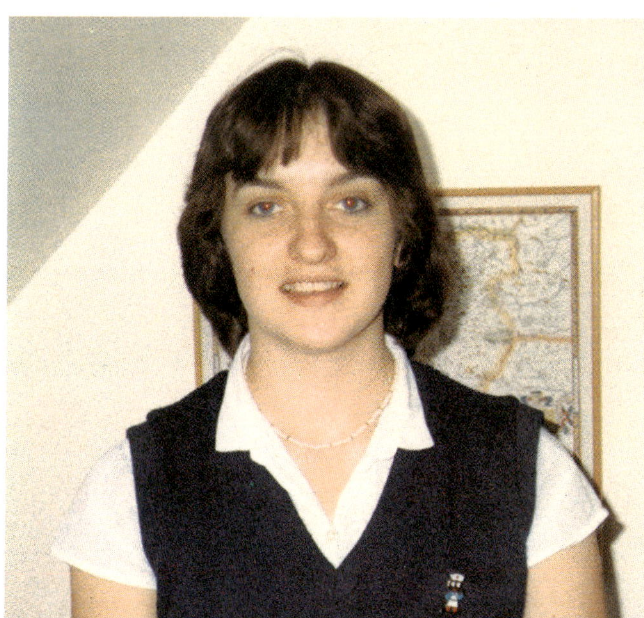

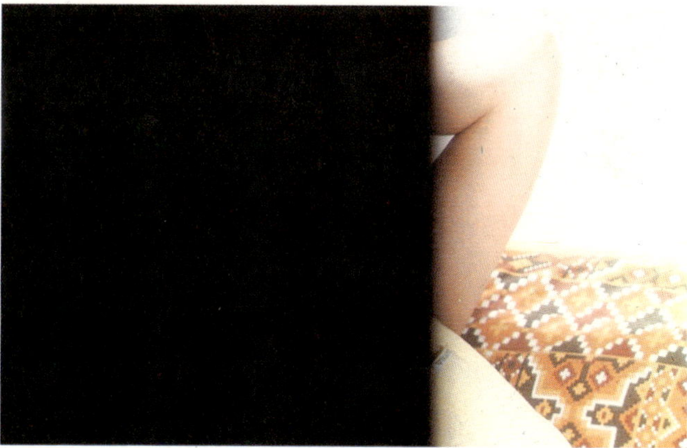

Flash operates so quickly, it's important to ensure the shutter is open at exactly the right moment (**top**). Using the wrong shutter speed (**bottom**) can give rise to flash synchronisation problems blanking out part of your picture

Automatic flash

Most modern flash units for SLR cameras are of the automatic or **computer** type. These vary the exposure, not by requiring you to alter the aperture size, but by altering the duration of the flash – shorter (down to $1/100,000$ second) for close subjects, longer (up to $1/100$ second) for distant subjects. And they do this automatically (a sensor measures how much light is reflected from the subject and switches off the flash when enough light has passed to the film to expose it correctly) so that you don't need to worry about working out how far your subjects are from the flash unit, or what aperture size you need to get the required flash range.

Even so, as there is a limit to how much variation there can be in flash duration, there is a limit to the variation in flash range you can get for a particular aperture: for example, a flash working with an aperture of f8 may allow you a range of between 1m and 5m (3ft to 16ft). Most computer flash units allow you to work with a choice of apertures – some with any aperture you like – so that you can cover a wide flash range. The ranges available with different apertures are likely to overlap, and you can take advantage of this to give you some flexibility in choosing a depth of field. Use this flexibility also, if you can, to avoid having to use very short flash durations as these may affect the colours in your photography.

Another plus point of computer flash (if it has what is called **thyristor circuitry**) is that you don't waste energy in producing a flash bigger than you need. So, unless you are working with the maximum flash duration, recycling times between flashes will be shorter, and the number of flashes you get from a set of batteries should be greater.

The main drawback is that the sensor system can be fooled into giving the wrong exposure – they tend not to be as clever as the metering systems for daylight exposure found in SLR cameras themselves (see page 52). Instead of taking a weighted reading, giving more importance to the centre of the picture, they simply take an average reading over the whole area. So if, for example, you photograph a bright subject in front of a dark wall the average reading will be fairly dull and a long flash duration will be used, probably making the subject over-exposed. On the other hand, a bright background will force a short duration, and will lead to under-exposure of the main subject if this is small and dark.

The answer is to alter the aperture manually, to compensate. Experience, and trial and error, is the only way you'll learn when and by how much you cannot trust the flash gun to give you the right exposure. But as a rough guide:
● use ½ stop *more* exposure out of doors at night or in very big rooms
● use ½ stop *less* exposure in light-coloured rooms or ones with reflecting surfaces.

These values are with slide film, and should be doubled if you are using print film.

The most automatic of the computer flash units is the **dedicated flash unit**. This is specially matched to the camera so every brand (and sometimes every model) has its own, slightly different dedicated unit. These do all the thinking for you, setting both shutter speed and apertures automatically, and signalling in the viewfinder when they are ready to fire. But you still need to correct aperture manually on difficult shots, and some of them are not very powerful.

Manual flash   A manual flash unit isn't one where you have to trigger the flash yourself – that's always done automatically because there is no way you could synchronise the flash to go off at exactly the split-second that the shutter opens. Rather, it's a unit where you have to work out what aperture size to use to give the correct exposure for the flash range you want, and the film speed you're using.

To take into account all these different points, the flash

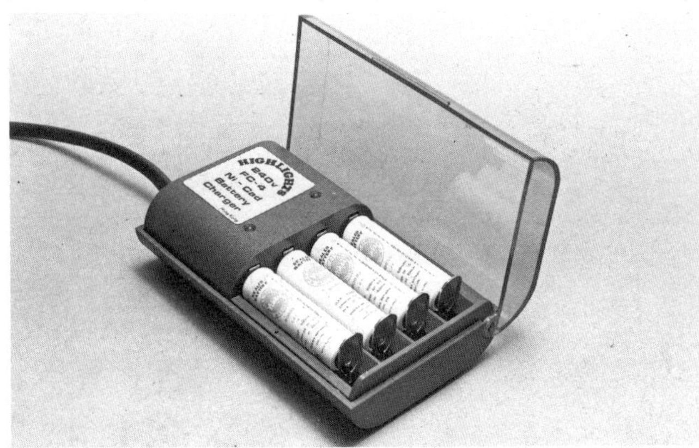

A ni-cad battery charging unit

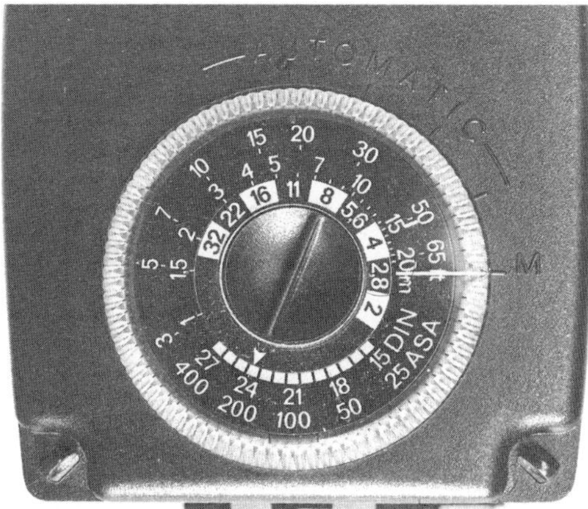

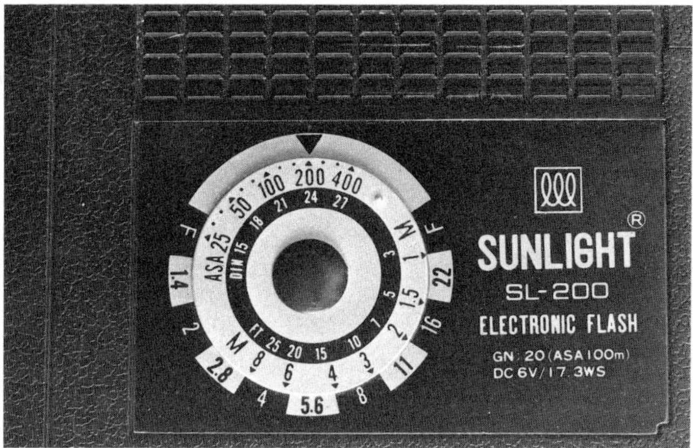

Aperture-setting dials on manual (**left**) and computer (**right**) flash units: essential for correct exposure with the manual unit; to give some choice in depth of field with computer units

unit is marked with a **guide number** which allows you to work out either the aperture required to achieve a particular range, or the range you get when working at a particular aperture. Where the guide number is quoted in metres, the calculations are:

$$\text{aperture needed} = \frac{\text{guide no}}{\text{range (in metres)}}$$

or

$$\text{range available (in metres)} = \frac{\text{guide no}}{\text{aperture}}$$

Note that these equations don't take into account the film speed. Guide numbers are quoted assuming you are using 100 ISO film: if you use slower film you need a larger aperture (lower f-number) or have to put up with a shorter available range; if you use a faster film, you can manage with a smaller aperture (higher f-number) or get a greater range. The rule is that *quartering* the film speed requires an increase in aperture of one stop, or *halves* the range; *quadrupling* the film speed allows a decrease in aperture of one stop or *doubles* the range. You don't want to have to carry a pocket calculator and measuring tape around with you on your photographic expeditions. And you don't have to. Most manual flash units have a built-in calculator to help you set the aperture you

need. You set your film speed on a dial or scale, then read off the correct aperture to use for whatever distance your subject is from the camera. You need never even know what guide number your flash unit has (except that you'll know if it's low by the restrictions it places on range or aperture settings allowable).

Three problems: how do you work out easily how far away your subject is; what do you do when – as is usually the case – important parts of the scene are all at differing distances from the camera; and how do you control depth of field? The first problem can be easily solved on an SLR camera by focusing on your scene through the viewfinder, then reading off the subject distance from the scale on your lens – but remember that focusing through the viewfinder is difficult in poor light (and the light is likely to be poor if you are intending to use flash). The second problem has no real solution – with a flash picture, you must keep all the subjects at about the same distance from the camera if you want them to be equally exposed (as the pictures on page 118 show). As usual, you probably have a bit more leeway with film for prints rather than slides – though even here, processing will either give you correct exposure for closer subjects or for more distant subjects, not both at once.

The third problem may be a matter of tough luck, too. With many cameras you have little control over the shutter speed (see 'Synchronisation and shutter speed', below) so you're stuck with whatever aperture size the flash requires you to use for any particular subject distance, and therefore with

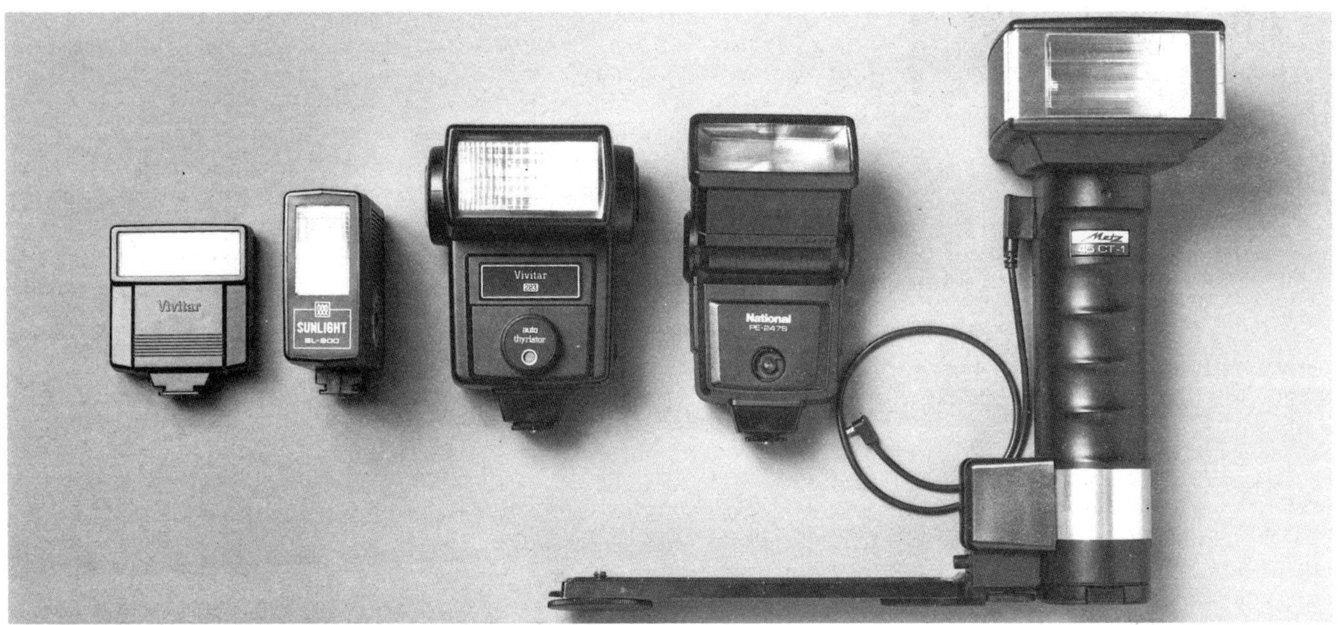

A selection of different types of separate flash gun, designed for use with SLR cameras

whatever depth of field that aperture gives you. The only way you could alter the depth of field is to change your camera position. You might be able to use a lens with a different focal length, but this brings problems too – see page 129.

Synchronisation and shutter speeds

The burst of light from a flash unit lasts for a thousandth of a second or less – so from the point of view of exposure it doesn't really matter what shutter speed you use (you're using flash because there isn't enough natural light, remember, so even if the shutter is open for some time after the flash has gone out, this is unlikely to affect the overall exposure on the film).

However, given the short time that the flash is operational, it is absolutely essential to ensure that the shutter is properly open during this brief instant – so good synchronisation between shutter and flash is vital. Fabric blind shutters are usually synchronised for flash at speeds of $\frac{1}{60}$ or $\frac{1}{125}$ second (check your camera's instructions) though you can use a slower speed with no problem. If you use a faster speed, you will find that the blind does not completely uncover the film and part of your picture will be cut off (see page 119). Between-the-lens shutters are usually synchronised for flash at all speeds. This can be useful if you are using flash merely to fill in shadows on a scene that otherwise would have enough natural light not to need flash and on which you would normally be using a fast shutter speed such as action shots.

Another problem with synchronisation is that different types of flash reach their maximum light level at different times. Electronic flash, for example, discharges almost immediately; with bulb flash it takes about $\frac{1}{60}$ second before they fire. So, unless the shutter speed is very slow, the start of the shutter opening must be delayed by a fraction of a second when bulb flash is used. Cameras that can cater for both types of flash therefore have two synchronisation sockets or 'contacts' – the X contact for electronic flash, and the M contact for bulb flash.

Solving the shadows problem

Snapshots taken with flash always seem to have very harsh shadows in them – not at all the sort of effect you see in real life. This is because in the majority of flash shots the lighting unit is mounted on the camera itself, pointing directly at the subject and only a couple of metres away. So the subject is lit with only one source of harsh, direct light. Compare that with natural light – millions of miles away, diffused by the atmosphere and reflected off the ground, buildings, even trees. Your flash pictures will look better if you can get some of those effects into them.

The photographs starting on this page, and continuing over the next few pages show the sort of effects that various types of flash lighting and lighting angles will bring to your pictures, and the drawings illustrate how the lighting was set up for each shot.

Direct lighting

Direct, unangled flash mounted on the camera and pointing straight at your subjects will give a flattened look to your picture. If shadows can be seen in the picture, they will be very harsh.

A particular problem with direct flash in colour photographs is *red-eye* – the people in your photograph appear to have red spots in their eyes (because the flash is reflecting off the retina straight back on to the camera film). The effect is most likely to occur when the flash is very close to the camera lens; with Magicubes, you can help prevent it by using an extender which lifts the flash away from the lens: with built-in flash, keep the room lights on, and don't let your subjects stare directly into the camera lens.

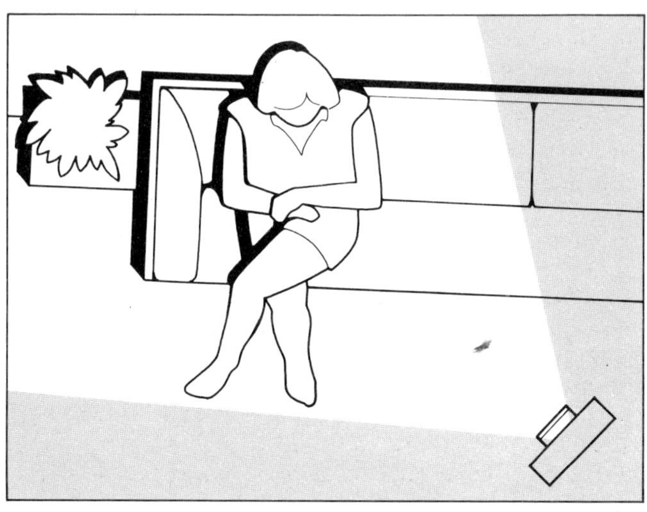

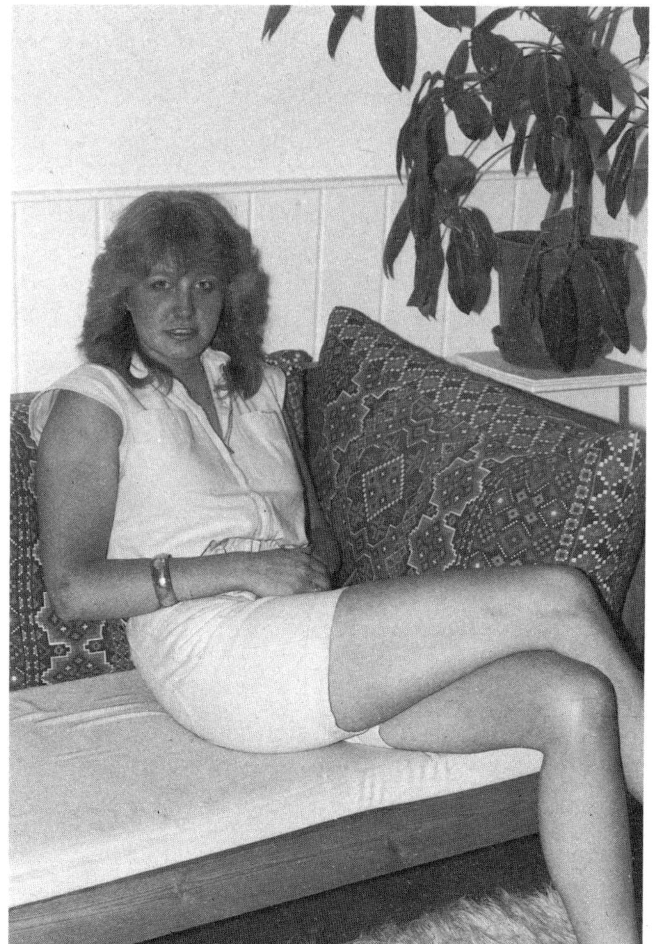

Angled flash

If you can use the flash unit off-camera, do so (though it will not be anywhere near as convenient). You'll need a lead to run from the socket on the camera to the one on the flash. The simplest solution is to hold the flash at arm's length, and at an angle to the camera. You won't get rid of the harsh shadows (indeed, they may be more visible) but it will give a degree of modelling in the picture which will make it more interesting and life-like. Carefully positioning the flash unit will help ensure any shadows that are produced are not too distracting – our pictures show the different effects you get simply by holding the flash first in one hand and then in the other.

A *diffuser* fitted over the flash will break up the light and soften the shadows to some extent. But it will reduce output – a computer flash will compensate for this automatically, but with a manual unit, you'll have to guess by how much to increase the aperture (or reduce the distance) to get a properly-exposed picture. Diffuses for different flash guns can be bought, but something as simple as a white handkerchief will do.

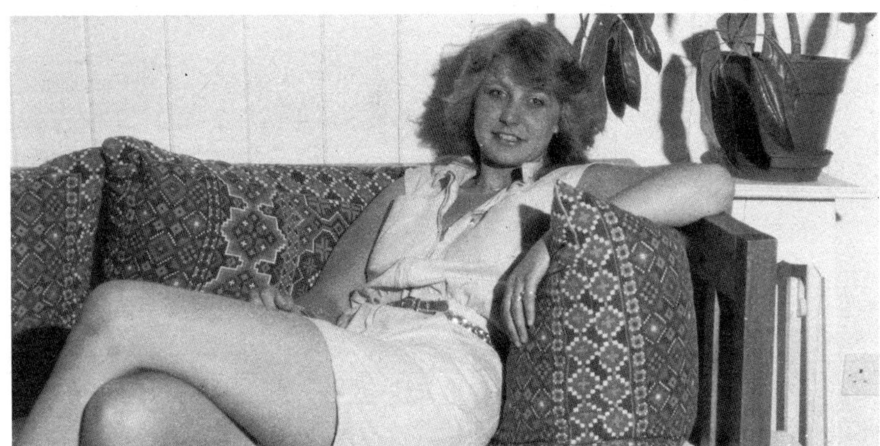

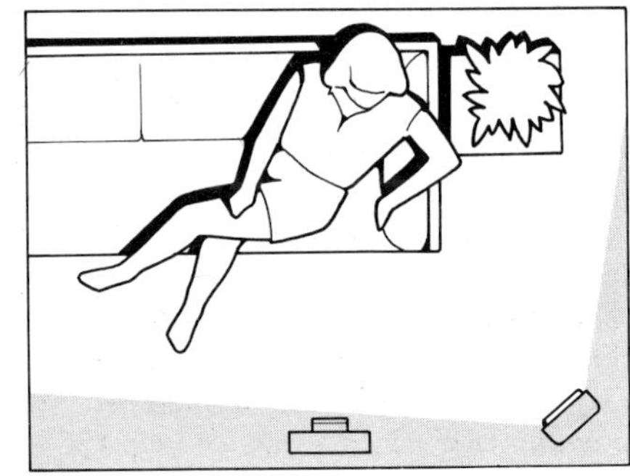

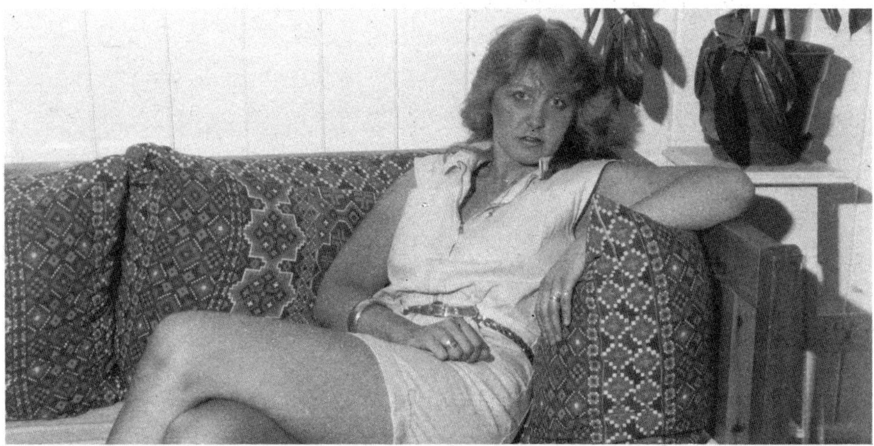

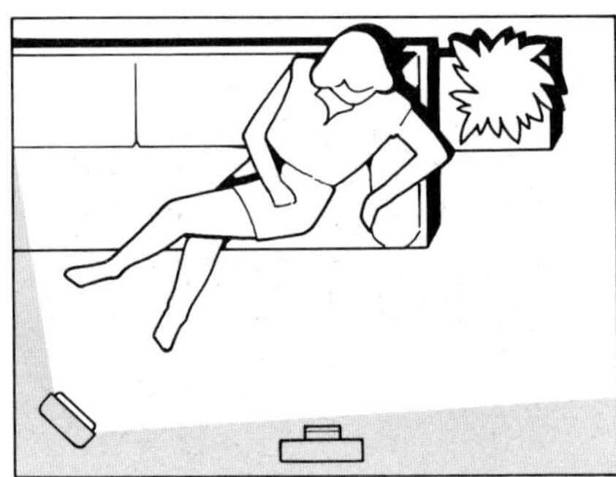

Bounce flash

Bouncing the flash off walls or ceilings is a good way to remove hard edges, and to introduce some natural-looking reflections into the picture. Many flash units have a swivelling head so that you can set them to bounce without having to take them of the camera – which is more convenient.

Again, bouncing reduces the amount of light reaching the scene. A computer flash will compensate automatically for this if the sensor unit (which measures the light reflected from the scene) can be left pointing directly at the scene. If it moves with the flash head, then it will give an erroneous reading, and you will have to alter the aperture setting yourself, as you would with a manual unit.

Again, you'll have to guess by how much to increase the aperture – but as a start, bear in mind that the flash-to-subject distance is the total distance the flash light travels – from the flash to the ceiling (or wall) and from the ceiling to the subject. You will also lose some power as the light is diffused and absorbed by the ceiling – allow say a couple of f-stops if the surface is white, three if it is coloured.

As you will find out, you can use bounce flash only with a powerful unit (one with a large guide number); a low ceiling;

and a short subject distance. If you haven't got a handily-close wall or ceiling, bounce the flash off a piece of white card or board. Some flash units have an adaptor on to which you can clip a 'bounce board' – a sort of portable ceiling.

One final point on bouncing – the colours in your picture will be influenced by the colour of whatever you bounce the flash off. So white surfaces·are safest: bounce off coloured surfaces only if you are sure you want the colour effect they will give you.

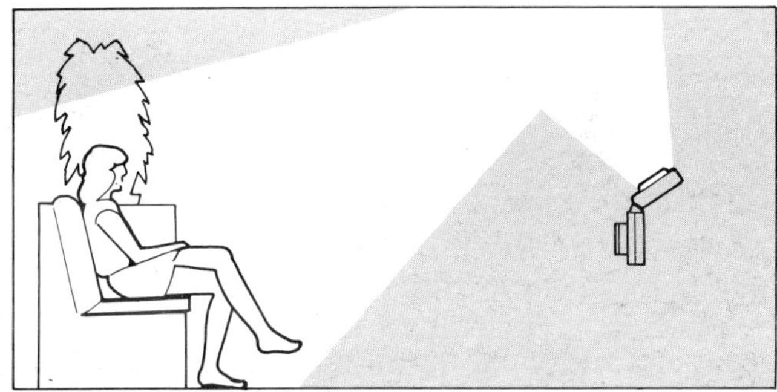

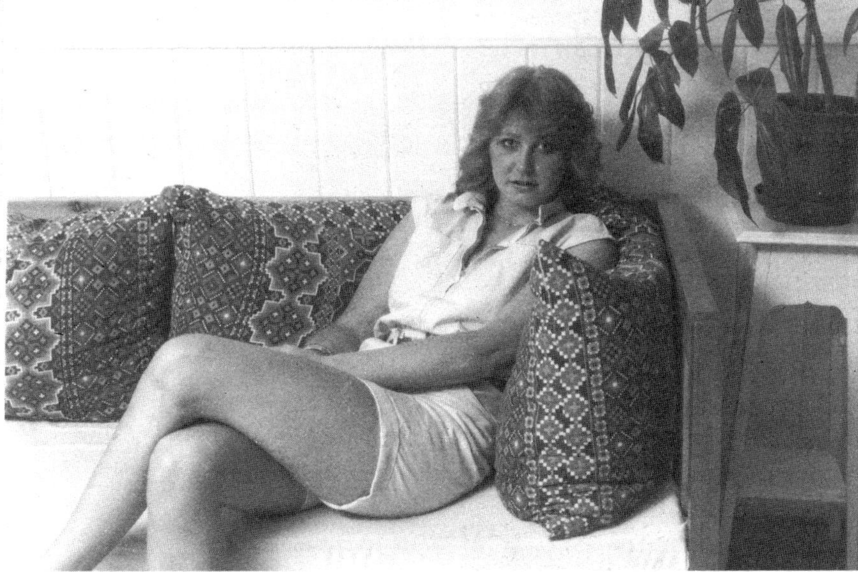

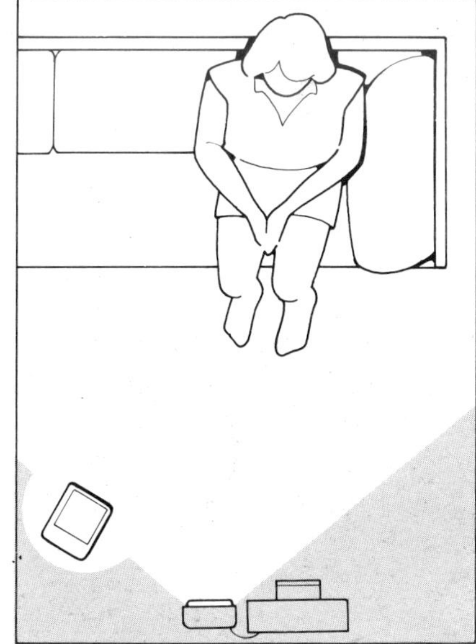

Multiple lighting

Two (or more) heads can be better than one – using multiple flash units is another way to reduce the harshness of shadows and increase the artistic effect of your pictures. You can connect the units together with cables, but generally you would use *slave units*. Each additional flash is fitted with a photo-electric cell which responds to the firing of the main flash by sending an electrical trigger to fire the slave flash unit. The whole operation is so rapid that are no problems with synchronisation or, on computer flashes, with the sensor reading incorrectly.

An alternative to using two or more flash guns is a single gun with two flash heads – one that can be swivelled for bounce flash, and another that can be used straight-on, for direct flash.

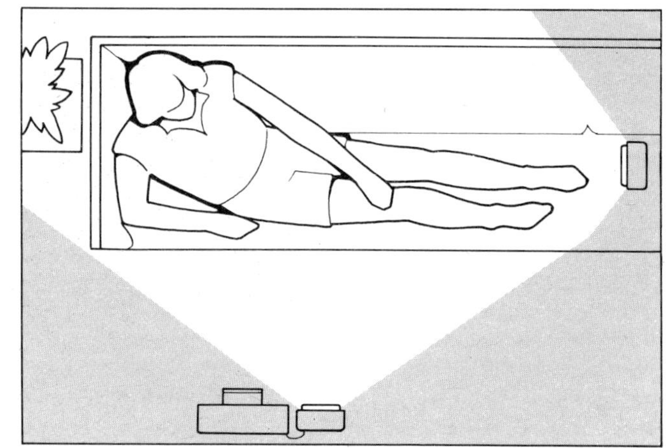

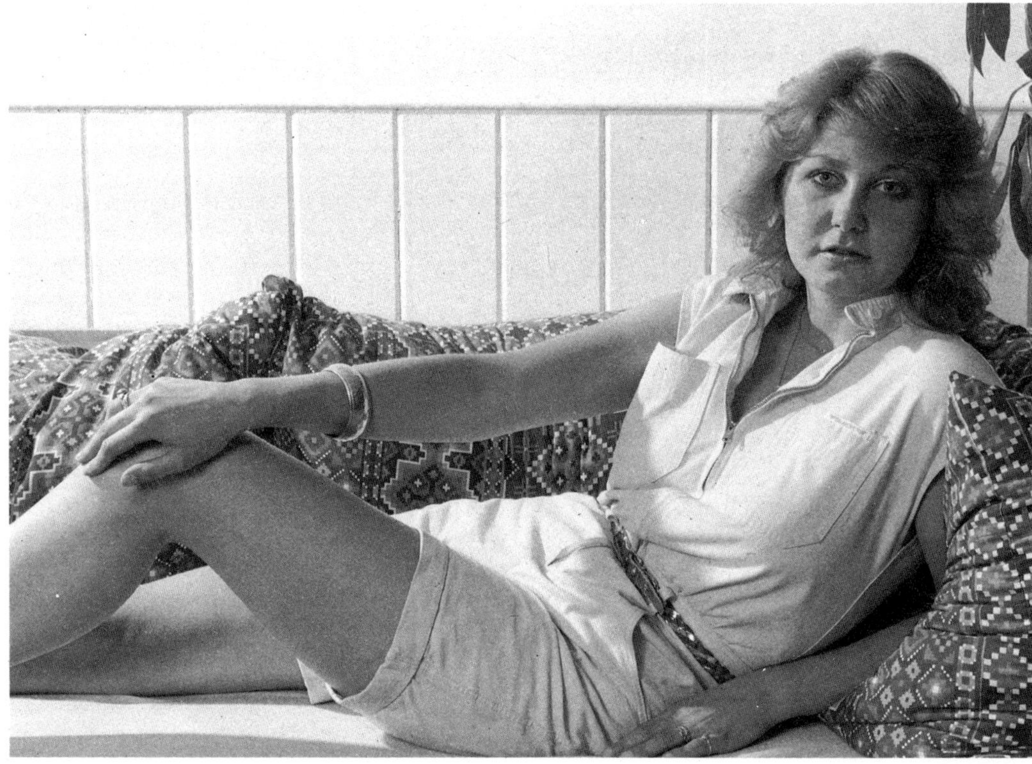

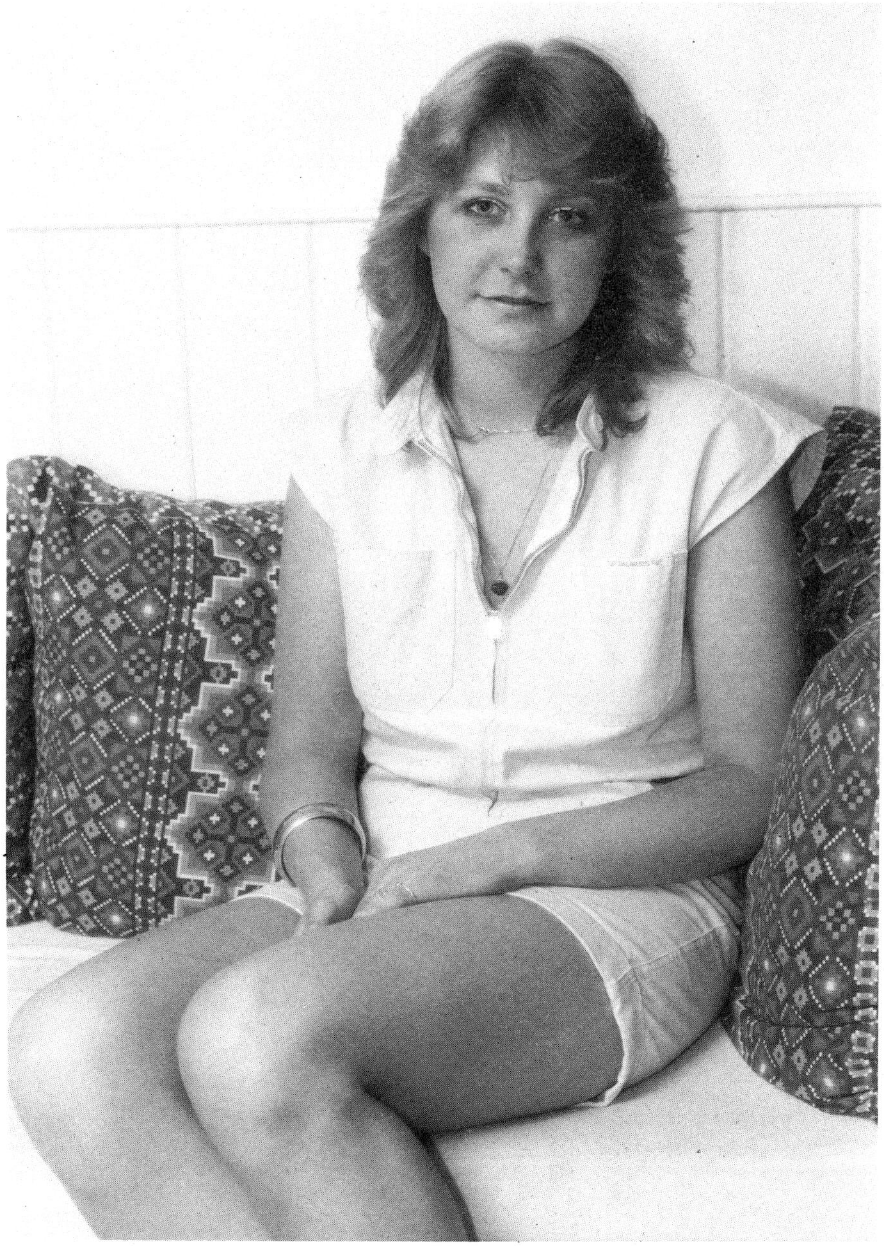

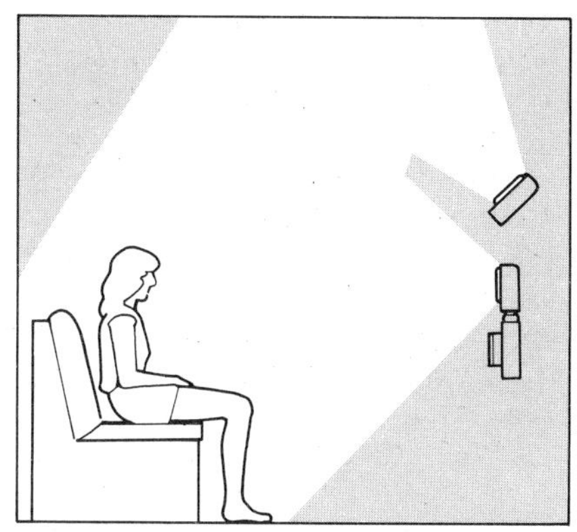

Fill-in flash

Don't keep flash purely for indoor or night-time shots. It can be used for fill-in lighting, to get rid of deep shadows, even in bright sunlight. You can get particularly attractive, and dramatic, pictures by *backlighting* your subject with the sunlight (that is, placing the subject so that the sunlight shines at its back) and using flash to pick out some detail at the front that would otherwise be in darkness.

To emphasise the backlighting, that is, to create more of a silhouette effect, choose a smaller aperture than one which would correctly expose the subject; to reduce the importance of the backlighting, use a bigger aperture.

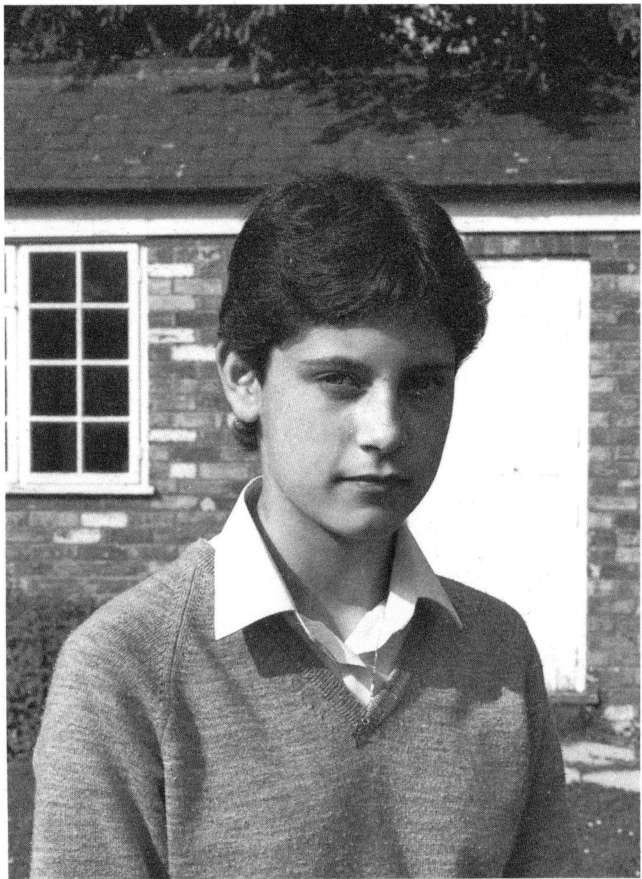

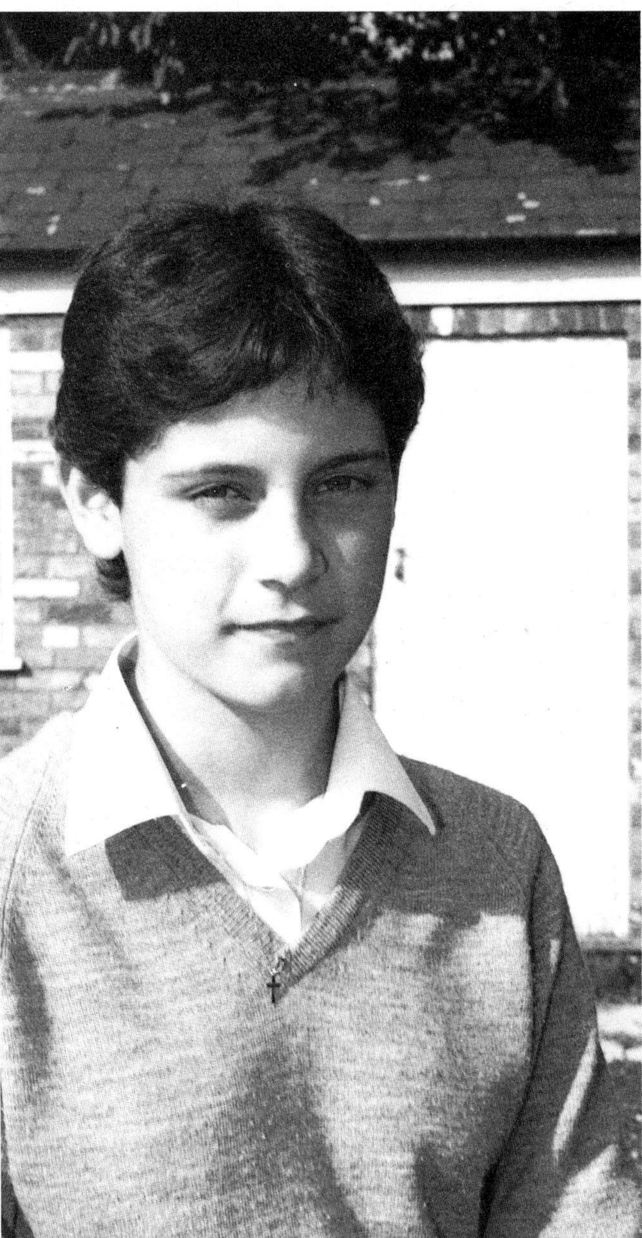

Different lenses

Flash units are designed mainly for use with standard lenses – their lighting angle is much the same as the 50° angle of view you get from a standard lens. So all the picture will (or should) be evenly lit. With a wide-angle lens, however, a standard flash unit won't light up as much of the scene as the lens sees, so the pictures you get will get darker at the edges and towards the corners – a bad case of 'vignetting'.

Most flash systems get round this problem by means of a wide-angle diffuser placed in front of the flash which spreads the flash light out over a wider angle. Spreading out the light like this effectively reduces the guide number of the flash unit; with computer flash, the sensor will take this into account automatically (because it works by sensing the amount of light returned to it, not the amount leaving the flash gun) otherwise you'll have to work out for yourself what extra exposure is needed.

If you really want to take flash pictures with a telephoto lens, you'll certainly get no problems with vignetting. But you'll probably be wanting a very long flash range and at the same time you will be wasting much of the power of the flash's light (because it will be lighting up a wider angle of view than will appear in your picture). You can solve both problems by fitting a long-focus lens to the front of the flash light – this concentrates the beam in a narrow angle and increases the flash range: it is possible to take successful flash pictures with a range of up to 20m (65ft). There are also zoom flash units with an angle of lighting that can be set to correspond with any lens between 80mm and 20mm focal length.

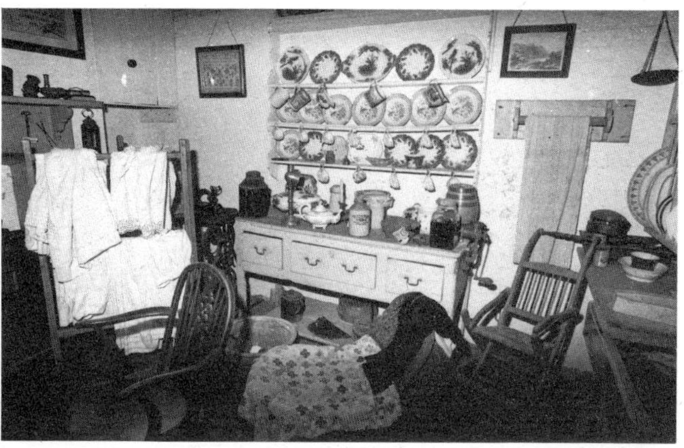

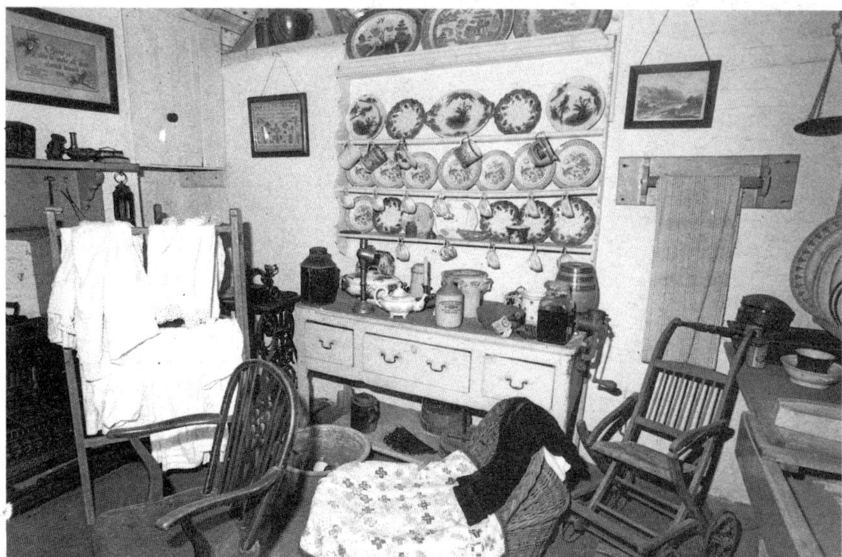

Flash and wide-angle lenses often go together – both are of use for indoor shots. But wide-angle lenses often take in more of the scene than an ordinary flash unit will cover, causing *vignetting* (**above**). Use a wide-angle flash gun or diffuser (**right**) to ensure the whole of scene is lit correctly

FLASH

You don't need an elaborate studio to take professional-quality portraits – use full-length curtains for a backdrop, and a minimum of lighting equipment. Here there is one flash gun on the camera for direct lighting; and side lighting is provided by a unit bounced, not off walls or ceiling, but off a lighting *umbrella* to produce a diffused and colour-free effect

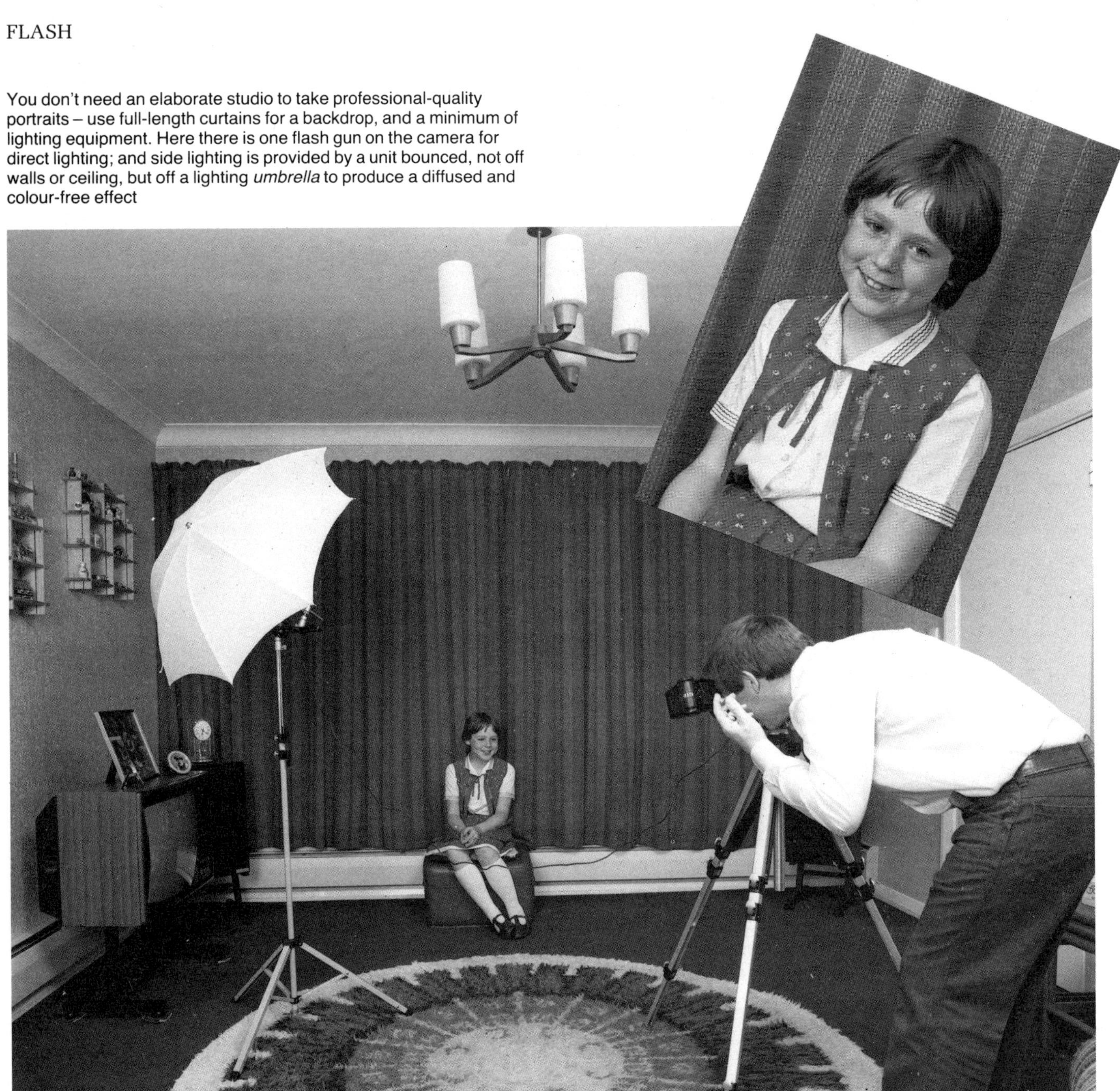

≣ BUYING GUIDE ≣

With simple cameras, you're unlikely to have much choice of flash unit. But all other things being equal, go for **built-in electronic** flash rather than Flipflash or Magicube, which are expensive to use.

If you have an SLR camera, the usual rule applies – you need something sophisticated enough to be able to stretch the limits of the format, otherwise there is no point in going for an SLR. Even so, automation is no drawback, and a **computer flash** will make life much easier but without restricting your creativity. Get one that enables you to alter the angle of the flash head without moving the sensor away from the lens, and go for the highest guide number you can afford – say between 28 and 36 for a guide number quoted in metres.

Units with a **thyristor circuit** are certainly cheaper in operation than others. More importantly, recycling times can be lower, and the number of flashes per battery greater.

Dedicated flash units are a little more automatic, and so even easier to use. Their cost is coming down now that independent brands are making them, and one would be worth buying if it was not much more expensive than a basic computer type.

CHAPTER ELEVEN

PROJECTORS

The main drawback of slides, or transparencies, is that you really need a projector to look at them properly – but a properly presented slide show can turn into a lot of fun

The picture on a slide is visible only when light is transmitted *through* it – unlike a print picture, where you see the light *reflected* off it. So to look at a slide you have to hold it up to the light. This is awkward and, in any case because the picture is so small, you cannot see much detail.

An improvement over holding up a slide and peering at it is to use a small hand-held viewer (see picture opposite). Here, the light from a small battery-powered bulb lights a translucent screen behind the slide, and an enlarging lens makes the image bigger. Rather larger, mains-powered viewers are also available, some with automatic changing of slides. The drawback of these viewers is that it's difficult for more than one person at a time to see the picture – and it still isn't very bright or large.

The best solution is to use a proper slide projector, in which a powerful bulb shines through the slide and a lens throws the image – very bright, and enlarged many times – on to a white wall or special screen placed two or three metres (or more) away.

Automation

In common with everything else, slide projectors are becoming more and more automatic in their operation, but a choice of degrees of automation does exist.

Fully manual   Here you drop a slide into a holder, and push the holder across into the path of the light rays from the projection lamp. That pushes another holder out of its place, so that you can remove the slide previously being shown, and replace it with another which you then pull into place – and so on. Projectors like these are almost museum pieces these days. They are cheap but tiresome to use.

Semi-automatic   You can load a large number of slides into a special holder, called a *magazine*, and show these one after the other in sequence, pausing on each one as long as you like. But you have to change the slides yourself.

Fully-automatic   Slides are also loaded into a magazine, but they are changed by an electric motor, which you operate with buttons on the projector or on a remote control unit.

Remote control

It's much nicer to be able to sit down among your company to watch a slide show, rather than having to be next to the projector working its controls. If you are giving a lecture, you clearly want to stand in front of your audience probably some distance away from the projector.

The answer, unless you want to hire a full-time projectionist, is a machine with **remote control** – a hand-held unit with buttons on it allows you to alter the projector's controls at some distance away.

There are two main types – some projectors come with both. With the *wired* type, the control unit is attached to the projector through a flex. The *infra-red* type works in the same way as the remote controls used for TVs. The control unit needs no wires to connect it to the projector, and is powered by a small battery which lasts for several years. Infra-red controls *tend* to be found only on the more expensive machines – you can get separate add-on infra-red units for some brands, but these can cost as much as many inexpensive projectors!

If you want to use your projector in a large lecture hall, make sure the remote control will work over large distances. Most infra-reds will operate over 15m (say 50ft) or more, but some down to only 4m (11ft). Flexes on wired control units are usually only about 1.5m to 2m long. Many of these you can extend, by plugging in extension cords, but some (and they include the very shortest cords) are wired directly into the projector so you cannot increase their length.

Check also what range of features the remote unit actually allows you to control – there may be some things that you still have to run back to the projector to do.

Focusing

A projector has a great deal in common with a camera. And, just as a camera lens has to be focused in order to throw a sharp image on to the film, the projector lens has to be focused so that the slide (that is, the developed film) throws a sharp image on to the viewing screen. The process is easier in one sense, because there's no depth of field to worry about – the image on the film is, of course, all in one plane (or nearly so: see 'Sharpness' on page 135).

However, there is one new complication. As the slide is

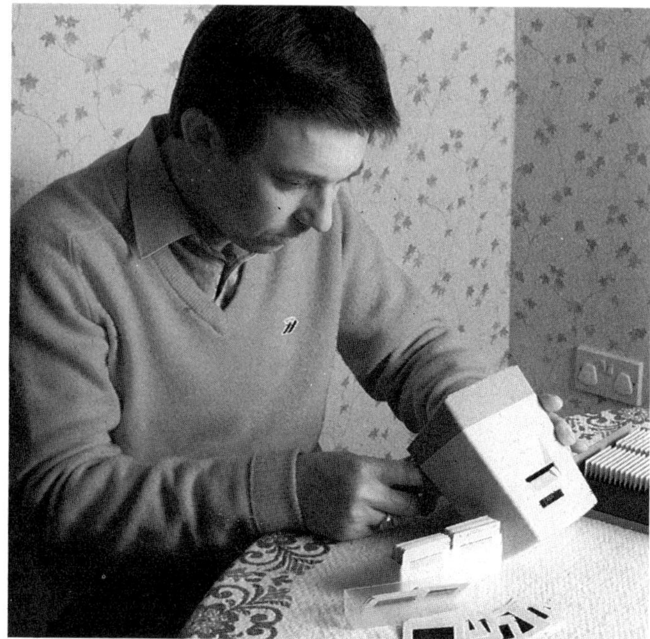

A hand-held viewer

shown heat from the projector's lamp tends to make it move, and to keep the picture sharp as this happens the focusing has to be continually altered slightly. With a **manual focus** machine you will have to do this yourself – and you'll probably find that you have to re-focus after each slide moves into position, and even while you are viewing a slide if you leave it on show for any length of time. But with an **autofocus** projector, the slides are kept sharp automatically – assuming you focus the first one accurately by hand.

Glazed mounts   The need for refocusing with a manual focus projector can be reduced by mounting all your slides between glass – you can buy special mounts for this.

These mounts keep the slide much flatter than the ordinary plastic or cardboard mount, so there is less curving and the slide stays in focus better. As a bonus, once mounted your slides are better protected against careless handling.

However, each mount costs about half as much as a developed slide, and the task of fitting them is quite time-consuming – mainly because each glass surface has usually to be cleaned first. And they can lead to other troubles. The picture may be distorted due to light patterns (called *Newton's rings*) between the surfaces, and the glass itself may seal in moisture, encouraging fungus growth in long-term storage.

Magazines

Although there is no single type of magazine for holding slides while they are being shown, there is one that can be used by the majority of projectors – the so-called *European Standard*, *Leitz* or *Universal* magazine. This is a straight magazine that holds either 36 or 50 slides. The cost is reasonably low – under £1 – so you might consider it worthwhile using the magazines as a storage system, and buying enough to hold *all* your slides. This would certainly cut out the tedious business of loading up a magazine from your stock of slides every time you wanted to show any of them. (But it is really better to select your slides for each particular audience.)

Perhaps the main drawback of the European Standard magazine is that all the slides will fall out if you turn it upside down. So a recent development is the compact straight magazine, which holds the slides tightly in position. There

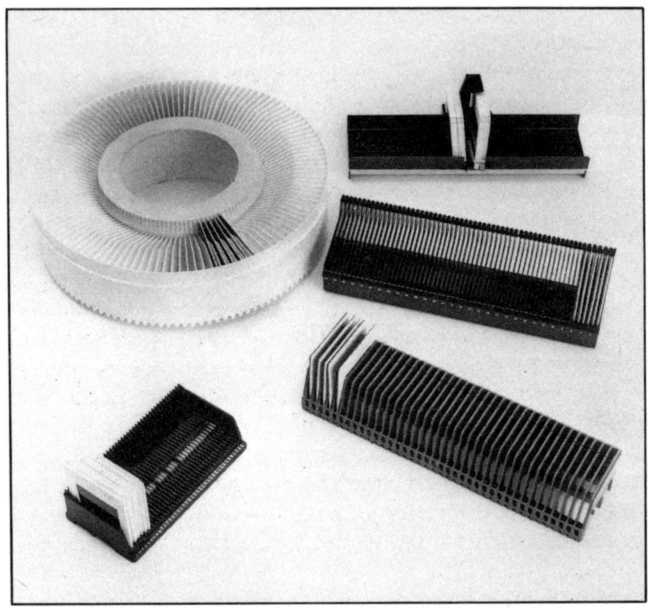

A selection of slide magazines. **Clockwise, from top left**: circular; stackloader; LKM; European Standard; Agfa CS

stack loader. You don't have to bother loading the slides individually into separate slots in the magazine, you simply pick up a stack of them and lay them on a carrier. But you cannot reverse direction to show a slide again, or show the whole lot in backwards order, as you can with a magazine.

Other features and facilities

Most of the features found on projectors are concerned with making slide-changing easy and slick. With some projectors, it is quick and easy to move the magazine forwards or backwards to a particular slide you want to pick out, but with others it is more difficult. Some projectors have a special arrangement for projecting a single slide without a magazine – which you can also usefully use for quickly turning around a slide that you find you have loaded the wrong way up.

The speed of slide-changing is much the same for all projectors – but one very expensive model uses a special system which moves two slides simultaneously for a particularly fast change-over. All projectors these days keep the screen dark between slides, but if you have a slide missing from your magazine at any position, most projectors will project a glaring white rectangle on to the screen – only some will black out the screen under these conditions. A remote dimmer control allows you to fade a slide out, change, and then slowly fade the next one up – very professional, but it's really only of use if you have two such projectors, so that one can be fading out while the other is fading in – the delay between slides is otherwise too slow to tolerate frequently.

Most people will want to linger over each slide for different lengths of time, depending on its interest – all projectors allow you to do this. Some projectors also have an automatic change system, where a timer changes slides at intervals – usually variable from about every five seconds to about every 45 seconds.

Many projectors have a small lighted screen – a *preview panel* – either on the body of the projector or on the remote control. You can hold a slide in front of this to check it before deciding whether to insert it into the projector's magazine.

With some projectors, you can project a lighted arrow on to the picture, and make it move around under remote control, so that you can point out different objects in the picture. It's intended mainly as a teaching aid.

are two types, one of which is the *LKM* which can hold any ordinary thin slide. The other is the *Agfa CS*, which can be used only with CS slide mounts because the edges of the mount have to be grooved; you can buy empty mounts for remounting those films that don't come with CS mounts, but this is a fiddly business. These compact magazines save space and can hold more slides than other straight magazines. They do work out rather more expensive per slide for storage than with the European Standard magazine, and few brands of projector use them.

Many projectors can also take one or other of the various *circular* magazines available. Again, these would work out expensive if used as a storage system, and in any case their shape makes them rather wasteful of storage space. But each magazine holds 80 or more slides – a greater number than a straight magazine. One brand of projector uses its own circular magazine which operates horizontally (the slides drop down into the projector by gravity).

Another brand of projector can use what is known as a

Audio-visual projectors

Some projectors have provisions for control systems to change slides in response to a signal recorded on a tape recorder, so a show can be entirely automatic. This is usually done with two projectors linked with a system to fade out one slide as the next one lights up. But this sort of equipment is very expensive for use in the home, and is normally intended for commercial or educational uses.

Lenses

The size of image that you will form on your screen depends on how far back you can site the projector, and the *focal length* of the lens it uses.

Most projectors come with a lens of 85mm focal length, which gives you a picture 1m wide and 667mm high (about 3ft 3in by 2ft 2in) at a distance of 2.5m (or a picture half this size at half this distance, and so on). Alternative focal lengths are usually available for projecting from other distances, and you may be able to get a zoom lens, so that you can change the size of the picture, or project the same-size picture from a range of distances.

Most projector manufacturers also offer a 90mm 'high-quality' lens designed to let through more light and to give a sharper image. These cost quite a bit extra – perhaps half as much again as the projector, even when bought *instead* of the usual lens. The better lens does help sharpness and brightness in many projectors, but you would probably notice the difference only if your slides were very good and you were using the projector in a large hall – in most cases, it is probably not worth spending the extra. A 90mm focal length lens gives a 1m-wide picture from a slightly greater distance than the 85mm lens – 2.75m as opposed to 2.5m.

The brightness of the picture depends also on the projector lamp being used. A 150W lamp is fitted to many projectors, and this is usually bright enough for most living rooms. For a hall or lecture theatre a projector using a 250W lamps will probably be an advantage.

Sharpness

One problem with an unglazed slide is not only that it moves when heated by the projector's lamp, but that it curls, so some parts of it are closer to the lens than others which makes it difficult to get the whole of a slide into focus – if you focus to get the centre of the picture sharp you may find that the edges and corners are blurred.

Individual slides will vary in the way that they curve, so even with an autofocus projector it is useful to have manual (or, more likely, remote) focus – then you can fine-tune focus so that the most important parts of the picture are sharp (this also helps, of course, if you have a slide that is itself not perfectly in focus all over).

If you want to get the best out of your slides and you don't want to put them all in glass mounts, then you could think about investing in a *curved field* lens which is designed to compensate for the curvature of unglazed slides. There are very few of these, and they fit only a few brands of projector. But they do get rid of much of the problem of poor sharpness.

To get the sharpest pictures it is important to set your projector up exactly at right angles to the screen. It is impossible to get both the top and the bottom of a picture in sharp focus if you have to prop up the front of the projector unless you also tilt the top of the screen forward (see drawing overleaf). Better, keep the screen perfectly vertical, and mount the projector on an adjustable projector stand. An easy way of telling if the screen and projector are at right angles is to check the edges of the picture – they should be exactly parallel to the edges of the screen all the way round.

Formats

Slide projectors are almost always designed for normal 35mm slides, set into a 50mm square mount. In case you use them, you'll find that 126 films can also be mounted in 50mm square mounts but some projectors will darken the edges of these 'super' slides. Half-frame 35mm slides are also normally mounted in 50mm square mounts. For 110 slides you can get special adaptor mounts to enable them to be used in normal projectors and magazines but you'll get better results from a special 110 projector. The 60mm square slides from 120 cameras also need special projectors.

Screens

You don't need to throw the image from your projector on to a screen. Any flat, white surface – a painted plaster wall, for example – will give a reasonable picture. But for the best results, a special projection screen is worth having. Besides, screens are portable and can be moved around to wherever is most convenient for viewing; house walls are less movable.

Projection screens are made of a cloth covered with a white or metallised coating or with crystals or beads of varying thickness. The most important feature of a screen is how bright and sharp a picture it gives. Different screens also have different *angles of view* – how far round off the 'axis' of the screen you can sit and still see a bright picture. Other points to be taken into account are how well the screen renders contrast (the difference between light and shade). All these factors depend to some extent on the type of screen – the main ones are described below.

Beaded screen   These give a bright picture but have a narrow angle of view; sharpness and contrast rendering are acceptable. But these screens are fragile and difficult to clean.

White screens   These give a bright picture with a wide angle of view. Sharpness, colour and contrast rendering are good to very good. They are easy to handle and maintain, and are probably the best choice for home use.

Metallic screens   These give a very bright picture, but a fairly restricted angle of view. Contrast is acceptable and sharpness is good. Maintenance is easy.

A better slide show

A good slide show is a lot of fun for you and your viewers; a poor one is very tedious and you're likely to find that friends will hastily make other appointments when you try to arrange the next showing. Follow these tips to improve your standing:
● be ruthless about eliminating any slide that is not sharp, or is over- or under-exposed (or is just plain boring)
● watch the rhythm of projection: some slides deserve more time than others

Choosing a screen Make sure that:
● the pads on the feet are securely attached
● the catches which hold the screen in its folded-up position work properly
● the casing is really strong (otherwise it will tend to twist when the screen is unrolled)
● the caps which form the end of the case are well secured
● the telescopic rod which supports the top of the screen, remains stable, does not revolve, and stays vertical when the screen is unrolled
● the hanging ring at the top of the screen is large enough

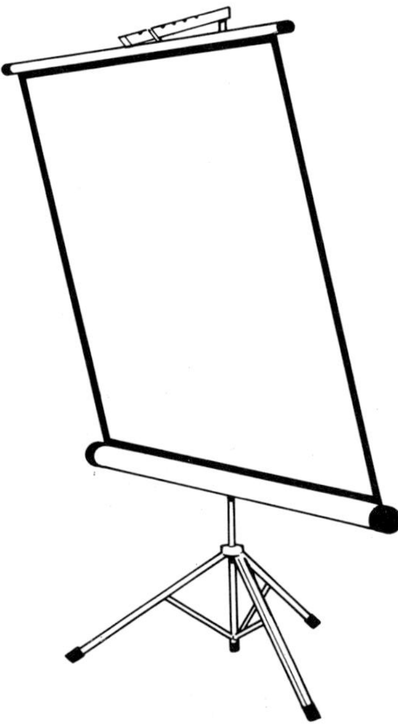

- try to arrange a theme for the presentation – it needn't be too rigorous – rather than simply showing a hotch-potch of different slides
- impose a time limit – don't have more than two 45-minute sessions if you ever want to see your guests again
- musical accompaniment – even if your projector has no audio synchronisation – can often help to increase the overall atmosphere of your show.

BUYING GUIDE

A slide projector is worth having if you want your photographs in the form of slides rather than prints. For ease of use it is worth while going for a fully-automatic projector with remote control and autofocus.

Page numbers in **bold** in this index
refer to illustrations

Page numbers in **bold** in this index
refer to illustrations

N

ND number 106
neutral density filter 106
   with slide film 95
non-reflex camera 9, 30-41
   autofocus **34**
   automatic **12**
   automatic exposure control 32
   coupled rangefinder 32, **33**
   date marking 38 **39**
   ease of use 40
   exposure control 30
   exposure indicator 38
   film 40
   film winding 39
   fixed focusing 32
   flash 35
   flash ready light 38
   focusing 32-34
   lenses 35
   loading film 30, **31**, 39
   motor wind 39 **40**
   parallax error 36, **37**
   picture quality 41
   rangefinder, coupled **33**
   scale focusing 32, **33**
   symbol focusing 32, **33**
   viewfinder accuracy **37**
   viewfinder information 36-38

P

parallax
   non-reflex camera 36, **37**
perspective
   choice of lens 72, **78**
perspective control lens **87**
picture quality
   110 camera 29, 92

disc camera 23, 92
   non-reflex camera 41
polarising filter **105**, 106
printing films see film processing
prints
   storing 100

R

rangefinder
   non-reflex camera **33**
   SLR camera   57
red-eye effect 21, **119**
   110 camera 27

S

screens for slide projectors 135
self timer
   disc camera 23
semi-automatic exposure control
   SLR camera 48
sensor flash
   disc camera 22
   non reflex camera 35
shutter priority exposure control
   SLR camera 49, **48**, **50**
shutter speed
   effect of different 47
   SLR camera 42
   with flash **119**
shutter speed range
   SLR camera 63
shutter speeds
   camera shake 79
shutters
   SLR camera 63
single lens reflex camera see SLR
camera

skylight filter 104
slide film
   110 camera 29
   colour balance 100
slide mounts 133
slide projector
   formats 135
   sharpness of pictures 135
   types 132
slide projector screens 135
   choosing 136
slide projectors 132-137
   audio visual 135
   focusing 133
   lenses 135
   magazines 133
slide show
   how to put together 136
slide viewer 132, **133**
slides
   storing 100
slow films 94, **94**
SLR camera 11, **13**, 42-65
   aperture priority exposure control
   48, **48**, **50**
   autofocus lens 59
   automatic exposure control 49, **49**,
   54
   checking depth of field 57
   closest focus distance 59
   depth of field scale **59**
   dual priority exposure control 49, **49**
   ease of use 64
   exposure compensation 52, **52**
   exposure control 42-57
   exposure correction 52-53, **56**
   exposure indicator 60
   exposure memory 53, **53**, **58**
   exposure meter **47**, 51-52
   film 64
   film loading 62
   film speed indicator **53**
   film winding 63

T, U

V

W, Z

Page numbers in **bold** in this index refer to illustrations